LIFELINES 2

LIFE2LINES

LETTERS FROM FAMOUS PEOPLE ABOUT THEIR FAVOURITE POEM

Compiled by

Ewan Gibson
Áine Jackson
Christopher Pillow

Edited by Niall MacMonagle

Foreword by Paul Durcan

Town House, Dublin

First published in Ireland by
Town House and Country House
Trinity House
Charleston Road
Ranelagh
Dublin 6
Ireland

British Library Cataloguing in Publication Data available

ISBNs: 0-948524-76-6 (pbk)
          0-948524-75-8 (hbk)

Cover illustration: *Saint Jerome Reading in a Landscape* by Giovanni Bellini. Courtesy of The National Gallery, London.

Design: Bill Murphy
Typeset by Typeform Ltd, Dublin
Printed in Ireland by Colour Books Ltd, Dublin

For the children of the Third World

And what did you want?
To call myself beloved, to feel myself
beloved on the earth.

Raymond Carver

CONTENTS

FOREWORD

War and Famine are raging in Rwanda. Day and night, confronted on our TV screens and in the photographs of courageous reporters such as Frank Miller of *The Irish Times*, we feel that we are helpless witnesses to unspeakable suffering.

Unspeakable? Therein lies the deadly temptation proposed to us by the Satan of War and Famine. We are tempted to feel that, in the face of War and Famine, art is irrelevant, futile, indecent, blasphemous.

The truth is that War and Famine are man-made: something that we in Ireland know and remember with anger and grief, if not with bitterness and remorse. The demons of evil that have been raging in Ethiopia, Somalia, Sudan and Rwanda are not freaks of Nature; they are the handiwork of evil men who can be overcome only by the power of art. The Satanic Tempter's deepest desire is that we lose faith in the power of art and surrender to despair. In his beautiful poem 'The Harvest Bow' Seamus Heaney quotes W B Yeats, who was in turn quoting Horace: 'The end of art is peace.'

Only in what we call art lies our salvation. 'If anything is sacred, the human body is sacred' — Whitman quoted by Steven Berkoff. Art is the last repository of humane values — one might say, African values. In the West our consumerism has caused a spiritual famine which is spreading into Russia and Siberia. Only in art have old, perennial, humane values survived. We look to Africa for spiritual aid just as Africa looks to us for economic aid.

These truths have been translated into a practical programme of uniquely outstanding poetry anthologies by the students of Wesley College. Not only have significant sums of money accrued but the very anthologies themselves embody a personality and an ethos which have provoked an immediate, urgent, attentive, magnanimous response from individual contributors as well as from the general reading public.

Normally there is no class of book more slipshod, more boring, more prejudiced, more snobbish, more exclusive, more incestuous, more narrow-minded, more arid, more ignorant, more canonical, more soulless, more soul destroying, more anti-poetic than a poetry anthology. The shelves of bookshops are stacked with the spines of these prodigies of spinelessness — poetry anthologies. So what is the magic recipe of the Wesley students?

It is their belief, first, in the personal, individual, social character of art; secondly, in art as a primarily subjective encounter. Absolute values — *pace* Yeats, Eliot, Kavanagh —

exist only in the context of subjective experience. What van Gogh wrote of painting is equally true of poetry: 'What lives in art and is eternally living is first of all the painter and then the painting.'

A work of art — a picture on the wall, a poem on the page, a nocturne in the concert hall, a film on the screen — is in itself only half-alive: that is to say, a poem ontologically (oops — but there is no other word for it) is only fifty per cent alive until it is read or heard by reader or auditor. It is only when art is encountered by audience that art is fully born, wholly alive.

Which is why each reader brings to the same poem a new life, and therefore no poem reads the same way twice; no poem exists frigidly intact on a pedestal in a classroom. 'Dualism be damned. This is where it's at' — Niall Stokes.

The curse of the teaching of poetry in our schools and colleges has been the Tyranny of the One Meaning: viz, that a poem means one thing and one thing only, and that reading the wretched thing is merely a question of finding the right key with which to unlock the locker and zap — the meaning of the poem slips out into your lap and you pick it up by the tail and carry the poor thing up to the po-faced, freckled, red-haired baldy old teacher who pats you on the pate and gives you a liquorice allsort and a kick in the pants. As well as needing to have many meanings, poetry needs to have no meaning. 'The pleasure you can take in them [words] that is nothing to do with their meaning' — Neil Jordan.

The letters in *Lifelines 2* are as vital and indispensable as the poems. Apart from the odd, stray, coy puff of conceit, the majority of the letters are passionate and startlingly honest: eg TV presenter Bibi Baskin — 'And yes, despite my profession, I do think the lovely evocative images of poetry do a much better job at it than the quick-flash images of television'; radio presenter Joe Duffy — 'I always came back to "The Windhover" mainly because it was the first poem to cast a sheltering shadow over my life'. Warm comic touches also, such as when that superb politician Mr Bertie Ahern TD, having chosen Kavanagh's Grand Canal poem, immediately protests his loyalty to the Royal Canal; or when Jeananne Crowley relates spending a week in Edinburgh, holding hands with Roger McGough.

Lifelines proved an extraordinarily popular book. How could the compilers of *Lifelines 2* hope to emulate it? They have surpassed themselves. This new anthology is even more exhilarating and distinctive.

Personally — how delighted I am to be able to wallow in that word aptly — I am astonished by the passages from Whitman, Poe, Lear, Millay, and Hill — none of whom featured in the first anthology. I rejoice in the ever-expanding recognition of Raymond Carver. I am grateful to contributors who are introducing me to poems I have not known before: eg Philip King

for 'I am Stretched On Your Grave'; Deirdre Madden for
'Vaucluse'; Art Cosgrove for 'The Song of the Strange Ascetic';
Mark Joyce for 'Not Ideas About The Thing But The Thing Itself';
Edna Longley for 'Old Man'; Gwen O'Dowd for 'Chicory Chicory
Dock'; Evelyn Conlon for 'I Gave Away That Kid'; James Hanley
for 'Uh-Oh'; Emma Cooke for 'The Chess Board'; Proinnsías Ó
Duinn for 'The Duck and the Kangaroo'; E Annie Proulx for
'Upon a Wasp Child With Cold'; Patrick McCabe for 'The Man
From God-Knows-Where'; Neil Astley for 'September Song'.

I am grateful also to those contributors who have brought me
back to rare poems read long ago: eg Pádraig J Daly for
'Swineherd'; Helen Dunmore for 'Buffalo Bill's'; Eilís Dillon for
'Bredon Hill'; Don Paterson for 'Soap Suds'; Bernard Farrell for
'The Cottage Hospital'; Charles Causley for 'The Faithless Wife'
(which I first read twenty-five years ago in a translation by
Michael Hartnett).

It is part of the unique recipe of *Lifelines 2* to be able to read all
these new and familiar poems side by side with great classics
such as 'The Lament for Art O'Leary' chosen by Seán Ó Tuama
and 'Epithalamion' chosen by Wendell Berry.

In the mid and late 1980s I was privileged to be invited to give
poetry recitals in Wesley College. The response of the students
was as memorable as it was moving, but most moving and
memorable of all was the spectacle of the relationship between
the students and their teachers. It was a palpable, visible current
of electric affection and it is something I have never ceased to
think about. When all is said and done, it is the individual school
teacher who is the keystone. If every teacher and arts
administrator was dedicated — in Dennis Potter's caustic,
romantic sense of 'dedication' — the world would be a world
without war and no child would go hungry.

When I was a boy I had the great good fortune to have a
dedicated teacher, Fr Joseph Veale SJ. Three of Ireland's most
popular writers — Brendan Kennelly, Roddy Doyle and Seamus
Heaney — have been renowned in their very different ways as
dedicated teachers. I think, and I am certain, that we owe an
immeasurable debt not only to the students of Wesley College
but to their teachers for throwing us — in a time of universal civil
war — *Lifelines 2*.

For the epitome of everything that is marvellous about *Lifelines
2*, listen to Tess Gallagher's words on her husband Raymond
Carver's poem 'What The Doctor Said': *I love its spiritual dimension
which is delivered so offhandedly that it takes hold of us the way sunlight
takes hold of roses and weeds alike.*

Paul Durcan
Ringsend
20 July 1994

PREFACE

The first little *Lifelines* booklet was compiled by Steven Given, Collette Lucy and Joy Marshall and produced in April 1985 on the school Gestetner machine. It sold out and inspired fifth-year students Julie Grantham, Jonathan Logue, Duncan Lyster, Joanne Bradish, Jackie Erskine, Carolyn Gibson, Paula Griffin, Nicola Hughes and Alice McEleney to compile three other booklets in 1987, 1989 and 1992. All four were initially published by The Underground Press, so named because the printing machine was in the school basement. A collected *Lifelines* with a foreword by Seamus Heaney was published by Town House in 1992 in aid of Concern, and was number one on the Irish bestsellers list for fourteen weeks. Penguin Books published a selected *Lifelines* in 1993, and we are happy to say that *Lifelines* has literally gone around the world. Most important of all is the fact that royalties from all *Lifelines* books are being sent to help people in the Developing World.

We began compiling *Lifelines 2* in 1993 and were astonished and delighted by the response. It was very exciting to see and open the envelopes, to read the letters and poems, and to put the book together. The result is this great, big, varied and beautiful *Lifelines 2*. Choosing a favourite poem is almost impossible, as is giving the reason why. We are very grateful to the huge number of people who replied. There were 223 contributors to *Lifelines,* and this is why we've continued into *Lifelines 2,* a companion volume, with number 224.

We also thank Paul Durcan who, with characteristic generosity, wrote the foreword to this volume, and Niall MacMonagle for overseeing the project. And lastly, thank you the reader for buying what we believe to be a most worthwhile book for a very worthwhile cause.

Ewan Gibson
Áine Jackson
Christopher Pillow

Wesley College
Dublin

Entries 1 to 223 appeared in *Lifelines*, which was published by
Town House and Country House in 1992.

JUNG CHANG   224

4 February 1994

Dear Ewan, Áine and Christopher,

Thank you for your letter. I would be happy to help you with your anthology, and enclose one of my favourite poems.

I first read this poem by the eighth century Chinese poet Tu Fu in 1969, when at the age of 16 I was sent to work as a peasant in a village at the edge of the Himalayas. My mother was in detention, and my father was in a labour camp. I was consumed by anxiety about what was happening to them. This poem gave expression to my longings to hear from them, and moreover, by transforming tragedy into great beauty, it helped keep me from feeling bitter or depressed.

Yours sincerely,
Jung Chang

Midnight

By the West Pavilion, on a thousand feet of cliff,
Walking at midnight under my latticed window.
Flying stars pass white along the water,
Transparent beams of moonset flicker on the sand.
At home in its tree, notice the secret bird:
Safe beneath the waves, imagine the great fishes.
From kinsmen and friends at the bounds of heaven and
    earth
Between weapon and buffcoat seldom a letter comes.

Tu Fu (712-770)

ROSE DOYLE   225

15 January 1994

Dear Ewan Gibson, Áine Jackson and Christopher Pillow:

It was lovely, and very flattering, to get your letter inviting me to be part of your next Lifelines *anthology. It's fearsome, in a way, to be asked for a favourite anything. I found it hard to choose a poem from amongst the many I've enjoyed over the years but, in the end, opted for William Blake's 'The Clod and the Pebble'.*

Blake's poem is short and perfect and says all there is to say about love. Which is that, like life, it is all things to all men, as selfish or as giving as we choose to make it. Interpretation apart, the sheer beauty and simplicity of the lyrics make it the sort of poem that is a joy to carry around in the head.

Hope this is more or less what you want. The best of good wishes with the anthology.

Regards,
Rose Doyle

The Clod and the Pebble
from *Songs of Experience*

'Love seeketh not Itself to please,
'Nor for itself hath any care,
'But for another gives its ease,
'And builds a Heaven in Hell's despair.'

So sung a little Clod of Clay
Trodden with the cattle's feet,
But a Pebble of the brook
Warbled out these metres meet:

'Love seeketh only Self to please,
'To bind another to Its delight,
'Joys in another's loss of ease,
'And builds a Hell in Heaven's despite.'
William Blake (1757–1827)

CHRISTOPHER FITZ-SIMON   226

16 February 1994

'The Wild Swans at Coole' *by William Butler Yeats*

I can speak many of Yeats's poems by heart, but I can not recall consciously sitting down to learn them. I've simply absorbed them — as any person growing up in Ireland might absorb and retain the sound of the surf on Erris Head, or the thick scent of meadowsweet after a shower of rain in a Monaghan sheugh, or the image of those all-seeing two-faced stone figures by the shores of Lough Erne. I suppose that my response to 'The Wild Swans at Coole' is tempered by many things: the story of the Gregory family, unusual in that its members were good landlords as well as distinguished people in public life; geology and topography, because of that extraordinary limestone landscape into which the Coole lakes are hollowed; ornithology, naturally — even if you exclude the mythological connotations of swans (which is impossible!) they are never anything short of being 'brilliant creatures'; and literary history, for it was at Coole Park that Yeats and Lady Gregory wrestled with the intractabilities of the Abbey Theatre. Almost twenty years after his first visit to Coole, we find the poet looking back on a period of intense creativity, on an era of cataclysmic political and social change in Ireland, on disillusion, broken dreams, and towards an uncertain future in which the imagination may not take flight in the way it used to do.

Christopher Fitz-Simon

The Wild Swans at Coole

The trees are in their autumn beauty,
The woodland paths are dry,
Under the October twilight the water
Mirrors a still sky;
Upon the brimming water among the stones
Are nine-and-fifty swans.

The nineteenth autumn has come upon me
Since I first made my count;
I saw, before I had well finished,
All suddenly mount
And scatter wheeling in great broken rings
Upon their clamorous wings.

I have looked upon those brilliant creatures,
And now my heart is sore.
All's changed since I, hearing at twilight,
The first time on this shore,
The bell-beat of their wings above my head,
Trod with a lighter tread.

Unwearied still, lover by lover,
They paddle in the cold
Companionable streams or climb the air;
Their hearts have not grown old;
Passion or conquest, wander where they will,
Attend upon them still.

But now they drift on the still water,
Mysterious, beautiful;
Among what rushes will they build,
By what lake's edge or pool
Delight men's eyes when I awake some day
To find they have flown away?

W B Yeats (1865–1939)

EDNA LONGLEY   227

School of English
The Queen's University of Belfast

My favourite poem is 'Old Man' by Edward Thomas.

This is a very complex poem in very simple language. It is also a poem that asks disconcerting questions about language itself. Written just after the Great War had begun, it explores the extent of our control over memory, history and meaning in a darkly problematic universe.

Edna Longley

Old Man

Old Man, or Lad's-Love — in the name there's nothing
To one that knows not Lad's-Love, or Old Man,
The hoar-green feathery herb, almost a tree,
Growing with rosemary and lavender.
Even to one that knows it well, the names
Half decorate, half perplex, the thing it is:
At least, what that is clings not to the names
In spite of time. And yet I like the names.

The herb itself I like not, but for certain
I love it, as some day the child will love it
Who plucks a feather from the door-side bush
Whenever she goes in or out of the house.
Often she waits there, snipping the tips and shrivelling
The shreds at last on to the path, perhaps
Thinking, perhaps of nothing, till she sniffs
Her fingers and runs off. The bush is still
But half as tall as she, though it is as old;
So well she clips it. Not a word she says;
And I can only wonder how much hereafter
She will remember, with that bitter scent,
Of garden rows, and ancient damson trees
Topping a hedge, a bent path to a door,
A low thick bush beside the door, and me
Forbidding her to pick.
                                        As for myself,
Where first I met the bitter scent is lost.
I, too, often shrivel the grey sheds,
Sniff them and think and sniff again and try
Once more to think what it is I am remembering,
Always in vain. I cannot like the scent,
Yet I would rather give up others more sweet,
With no meaning, than this bitter one.

I have mislaid the key. I sniff the spray
And think of nothing; I see and I hear nothing;
Yet seem, too, to be listening, lying in wait
For what I should, yet never can, remember:
No garden appears, no path, no hoar-green bush
Of Lad's-love, or Old Man, no child beside,
Neither father nor mother, nor any playmate;
Only an avenue, dark, nameless, without end.

Edward Thomas (1878–1917)

JEANANNE CROWLEY   228

3 February 1994

Dear Wesley College Students,

Yes I do know about Lifelines. *Indeed I even bought copies for my friends. As probably one of Ranelagh's Greatest Egoists, I was, I confess, a touch bothered that your former Fifth Years hadn't* deigned *to ask me for my Personal Poetry Choice before now. However, with the help of my local Parish Priest (presently chaplain to the Chippendales) I got over it and am duly humbled and grateful to finally be included.*

I'd love to choose Roger McGough, particularly 'Discretion is the Better Part of Valerie' because Roger was one of the first men I ever fell in love with. We held hands in Edinburgh for a whole week.

Not only is McGough an excellent poet but he also understands how poetry should be taught, besides which he's the only poet I've ever heard performing his own work properly. However, as I'm sure lots of your respondees will be choosing him, I'm prepared to offer an alternative.

Here are some short poems from one of the best anthologies I've ever come across. These are delicious translations by Graeme Wilson from the 7th, 8th and 9th century Japanese, which show how little in terms of human emotion ever seems to change. Something which delights and puzzles me at the same time.

With best regards to you all,
Jeananne Crowley

Discretion

Discretion is the better part of Valerie
(though all of her is nice)
lips as warm as strawberries
eyes as cold as ice
the very best of everything
only will suffice
not for her potatoes
and puddings made of rice

Not for her potatoes
and puddings made of rice
she takes carbohydrates
like God takes advice
a surfeit of ambition
is her particular vice
Valerie fondles lovers
like a mousetrap fondles mice

And though in the morning
she may whisper: 'it was nice'
you can tell by her demeanour
that she keeps her love on ice
but you've lost your hardearned heart
now you'll have to pay the price
for she'll kiss you on the memory
and vanish in a trice

Valerie is corruptible
but known to be discreet
Valerie rides a silver cloud
where once she walked the street.

Roger McGough (b.1937)

A Grain of Sand

No. I shall not die for love.
I lack the discipline
To face the waves and drown in them.
My nature is to spin
Around and around like a grain of sand
Whenever a tide flows in.

Anonymous (late seventh century)

Plum Trees

Those plum-slips that we planted
My darling wife and I.
Stand now in the garden
As thick around and high
As full-grown trees.

    I stare at them.

How high their branches float
Upon these tears which blind me
As grief thickens in my throat

Otomo no Tibito (665-731)

Pearl Diver

No one dives to the ocean-bottom
Just like that:
One does not learn the skills involved
At the drop of a hat
It's those skills slow-learnt in the depths of love
That I'm working at.

Lady Nakatomi (early eighth century)

MICHAEL COADY   229

16 January 1994

Dear Friends,

Thank you for your recent letter. I know of the very successful Lifelines *project and admire it. Thank you for your invitation to contribute towards a further collection.*

I would find it next to impossible to nominate any one particular poem as my favourite above all others, but I suggest one which has long been a favourite.

I remember being immediately entranced by John Montague's love-lyric 'All Legendary Obstacles' *when I opened the* Irish Times *to discover it one Saturday morning well over twenty years ago. Such potent memorability must be significant. The drama of Montague's poem is a primary one of journeying, of waiting and encounter, of hope and uncertainty and desire. Its personal intimacies are set against a great sweeping landscape — mountains, rain, the dark — and the poem's technique is strikingly cinematic. Its eye is one which has been consciously or unconsciously schooled by the camera, as we all have in this century. As in some classic film, the visual and emotional charge of the last 'scene' remains haunting and unforgettable.*

With best wishes,
Michael Coady

All Legendary Obstacles

All legendary obstacles lay between
Us, the long imaginary plain,
The monstrous ruck of mountains
And, swinging across the night,
Flooding the Sacramento, San Joaquin,
The hissing drift of winter rain.

All day I waited, shifting
Nervously from station to bar

As I saw another train sail
By, the *San Francisco Chief* or
Golden Gate, water dripping
From great flanged wheels.

At midnight you came, pale
Above the negro porter's lamp.
I was too blind with rain
And doubt to speak, but
Reached from the platform
Until our chilled hands met.

You had been travelling for days
With an old lady, who marked
A neat circle on the glass
With her glove, to watch us
Move into the wet darkness
Kissing, still unable to speak.

John Montague (b.1929)

CONOR FALLON   230

1 February — Bridget's Day — 1994

Dear Three,

Thank you for your letter. I know of and admire your work — Nancy my wife keeps your book by her bedside along with other treasured poetry.

My favourite poet is Czeslaw Milosz, now a very old man — we keep his Collected Poems *in the loo; with my father Padraic Fallon; Shakespeare's* Sonnets; *Housman's* A Shropshire Lad *and lately, Derek Walcott.*

My favourite poem is Milosz's series titled 'The World', about his boyhood in Poland — it's a long poem in many parts and I've chosen one almost at random — perhaps because of relevance to my work — I love the airiness, not clogged by poetic tone.

Yours sincerely,
Conor Fallon

The Bird Kingdom
from *The World*

Flying high the heavy wood grouse
Slash the forest sky with their wings
And a pigeon returns to its airy wilderness
And a raven gleams with airplane steel.

What is the earth for them? A lake of darkness.
It has been swallowed by the night forever.
They, above the dark as above black waves,
Have their homes and islands, saved by the light.

If they groom their long feathers with their beaks
And drop one of them, it floats a long time
Before it reaches the bottom of the lake
And brushes someone's face, bringing news
From a world that is bright, beautiful, warm, and free.

Czeslaw Milosz (b.1911) (translated by the author)

HERMIONE LEE   231

2 February 1994

Dear Ewan Gibson, Áine Jackson and Christopher Pillow:

Thank you for asking me to choose my favourite poem for Lifelines. *In response, I realized that many of my favourite poems are elegies: Tennyson's 'In Memoriam', Milton's 'Lycidas', Auden's magnificent 'In Memory of W.B. Yeats' (the un-cut version), Donne's heartbreakingly formal 'Nocturnall Upon S. Lucies Day', Henry King's poignant 'The Exequy', and Peter Porter's beautiful echoing of it in 'An Exequy'; Hardy's 1912–1913 Poems, love-poems for the wife he had stopped loving; and Stevie Smith's 'Harold's Leap', a dignified tribute to a brave failure. I like these poems in memory of dead wives, friends and poets because, like a biography or a love-letter, they tell the story of a relationship between the writer and the lost subject, who is re-found in the poem; and because of the problem they all confront, of turning a grief into a shape. I chose Emily Dickinson's extraordinary version of elegy, which boldly abandons the conventions for a ruthlessly detailed, exact account of the moment of death, and its effect on the living. As in all her greatest poems, what looks domestic, small, and 'narrow', opens out into a terrifying, 'awful' space. The poem has no title. It was written in about 1866 and first published in 1890.*

With best wishes for the success of Lifelines.

Yours sincerely,
Hermione Lee

The last Night that She lived
It was a Common Night
Except the Dying — this to Us
Made Nature different

We noticed smallest things —
Things overlooked before
By this great light upon our Minds
Italicized — as 'twere.

As We went out and in
Between Her final Room
And Rooms where Those to be alive
Tomorrow were, a Blame

That Others could exist
While She must finish quite
A Jealousy for Her arose
So nearly infinite —

We waited while She passed —
It was a narrow time —
Too jostled were Our Souls to speak
At length the notice came.

She mentioned, and forgot —
Then lightly as a Reed
Bent to the Water, struggled scarce —
Consented, and was dead —

And We — We placed the Hair —
And drew the Head erect —
And then an awful leisure was
Belief to regulate —

Emily Dickinson (1830-1886)

BERTIE AHERN   232

Oifig an Aire Airgeadais
(Office of the Minister for Finance)
Baile Átha Cliath 2 (Dublin 2)

25 February 1994

Dear Mr Gibson,

*The Minister for Finance, Mr Bertie Ahern, TD, has asked me to refer
to your request for a favourite poem from him for your publication for
the Third World.*

*The Minister has asked me to forward the enclosed to you and has asked
me to pass on his best wishes for your upcoming publication.*

Yours sincerely,
Hannah O'Riordan
Private Secretary

Canal Bank Walk

Leafy-with-love banks and the green waters of the canal
Pouring redemption for me, that I do
The will of God, wallow in the habitual, the banal,
Grow with nature again as before I grew.
The bright stick trapped, the breeze adding a third
Party to the couple kissing on an old seat,
And a bird gathering materials for the nest for the Word
Eloquently new and abandoned to its delirious beat.
O unworn world enrapture me, encapture me in a web
Of fabulous grass and eternal voices by a beech,
Feed the gaping need of my senses, give me ad lib
To pray unselfconsciously with overflowing speech
For this soul needs to be honoured with a new dress woven
From green and blue things and arguments that cannot
    be proven.

Patrick Kavanagh (1904–1967)

Like most other schoolboys I suppose I did not really appreciate poetry at an early age. Having to learn line upon line of verse never really knowing what it meant was probably not the greatest way to instil an appreciation of poetry in a tender mind. However, like a good wine, an appreciation of poetry develops as the years go by. One of my children bought me a birthday present of the Complete Poems of Patrick Kavanagh *some years back. 'Canal Bank Walk' became one of my favourites. This is not to say that I do not have a deep love of the Royal Canal which flows through my native Northside but I passed by that very area which Kavanagh wrote about every day for five years when I was Minister for Labour. I can certainly tell you there were many evenings of long negotiations when I looked out my window and wished that I was walking up its leafy banks which seem to have a distinctive colour for every season. Kavanagh seems to capture all the movement and emotion of the canal which he so eloquently put to verse. I am obviously not the only one who has been attracted by its beauty, it has always proved a popular place for walkers, lunchtimers or those who simply want to sit and watch the world go by.*

Bertie Ahern, TD
Minister for Finance

NEIL JORDAN   233

7 February 1994

'Hugh Selwyn Mauberley' *by Ezra Pound*

The reason this is my favourite poem is because through the first three stanzas I became aware of the musical possibilities of words. The pleasure you can take in them that is nothing to do with their meaning.

'The Chopped seas held him, therefore, that year. . .'

Neil Jordan

[The publishers were unable to obtain permission to print 'Hugh Selwyn Mauberley'.]

GEMMA HUSSEY   234

19 January 1994

Dear Lifelines Collectors,

The Seamus Heaney poem that I've chosen (from his volume Seeing Things*) is the simplest but most vivid image which makes you think and think again about its implications. Perhaps it will be suitable for the admirable purpose behind your* Lifelines *project. I wish you great success.*

Kindest regards,
Gemma Hussey

from *Lightenings*

viii
The annals say: when the monks of Clonmacnoise
Were all at prayers inside the oratory
A ship appeared above them in the air.

The anchor dragged along behind so deep
It hooked itself into the altar rails
And then, as the big hull rocked to a standstill,

A crewman shinned and grappled down the rope
And struggled to release it. But in vain.
'This man can't bear our life here and will drown',

The abbot said, 'unless we help him'. So
They did, the freed ship sailed, and the man climbed back
Out of the marvellous as he had known it.

Seamus Heaney (b.1939)

MICHAEL DAVITT   235

7 Feabhra 1994

Dear Ewan,

I enclose two poems in Irish, one with English translation.

'Fiabhras' (Fever) by Seán Ó Ríordáin is a masterpiece. Although set in a TB sanatorium in the fifties, as a university student in the late sixties I always thought of it as part of the whole 'psychedelic' era, with the hallucinatory imagery like the swelling picture and melting frame, and the last two intriguing lines:

> Tá ba ar an mbóthar ó thuaidh,
> Is níl ba na síoraíochta chomh ciúin.

> There are cows on the road to the north
> And the cows of eternity aren't as quiet.

Everytime I read it, it continues to radiate off the page.
From my own work I've chosen 'Urnaí Maidne' *translated by Philip Casey as* 'Morning Prayer'. *I have two kinds of morning prayers: (i) Good morning, God (ii) Good God, morning! This poem belongs to the latter category and I often begin readings with it. Each verse has its own mood and rhythm and it just flowed off the pen one grey morning back in 1982.*

I hope this fits the bill.

le gach dea-ghuí,
Michael Davitt

Fiabhras

Tá sléibhte na leapa mós ard,
Tá breoiteacht 'na brothall 'na lár,
Is fada an t-aistear urlár,
   Is na mílte is na mílte i gcéin
   Tá suí agus seasamh sa saol.

Atáimid i gceantar braillín.
Ar éigean más cuimhin linn cathaoir,
Ach bhí tráth sar ba mhachaire sinn,
   In aimsir choisíochta fadó,
   Go mbímis chomh hard le fuinneog.

Tá pictiúir ar an bhfalla ag at,
Tá an fráma imithe ina lacht,
Ceal creidimh ní féidir é bhac,
   Tá nithe ag druidim fém dhéin,
   Is braithim ag titim an saol.

Tá ceantar ag taisteal ón spéir,
Tá comharsanacht suite ar mo mhéar,
Dob fhuirist dom breith ar shéipéal,
  Tá ba ar an mbóthar ó thuaidh,
  Is níl ba na síoraíochta chomh ciúin.

Seán Ó Ríordáin (1916–1977)

Urnaí Maidne

Slogann dallóg na cistine a teanga de sceit
caochann an mhaidin liathshúil.
Seacht nóiméad déag chun a seacht
gan éan ar chraobh
ná coileach ag glaoch
broidearnach im shúil chlé
is blas bréan im bhéal.

Greamaíonn na fógraí raidió den bhfo-chomhfhios
mar a ghreamódh
buíocán bogbheirithe uibh
de chois treabhsair dhuibh
mar a ghreamódh cnuimh de chneá.
Na héisteodh sibh
in ainm dílis Dé ÉISTÍG . . .

Tagann an citeal le blubfhriotal miotalach
trí bhuidéal bainne ón gcéim
dhá mhuga mhaolchluasacha chré.
Dúisigh a ghrá
tá sé ina lá. Seo, cupán tae
táim ag fáil bháis
conas tánn tú fhéin?

Michael Davitt (b.1950)

Morning Prayer

The kitchen blind gulps its tongue in fright
morning winks a grey eye.
Seventeen minutes to seven
not a bird on a branch
not a cock crowing
my left eye is pounding
there's a foul taste in my mouth.

Radio commercials cling to the id
like the yolk
of a halfboiled egg
to a black trouser leg
like a speck to a wound.
Will you not listen
in the name of sweet Christ *SHUT UP* . . .

The kettle comes with metallic splutters
three bottles of milk from the step
two abashed clay mugs.
Wake up my love
it's morning. Here's a cup
of tea. I'm dying.
How are you?
Translated by Philip Casey

KEVIN HOUGH   236

RTE
11 January 1994

Dear Ewan, Áine and Christopher,

Thank you so much for inviting me to select my favourite poem for your publication. I enclose a copy and hope that not many have chosen the same piece.

My reason for selecting this one is because when I was at school I found it very difficult to memorize a lot of poems, but funnily enough 'To Daffodils' was very easy for me to learn and to this day I can remember it all. My mother also loved this poem and included it in her favourite pieces. Poetry was very special to her and indeed she has had a number of poems published.

Yours sincerely,
Kevin Hough

To Daffodils

Fair daffodils, we weep to see
    You haste away so soon;
As yet the early rising sun
    Has not attained his noon.
      Stay, stay,
    Until the hasting day
      Has run
    But to the even-song:
And, having prayed together, we
    Will go with you along.

We have short time to stay as you,
    We have as short a spring;
As quick a growth to meet decay,
    As you, or anything.
      We die,

As your hours do, and dry
   Away,
Like to the summer's rain,
Or as the pearls of morning's dew,
   Ne'er to be found again.

Robert Herrick (1591–1674)

MATTHEW SWEENEY   237

4 February 1994

Dear Ewan, Áine and Christopher,

Thanks for your letter and apologies for taking a while to get back to you.

As with many of your contributors, I find it impossible to come up with a favourite poem, as I have many favourites. I have gone for a Sylvia Plath poem, however, 'Death & Co.', because she was the first contemporary poet who was important to me, and is still possibly my favourite.

What I like about this poem, in particular — apart from the sinister edge, the chilling elegance of it, and the spare well-madeness — is the feeling you get of imagination being given its head and coming up with another realism the other side of surrealism. This kind of transforming imagination is something I value in poetry, and is an example to any young poet.

I could just as easily have gone for several other Plath poems, as I have many favourites among her work alone.

Good luck with your project, it's a good one. The big Lifelines *book was fascinating.*

All best wishes,
Matthew Sweeney

Death & Co.

Two, of course there are two.
It seems perfectly natural now —
The one who never looks up, whose eyes are lidded
And balled, like Blake's,
Who exhibits

The birthmarks that are his trademark —
The scald scar of water,
The nude
Verdigris of the condor.
I am red meat. His beak

Claps sidewise: I am not his yet.
He tells me how badly I photograph.
He tells me how sweet
The babies look in their hospital
Icebox, a simple

Frill at the neck
Then the flutings of their Ionian
Death-gowns,
Then two little feet.
He does not smile or smoke.

The other does that,
His hair long and plausive.
Bastard
Masturbating a glitter,
He wants to be loved.

I do not stir.
The frost makes a flower,
The dew makes a star,
The dead bell,
The dead bell.

Somebody's done for.

Sylvia Plath (1932–1963)

NEIL ASTLEY   238

Bloodaxe Books
Newcastle Upon Tyne

5 February 1994

Dear Ewan, Áine & Christopher,

Thank you for your letter about the new edition of Lifelines. *The poem I'd choose is 'September Song' by Geoffrey Hill, from his collection* King Log. *I'm not sure I'd call it a 'favourite' poem, but of the poems I admire it seems the most appropriate for a book produced in response to the unnecessary deaths of millions of children in the Third World. Here's my comment:*

'September Song' remembers an unknown ten-year-old child who died anonymously some time after 24 September 1942 in one or other Nazi concentration camp: these bare facts are given only in the epigraph. Born in 1932, the same year as the poet Geoffrey Hill, the child could have been him ('an elegy for myself'), or any of us: any child's death diminishes us all. The poem is understated and oblique. The more you read it, the more terrifying it becomes, as further implications rise to the surface, as you notice how the meaning of each line changes, or shifts, with each line break. Geoffrey Hill knows how the Nazis perfected the art of misusing language to disguise the nature of what they called their

'Final Solution': throughout this short poem, he simultaneously masks and reveals the horror behind that phrase through painful irony, through awful double-meanings and juxtapositions ('routine cries'). When you reach his description of autumn bonfire smoke, you can't help thinking of less 'harmless fires', of the child who died; of the millions who died. Just the thought of drifting smoke makes your eyes sting. But you're alive. You start to cry.

With all good wishes for the new Lifelines.

Yours sincerely,
Neil Astley

September Song
born 19.6.32 — deported 24.9.42

Undesirable you may have been, untouchable
you were not. Not forgotten
or passed over at the proper time.

As estimated, you died. Things marched,
sufficient, to that end.
Just so much Zyklon and leather, patented
terror, so many routine cries.

(I have made
an elegy for myself it
is true)

September fattens on vines. Roses
flake from the wall. The smoke
of harmless fires drifts to my eyes.

This is plenty. This is more than enough.
Geoffrey Hill (b.1932)

INGRID CRAIGIE   239

26 January 1994

Dear Ewan, Áine and Christopher,

Thank you very much for your letter, asking me to contribute to your anthology. I am delighted to do so, and enclose my selection for your attention. I have a framed copy of this poem, a present from the director, Garry Hynes, which she gave to me on the first night of Lover's Meeting, *a play we did together.*
It could have been written about the character I played, who is haunted and distracted by an obsessive love. This is the dark side of love. From the shocking and surprising image of the first stanza, it is love turned inside out.

Yours sincerely,
Ingrid Craigie

Symptoms of Love

Love is a universal migraine,
A bright stain on the vision
Blotting out reason.

Symptoms of true love
Are leanness, jealousy,
Laggard dawns;

Are omens and nightmares —
Listening for a knock,
Waiting for a sign:

For a touch of her fingers
In a darkened room,
For a searching look.

Take courage, lover!
Could you endure such grief
At any hand but hers?

Robert Graves (1895–1985)

LOUISE GLÜCK   240

March 1993

Dear People,

Your anthology seems a wonderful one; I am honored to be invited to contribute.

Impossible, though, to name a favorite poem. Instead, I'll name the first poems I loved (which still move me). I learned to read, was taught to read, very early, and found my way into various anthologies; I loved best Shakespeare's songs (was most haunted by 'O Mistress Mine') and Blake's Songs of Innocence *(most, 'The Little Black Boy'). I understood, probably, very little of them, in terms of sense. I couldn't have been more than five or six years old. But the tone spoke; I heard the sorrow in Shakespeare's music, the grave heartbreaking simplicity of Blake, and in both an (apparently) artless directness, which came to seem to me the ideal of art.*

These reasons are simple-minded; the poems, of course, are amazements.

Sincerely,
Louise Glück

from *Twelfth Night II (iii)*

O mistress mine, where are you roaming?
O stay and hear, your true love's coming,

That can sing both high and low.
Trip no further, pretty sweeting;
Journeys end in lovers' meeting,
    Every wise man's son doth know.

What is love? 'Tis not hereafter;
Present mirth hath present laughter;
                                    What's to come is still unsure.
In delay there lies no plenty,
Then come kiss me, sweet and twenty;
                                    Youth's a stuff will not endure.

William Shakespeare (1564–1616)

The Little Black Boy
from *Songs of Innocence*

My mother bore me in the southern wild,
And I am black, but O! my soul is white;
White as an angel is the English child:
But I am black as if bereav'd of light.

My mother taught me underneath a tree,
And sitting down before the heat of day,
She took me on her lap and kisséd me,
And pointing to the east, began to say:

'Look on the rising sun: there God does live,
And gives his light, and gives his heat away;
And flowers and trees and beasts and men receive
Comfort in morning, joy in the noon day.

'And we are put on earth a little space,
That we may learn to bear the beams of love,
And these black bodies and this sun-burnt face
Is but a cloud, and like a shady grove.

'For when our souls have learn'd the heat to bear,
The cloud will vanish; we shall hear his voice,
Saying: "Come out from the grove, my love & care,
And round my golden tent like lambs rejoice." '

Thus did my mother say, and kisséd me;
And thus I say to little English boy.
When I from black and he from white cloud free,
And round the tent of God like lambs we joy,

I'll shade him from the heat till he can bear
To lean in joy upon our father's knee;
And then I'll stand and stroke his silver hair,
And be like him, and he will then love me.

William Blake (1757–1827)

PADDY COLE   241

My favourite poem is a W B Yeats. It's called 'The Lake Isle of Innisfree'.

As I lead a very hectic life, with a lot of travelling, this poem to me depicts everything that is relaxing and tranquil:

> I will arise and go now, and go to Innisfree,
> And a small cabin build there, of clay and wattles made:
> Nine bean-rows will I have there, a hive for the honey-bee,
> And live alone in the bee-loud glade.

I think the last line in this verse is fabulous as I can just imagine a 'bee-loud glade'. I love to fish, and have done since I was a young boy with my father, so this poem is about everything outdoors, that I love to get away to.

> And I shall have some peace there, for peace comes dropping slow,

I often would think of that line, and of course 'Evening full of the linnet's wings'.

Thank you,
Paddy Cole

The Lake Isle of Innisfree

I will arise and go now, and go to Innisfree,
And a small cabin build there, of clay and wattles made:
Nine bean-rows will I have there, a hive for the honey-bee,
And live alone in the bee-loud glade.

And I shall have some peace there, for peace comes dropping
    slow,
Dropping from the veils of the morning to where the cricket
    sings;
There midnight's all a glimmer, and noon a purple glow,
And evening full of the linnet's wings.

I will arise and go now, for always night and day
I hear lake water lapping with low sounds by the shore;
While I stand on the roadway, or on the pavements grey,
I hear it in the deep heart's core.

W B Yeats (1865–1939)

['The Lake Isle of Innisfree' was also chosen by Chaim Herzog,
the President of Israel, in *Lifelines*.]

MARITA CONLON-McKENNA   242

29 January 1994

Dear Áine, Ewan and Christopher,

Thank you for your letter, I am delighted that there will be a new edition of Lifelines. *'Nightfeed' by Eavan Boland is one of my old favourites.*

I first read this poem when I was awash with babies and buggies and sticky fingers — my own fine collection of 'daisies'. Its sheer simplicity took my breath away, and to hear a poet speak of life's cycle and that love which is so often ignored in poetry — mother and child.

My second poem would be 'Digging' by Seamus Heaney. His poetry tends to leave an invisible bruise that hurts for a long long time afterwards.

Good luck with the book.

Yours truly,
Marita Conlon-McKenna

Night Feed

This is dawn.
Believe me
This is your season, little daughter.
The moment daisies open,
The hour mercurial rainwater
Makes a mirror for sparrows.
It's time we drowned our sorrows.

I tiptoe in.
I lift you up
Wriggling
In your rosy, zipped sleeper.
Yes, this is the hour
For the early bird and me
When finder is keeper.

I crook the bottle.
How you suckle!
This is the best I can be,
Housewife
To this nursery
Where you hold on,
Dear life.

A silt of milk
The last suck.
And now your eyes are open,
Birth-coloured and offended.

Earth wakes.
You go back to sleep.
The feed is ended.

Worms turn.
Stars go in.
Even the moon is losing face.
Poplars stilt for dawn
And we begin
The long fall from grace.
I tuck you in.

Eavan Boland (b.1944)

Digging

Between my finger and my thumb
The squat pen rests; snug as a gun.

Under my window, a clean rasping sound
When the spade sinks into gravelly ground:
My father, digging. I look down

Till his straining rump among the flowerbeds
Bends low, comes up twenty years away
Stooping in rhythm through potato drills
Where he was digging.

The coarse boot nestled on the lug, the shaft
Against the inside knee was levered firmly.
He rooted out tall tops, buried the bright edge deep
To scatter new potatoes that we picked
Loving their cool hardness in our hands.

By God, the old man could handle a spade.
Just like his old man.

My grandfather cut more turf in a day
Than any other man on Toner's bog.
Once I carried him milk in a bottle
Corked sloppily with paper. He straightened up
To drink it, then fell to right away
Nicking and slicing neatly, heaving sods
Over his shoulder, going down and down
For the good turf. Digging.

The cold smell of potato mould, the squelch and slap
Of soggy peat, the curt cuts of an edge
Through living roots awaken in my head.
But I've no spade to follow men like them.

Between my finger and my thumb
The squat pen rests.
I'll dig with it.

Seamus Heaney (b.1939)

DON PATERSON   243

Dear Ewan,

Re your enquiry for Lifelines *anthology — one of my favourite poems is MacNeice's 'Soap Suds'; from the poet's point of view it's a technical miracle, MacNeice's foot hard on the brakes one minute, hard on the accelerator the next, freezing time then speeding it up outrageously and most importantly, taking the reader along for the ride. Poems, like cars, are really time-machines, and no poem I can think of demonstrates better the terrifying capabilities they possess.*

Best wishes,
Don Paterson

Soap Suds

This brand of soap has the same smell as once in the big
House he visited when he was eight: the walls of the
     bathroom open
To reveal a lawn where a great yellow ball rolls back
     through a hoop
To rest at the head of a mallet held in the hands of a child.

And these were the joys of that house: a tower with a telescope;
Two great faded globes, one of the earth, one of the stars;
A stuffed black dog in the hall; a walled garden with bees;
A rabbit warren; a rockery; a vine under glass; the sea.

To which he has now returned. The day of course is fine
And a grown-up voice cries Play! The mallet slowly swings,
Then crack, a great gong booms from the dog-dark hall and
     the ball
Skims forward through the hoop and then through the next
     and then

Through hoops where no hoops were and each dissolves in
     turn
And the grass has grown head-high and an angry voice
     cries Play!
But the ball is lost and the mallet slipped long since from
     the hands
Under the running tap that are not the hands of a child.

Louis MacNeice (1907–1963)

MAURA TREACY   244

4 March 1994

Dear Ewan, Áine and Christopher,

Thank you for your letter inviting me to choose my favourite poem. With so many long-standing favourites already spoken for in the other Lifelines, I've chosen a comparatively recent discovery: 'And now the leaves suddenly lose strength' *by Philip Larkin.*

Though written in 1961, this poem wasn't published until after Larkin's death in 1985 — which suggests that he had some reservations about it. Now, I don't mean to vex his ghost by choosing a poem he wouldn't publish himself, but I love this one.

And I'm intrigued as to why he withheld it all those years. It's not as if there's anything too gruesomely personal here. And I'm sure it wasn't mislaid — it hadn't slipped down behind a drawer or anything — because he methodically filed everything. Maybe he was jaded, even a little embarrassed: maybe he thought, Autumn leaves, they've been done to death. And indeed that is so. But he needn't have let that stop him: it's not everybody can make dead leaves 'chase warm buses, speckle statued air. . .'

I think this is a fine poem from beginning to end, and — apart from anything else — an impeccable setting for that brilliant, faceted word, 'rubricate', which encapsulates not just the colours of Autumn but all the ritual that attends the dying year.

With best wishes,
Maura Treacy

And now the leaves suddenly lose strength

And now the leaves suddenly lose strength.
Decaying towers stand still, lurid, lanes-long,
And seen from landing windows, or the length
Of gardens, rubricate afternoons. New strong
Rain-bearing night-winds come: then
Leaves chase warm buses, speckle statued air,
Pile up in corners, fetch out vague broomed men
Through mists at morning.

          And no matter where goes down
The sallow lapsing drift in fields
Or squares behind hoardings, all men hesitate
Separately, always, seeing another year gone —
Frockcoated gentleman, farmer at his gate,
Villein with mattock, soldiers on their shields,
All silent, watching the winter coming on.

Philip Larkin (1922–1985)

STEVEN BERKOFF   245

29 January 1994

Dear Friends,

I hope I can squeeze a few lines out, giving reasons for the choice of one of my favourite poems, which is 'I Sing the Body Electric' by Walt Whitman.

One of the reasons I like the poem so much is that it completely encapsulates a man's passion for his fellow man or woman, and shows such an enthusiasm, such a basic, whole-hearted love for humanity that manifests itself in line after line of the most exquisite language. I never tire of reading this poem and it happily eschews the preciousness of poetry and gives poetry a powerful masculinity and passion and lack of self-consciousness that makes 'I Sing the Body Electric' one of my all-time favourites.

I hope this will do.

Yours sincerely,
Steven Berkoff

I Sing the Body Electric

I
I sing the body electric,
The armies of those I love engirth me and I engirth them,
They will not let me off till I go with them, respond to
        them,
And discorrupt them, and charge them full with the charge of
        the soul.

Was it doubted that those who corrupt their own bodies
        conceal themselves?
And if those who defile the living are as bad as they who
        defile the dead?
And if the body does not do fully as much as the soul?
And if the body were not the soul, what is the soul?

II
The love of the body of man or woman balks account, the
        body itself balks account,
That of the male is perfect, and that of the female is perfect.

The expression of the face balks account,
But the expression of a well-made man appears not only in
        his face,
It is in his limbs and joints also, it is curiously in the joints of
        his hips and wrists,
It is in his walk, the carriage of his neck, the flex of his waist
        and knees, dress does not hide him,

The strong sweet quality he has strikes through the cotton
 and broad-cloth,
To see him pass conveys as much as the best poem, perhaps
 more,
You linger to see his back, and the back of his neck and
 shoulder-side.

The sprawl and fullness of babes, the bosoms and heads of
 women, the folds of their dress, their style as we pass in the
 street, the contour of their shape downwards,
The swimmer naked in the swimming-bath, seen as he
 swims through the transparent green-shine, or lies with his
 face up and rolls silently to and fro in the heave of the water,
The bending forward and backward of rowers in row-boats,
 the horseman in his saddle,
Girls, mothers, house-keepers, in all their performances,
The group of laborers seated at noon-time with their open
 dinner kettles, and their wives waiting,
The female soothing a child, the farmer's daughter in the
 garden or cow-yard,
The young fellow hoeing corn, the sleigh-driver driving his
 six horses through the crowd,

The wrestle of wrestlers, two apprentice-boys, quite grown,
 lusty, good-natured, native-born, out on the vacant lot
 at sundown after work,
The coats and caps thrown down, the embrace of love and
 resistance,
The upper-hold and under-hold, the hair rumpled over and
 blinding the eyes;
The march of firemen in their own costumes, the play of
 masculine muscle through clean-setting trowsers and
 waist-straps,
The slow return from the fire, the pause when the bell strikes
 suddenly again, and the listening on the alert,
The natural, perfect, varied attitudes, the bent head, the
 curv'd neck and the counting;
Such-like I love—I loosen myself, pass freely, am at the
 mother's breast with the little child,
Swim with the swimmers, wrestle with wrestlers, march in
 line with the firemen, and pause, listen, count.

III
I knew a man, a common farmer, the father of five sons,
And in them the fathers of sons, and in them the fathers of
 sons.

This man was of wonderful vigor, calmness, beauty of person,
The shape of his head, the pale yellow and white of his hair
 and beard, the immeasurable meaning of his black eyes, the
 richness and breadth of his manners,
These I used to go and visit him to see, he was wise also,

He was six feet tall, he was over eighty years old, his sons
    were massive, clean, bearded, tan-faced, handsome,
They and his daughters loved him, all who saw him loved him,
They did not love him by allowance, they loved him with
    personal love,
He drank water only, the blood show'd like scarlet through
    the clear-brown skin of his face,
He was a frequent gunner and fisher, he sail'd his boat him-
    self, he had a fine one presented to him by a ship-joiner,
    he had fowling-pieces presented to him by men that
    loved him,
When he went with his five sons and many grand-sons to
    hunt or fish, you would pick him out as the most beauti-
    ful and vigorous of the gang,
You would wish long and long to be with him, you would
    wish to sit by him in the boat that you and he might
    touch each other.

IV

I have perceiv'd that to be with those I like is enough,
To stop in company with the rest at evening is enough,
To be surrounded by beautiful, curious, breathing, laughing
    flesh is enough,
To pass among them or touch any one, or rest my arm ever
    so lightly round his or her neck for a moment, what is
    this then?
I do not ask any more delight, I swim in it as in a sea.

There is something in staying close to men and women and
    looking on them, and in the contact and odor of them,
    that pleases the soul well,
All things please the soul, but these please the soul well.

V

This is the female form,
A divine nimbus exhales from it from head to foot,
It attracts with fierce undeniable attraction,
I am drawn by its breath as if I were no more than a helpless
    vapor, all falls aside but myself and it,
Books, art, religion, time, the visible and solid earth, and
    what was expected of heaven or fear'd of hell, are now
    consumed,
Mad filaments, ungovernable shoots play out of it, the
    response likewise ungovernable,
Hair, bosom, hips, bend of legs, negligent falling hands all
    diffused, mine too diffused,
Ebb stung by the flow and flow stung by the ebb, love-flesh
    swelling and deliciously aching,
Limitless limpid jets of love hot and enormous, quivering
    jelly of love, white-blow and delirious juice,

Bridegroom night of love working surely and softly into the
    prostrate dawn,
Undulating into the willing and yielding day,
Lost in the cleave of the clasping and sweet-flesh'd day.

This the nucleus—after the child is born of woman, man is
    born of woman,
This the bath of birth, this the merge of small and large, and
    the outlet again.

Be not ashamed women, your privilege encloses the rest, and
    is the exit of the rest,
You are the gates of the body, and you are the gates of the soul.

The female contains all qualities and tempers them,
She is in her place and moves with perfect balance,
She is all things duly veil'd, she is both passive and active,
She is to conceive daughters as well as sons, and sons as well
    as daughters.

As I see my soul reflected in Nature,
As I see through a mist, One with inexpressible completeness,
    sanity, beauty,
See the bent head and arms folded over the breast, the
    Female I see.

VI
The male is not less the soul nor more, he too is in his place,
He too is all qualities, he is action and power,
The flush of the known universe is in him,
Scorn becomes him well, and appetite and defiance become
    him well,
The wildest largest passions, bliss that is utmost, sorrow that is
    utmost become him well, pride is for him,
The full-spread pride of man is calming and excellent to the
    soul,
Knowledge becomes him, he likes it always, he brings every
    thing to the test of himself,
Whatever the survey, whatever the sea and the sail he strikes
    soundings at last only here,
(Where else does he strike soundings except here?)

The man's body is sacred and the woman's body is sacred,
No matter who it is, it is sacred—is it the meanest one in the
    laborer's gang?
Is it one of the dull-faced immigrants just landed on the
    wharf?
Each belongs here or anywhere just as much as the well-off,
    just as much as you,
Each has his or her place in the procession.

(All is a procession,
The universe is a procession with measured and perfect
    motion.)

Do you know so much yourself that you call the meanest
      ignorant?
Do you suppose you have a right to a good sight, and he or
      she has no right to a sight?
Do you think matter has cohered together from its diffuse
      float, and the soil is on the surface, and water runs and
      vegetation sprouts,
For you only, and not for him and her?

VII

A man's body at auction,
(For before the war I often go to the slave-mart and watch the
      sale,)
I help the auctioneer, the sloven does not half know his
      business.

Gentlemen look on this wonder,
Whatever the bids of the bidders they cannot be high enough
      for it,
For it the globe lay preparing quintillions of years without
      one animal or plant,
For it the revolving cycles truly and steadily roll'd.

In this head the all-baffling brain,
In it and below it the makings of heroes.

Examine these limbs, red, black, or white, they are cunning in
      tendon and nerve,
They shall be stript that you may see them.

Exquisite senses, life-lit eyes, pluck, volition,
Flakes of breast-muscle, pliant backbone and neck, flesh not
      flabby, good-sized arms and legs,
And wonders within there yet.

Within there runs blood,
The same old blood! the same red-running blood!
There swells and jets a heart, there all passions, desires,
      reachings, aspirations,
(Do you think they are not there because they are not
      express'd in parlors and lecture-rooms?)

This is not only one man, this the father of those who shall
      be fathers in their turns,
In him the start of populous states and rich republics,
Of him countless immortal lives with countless embodiments
      and enjoyments.

How do you know who shall come from the offspring of his
      offspring through the centuries?
(Who might you find you have come from yourself, if you
      could trace back through the centuries?)

VIII

A woman's body at auction,

She too is not only herself, she is the teeming mother of
    mothers,
She is the bearer of them that shall grow and be mates to the
    mothers.

Have you ever loved the body of a woman?
Have you ever loved the body of a man?
Do you not see that these are exactly the same to all in all
    nations and times all over the earth?

If any thing is sacred the human body is sacred,
And the glory and sweat of a man is the token of manhood
    untainted,
And in man or woman a clean, strong, firm-fibred body, is
    more beautiful than the most beautiful face.

Have you seen the fool that corrupted his own live body? or
    the fool that corrupted her own live body?
For they do not conceal themselves, and cannot conceal
    themselves.

IX
O my body! I dare not desert the likes of you in other men
    and women, nor the likes of the parts of you,
I believe the likes of you are to stand or fall with the likes of
    the soul, (and that they are the soul,)
I believe the likes of you shall stand or fall with my poems, and
    that they are my poems,
Man's, woman's, child's, youth's, wife's, husband's, mother's,
    father's, young man's, young woman's poems,
Head, neck, hair, ears, drop and tympan of the ears,
Eyes, eye-fringes, iris of the eye, eyebrows, and the waking or
    sleeping of the lids,
Mouth, tongue, lips, teeth, roof of the mouth, jaws, and the
    jaw-hinges,
Nose, nostrils of the nose, and the partition,
Cheeks, temples, forehead, chin, throat, back of the neck,
    neck-slue,
Strong shoulders, manly beard, scapula, hind-shoulders, and
    the ample side-round of the chest,
Upper-arm, armpit, elbow-socket, lower-arm, arm-sinews,
    arm-bones,
Wrist and wrist-joints, hand, palm, knuckles, thumb, fore-
    finger, finger-joints, finger-nails,
Broad breast-front, curling hair of the breast, breast-bone,
    breast-side,
Ribs, belly, backbone, joints of the backbone,
Hips, hip-sockets, hip-strength, inward and outward round,
    man-balls, man-root,
Strong set of thighs, well carrying the trunk above,
Leg-fibres, knee, knee-pan, upper-leg, under-leg,
Ankles, instep, foot-ball, toes, toe-joints, the heel;

All attitudes, all the shapeliness, all the belongings of my or
     your body or of any one's body, male or female,
The lung-sponges, the stomach-sac, the bowels sweet and
     clean,
The brain in its folds inside the skull-frame,
Sympathies, heart-valves, palate-valves, sexuality, maternity,
Womanhood and all that is a woman, and the man that comes
     from woman,
The womb, the teats, nipples, breast-milk, tears, laughter,
     weeping, love-looks, love-perturbations and risings,
The voice, articulation, language, whispering, shouting aloud,
Food, drink, pulse, digestion, sweat, sleep, walking, swimming,
Poise on the hips, leaping, reclining, embracing, arm-curving
     and tightening,
The continual changes of the flex of the mouth, and around
     the eyes,
The skin, the sunburnt shade, freckles, hair,
The curious sympathy one feels when feeling with the hand
     the naked meat of the body,
The circling rivers the breath, and breathing it in and out,
The beauty of the waist, and thence of the hips, and thence
     downward toward the knees,
The thin red jellies within you or within me, the bones and
     the marrow in the bones,
The exquisite realization of health;
O I say these are not the parts and poems of the body only,
     but of the soul,
O I say now these are the soul!

Walt Whitman (1819–1892)

CECILY BRENNAN   246

1 February 1994

Dear Ewan, Áine, and Christopher,

Thank you for asking me to contribute to Lifelines. *The poem that I have chosen is by Emily Dickinson.*

Volcanoes be in Sicily
And South America
I judge from my Geography—
Volcanoes nearer here
A Lava step at any time
Am I inclined to climb—
A Crater I may contemplate
Vesuvius at Home.

Emily Dickinson (1830–1886)

In 1989, I travelled to Iceland to paint. I chose Iceland because of its explosive and volcanic landscape and hence its enormous difference to the Irish landscape which we generally view as unchanging. The instability and volatility of the landscape was paralleled for me in physical terms during the pregnancy and birth of my son. I love this poem by Emily Dickinson because what she seems to me to be saying is that while the world is full of strange and awe-inspiring sights and events, you don't have to travel far from home to experience awe and intensity. Good luck with your project.

With best wishes,
Cecily Brennan

JIM KEMMY   247

Dáil Éireann
1 February 1994

Dear Ewan, Áine, and Christopher,

Thank you for your letter and for your kind invitation to contribute to your next edition of Lifelines.

I enclose a copy of my favourite poem, 'Limerick Town' *by John Francis O'Donnell, and my reasons for selecting this poem.*

With best wishes for the success of your next edition of Lifelines.

Yours sincerely,
Ald. Jim Kemmy, TD

John Francis O'Donnell, a journalist and one of the Nation *poets, was born in Limerick in 1837 and died in London in 1874. 'Limerick Town' is a delightful celebration of the sights, sounds and smells of the 'things I long have longed to see' in the city's market-place, as the poet recalled it from his boyhood memories. I often reflect on the last two lines and on the inevitability of life's journey into oblivion for the generality of mankind.*

Limerick Town

Here I've got you, Philip Desmond, standing in the market-place,
'Mid the farmers and the corn sacks, and the hay in either space,
Near the fruit stalls, and the women knitting socks and selling
    lace.

There is High Street up the hillside, twenty shops on either side,
Queer, old-fashioned, dusky High Street, here so narrow, there
    so wide,
Whips and harness, saddles, signboards, hanging out in quiet
    pride.

Up and down the noisy highway, how the market people go!
Country girls in Turkey kerchiefs— poppies moving to and fro—
Frieze-clad fathers, great in buttons, brass and watch seals all
    a-show.

Merry, merry are their voices, Philip Desmond, unto me,
Dear the mellow Munster accent, with its intermittent glee;
Dear the blue cloaks, and the grey coats, things I long have
    longed to see.

Even the curses, adjurations, in my senses sound like rhyme,
And the great, rough-throated laughter of that peasant in his
    prime,
Winking from the grassbound cart-shaft, brings me back the
    other time.

Not a soul, observe you, knows me, not a friend a hand will
    yield,
Would they know, if to the landmarks all around them I
    appealed?
Know me? If I died this minute, dig for me the Potter's Field!

** ** ** **

'Pshaw! you're prosy'. Am I prosy? Mark you then this sunward
    flight:
I have seen this street and roof tops ambered in the morning's
    light,
Golden in the deep of noonday, crimson on the marge of night.

Continents of gorgeous cloudland, argosies of blue and flame,
With the sea-wind's even pressure, o'er this roaring faubourg
    came.
This is fine supernal nonsense. Look, it puts my cheek to shame!

Come, I want a storm of gossip, pleasant jests and ancient chat;
At that dusky doorway yonder my grandfather smoked and sat,
Tendrils of the wind-blown clover sticking in his broad-leafed
    hat.

There he sat and read his paper, Fancy I recall him now!
All the shadow of the house front slanting up from knee to brow;
Critic he of far convulsions, keen-eyed judge of sheep and cow.

** ** ** **

Many a night from race and market down this street six brothers
    strode,
Finer, blighter, truer fellows never barred a country road.
Shouting, wheeling, fighting, scorning watchman's law and
    borough code.

** ** ** **

Rolled the waggons, swore the carters, outside in the crowded
    street,
Horses reared and cattle stumbled, dogs barked high from loads
    of wheat;
But inside the room was pleasant, and the air with thyme was
    sweet.

Others now are in their places, honest folks who know us not;
Do I chafe at the transition? Philip 'tis the common lot —
Do your duty, live your lifetime, say your prayers and be forgot.

John Francis O'Donnell (1837–1874)

HUGO WILLIAMS   248

4 February, 1994

'A Nun Takes the Veil' *by Bernard O'Donoghue from his (first) book*
The Weakness.

*Natural speaking language packed with vivid casual detail and hence
feeling. Brilliant subject — the collision of the old days and the new as
a country girl makes the journey to town to go into a convent and catches
sight as she does so of her first car 'but I couldn't forget/The morning's
vision, and I fell asleep/With the engine, humming through the open
window'.*

*Such a gentle delivery and yet that final image holds so much: the irony
that the vision is not of the Virgin Mary or something, but the 20th
century monster, the automobile. So we hear Yeats humming in the
background: 'A terrible beauty is born'. You feel that the car might have
been a good thing too, so there is terrible sadness lurking, as the girl says
goodbye to the world. The poem has everything, a public and a private
life, each leaning up against the other to make a perfectly satisfying
whole.*

Hugo Williams

A Nun Takes the Veil

That morning early I ran through briars
To catch the calves that were bound for market.
I stopped the once, to watch the sun
Rising over Doolin across the water.

The calves were tethered outside the house
While I had my breakfast: the last one at home
For forty years. I had what I wanted (they said
I could), so we'd loaf bread and Marie biscuits.

We strung the calves behind the boat,
Me keeping clear to protect my style:
Confirmation suit and my patent sandals.
But I trailed my fingers in the cool green water,

Watching the puffins driving homeward
To their nests on Aran. On the Galway mainland
I tiptoed clear of the cow-dunged slipway
And watched my brothers heaving the calves

As they lost their footing. We went in a trap,
Myself and my mother, and I said goodbye
To my father then. The last I saw of him
Was a hat and jacket and a salley stick,

Driving cattle to Ballyvaughan.
He died (they told me) in the county home,
Asking to see me. But that was later:
As we trotted on through the morning mist,

I saw a car for the first time ever,
Hardly seeing it before it vanished.
I couldn't believe it, and I stood up looking
To where I could hear its noise departing

But it was only a glimpse. That night in the convent
The sisters spoilt me, but I couldn't forget
The morning's vision, and I fell asleep
With the engine humming through the open window.

Bernard O'Donoghue (b.1945)

DONALD CAIRD   249

The See House, Dublin 6
4 March 1994

Dear Pupils,

The Archbishop has asked me to thank you for your letter and as requested has pleasure in enclosing his choice of poetry with an accompanying note.

He sends you his very best wishes for the success of this project and looks forward to reading the completed book in due course. With kindest regards,

Yours faithfully,
Helen R O'Neill
Secretary to the Archbishop

My Grief on the Sea

My grief on the sea,
How the waves of it roll!
For they heave between me
And the love of my soul!

Abandoned, forsaken,
To grief and to care,
Will the sea ever waken
Relief from despair?

My grief, and my trouble!
Would he and I were
In the province of Leinster,
Or county of Clare.

Were I and my darling —
Oh, heart-bitter wound! —
On board of the ship
For America bound.

On a green bed of rushes
All last night I lay,
And I flung it abroad
With the heat of the day.

And my love came behind me —
He came from the south;
His breast to my bosom,
His mouth to my mouth.

Translated by Douglas Hyde (1862–1946)

This is a lovely translation of an Irish poem which Douglas Hyde heard spoken by an old woman in the West of Ireland when as a young man he was collecting remnants of Irish poetry before, as he felt, it would disappear and be lost for ever. He catches in this translation exactly both the form and metre of the Irish and also the delicate pathos of the thought and feeling. It encapsulates for me the sense of desolate loneliness felt by a wife or a fiancée left behind in the West of Ireland when circumstances have forced her husband or fiancé to sail to America with all the dangers which that involved at that time and with the strong possibility that they would not see one another again. The sense of desolate loneliness mingled with utter commitment in love must have been a not infrequent experience for many couples in the 18th Century or early 19th Century in Ireland.

The Most Reverend Dr D A R Caird
Archbishop of Dublin

GARRY HYNES   250

Dear Ewan,

The poem I've chosen for Lifelines *is* 'A Woman Dead in her Forties' *by Adrienne Rich.*

Apart from the fact that it is a magnificent collection of poetry the great joy of reading Adrienne Rich's The Fact of a Doorframe Poems Selected and New 1950-1984 *is to witness the maturing of a poet. Her early work is intelligent, formal, controlled. Then as the certainties shift the work reflects this in both form and content.* 'A Woman Dead in Her Forties' *is brutal complex elusive; it haunts me. I read it endlessly.*

Good luck and keep up the good work.
Garry Hynes

A Woman Dead in Her Forties

1
Your breasts/   sliced-off   The scars
dimmed   as they would have to be
years later

All the women I grew up with are sitting
half-naked on rocks   in sun
we look at each other and
are not ashamed

and you too have taken off your blouse
but this was not what you wanted:

to show your scarred, deleted torso

I barely glance at you
as if my look could scald you
though I'm the one who loved you

I want to touch my fingers
to where your breasts had been
but we never did such things

You hadn't thought everyone
would look so perfect
unmutilated

you pull on
your blouse again: stern statement:

There are things I will not share
with everyone

2
You send me back to share
My own scars   first of all
with myself

What did I hide from her
what have I denied her
what losses suffered

how in this ignorant body
did she hide

waiting for her release
till uncontrollable light began to pour

from every wound and suture
and all the sacred openings

3
Wartime.   We sit on warm
weathered, softening grey boards

the ladder glimmers where you told me
the leeches swim

I smell the flame
of kerosene   the pine

boards where we sleep side by side
in narrow cots

the night-meadow exhaling
its darkness   calling

child into woman
child into woman
woman

4
Most of our love from the age of nine
took the form of jokes and mute

loyalty: you fought a girl
who said she'd knock me down

we did each other's homework
wrote letters   kept in touch, untouching

lied about our lives: I wearing
the face of the proper marriage

you the face of the independent woman
We cleaved to each other across that space

fingering webs
of love and estrangement   till the day

the gynecologist touched your breast
and found a palpable hardness

5
You played heroic, necessary
games with death

since in your neo-protestant tribe the void

was supposed not to exist

except as a fashionable concept
you had no traffic with

I wish you were here tonight   I want
to yell at you

Don't accept
Don't give in

But would I be meaning your brave
irreproachable life, you dean of women, or

your unfair, unfashionable, unforgivable
woman's death?

6
You are every woman I ever loved
and disavowed

a bloody incandescent chord strung out
across years, tracts of space

How can I reconcile this passion
with our modesty

your calvinist heritage
my girlhood frozen into forms

how can I go on this mission
without you

you, who might have told me
everything you feel is true?

7
Time after time in dreams you rise
reproachful

once from a wheelchair pushed by your father
across a lethal expressway

Of all my dead it's you
who come to me unfinished

You left me amber beads
strung with turquoise from an Egyptian grave

I wear them wondering
How am I true to you?

I'm half-afraid to write poetry
for you   who never read it much

and I'm left laboring
with the secrets and the silence

in plain language: I never told you how I loved you
we never talked at your deathbed of your death

8
One autumn evening in a train
catching the diamond-flash of sunset

in puddles along the Hudson
I thought: *I understand*

life and death now, the choices
I didn't know your choice

or how by then you had no choice
how the body tells the truth in its rush of cells

Most of our love took the form
of mute loyalty

we never spoke at your deathbed of your death

but from here on
I want more crazy mourning, more howl, more keening

We stayed mute and disloyal
because we were afraid

I would have touched my fingers
to where your breasts had been
but we never did such things

Adrienne Rich (b.1929)

BARRIE COOKE   251

New York

7 February 1994

Dear Ewan, Áine and Christopher,

Thank you for your letter which has been forwarded to me.

I'm delighted to be offered a second chance. I chose a poem for the first Lifelines, *wrote a note about it and then shamefully forgot to post it.*

I'll choose the same poem 'Tyger Tyger Burning Bright' *by William Blake (to my surprise no one else chose it for the first volume).*

Here are some reasons: first of all it has such compression; it sounds as clenched and muscular and fluid as a tiger. It is as ringingly memorable as a nursery rhyme and as apparently simple but full of complication — a lot of matter packed in a small container.

With best wishes toward another odd and wonderful anthology,
Barrie Cooke

The Tyger
from *Songs of Experience*

Tyger! Tyger! burning bright
In the forests of the night,
What immortal hand or eye
Could frame thy fearful symmetry?

In what distant deeps or skies
Burnt the fire of thine eyes?
On what wings dare he aspire?
What the hand dare seize the fire?

And what shoulder, and what art,
Could twist the sinews of thy heart?
And when thy heart began to beat,
What dread hand? and what dread feet?

What the hammer? what the chain?
In what furnace was thy brain?
What the anvil? what dread grasp
Dare its deadly terrors clasp?

When the stars threw down their spears,
And water'd heaven with their tears,
Did he smile his work to see?
Did he who made the Lamb make thee?

Tyger! Tyger! burning bright
In the forests of the night,
What immortal hand or eye,
Dare frame thy fearful symmetry?

William Blake (1757–1827)

MICHÈLE ROBERTS   252

*My favourite poem is impossible to pick out of the many poems I like
and often re-read. One poem I like a lot is the one by Thomas Wyatt
which begins: 'My galley charged with forgetfulness/Thorough sharp
seas in winter nights doth pass' — because it represents the creation of
form and beauty out of chaos and despair.*

Michèle Roberts

Sonnet XIX

My galley charged with forgetfulness
Thorough sharp seas in winter nights doth pass
'Tween rock and rock; and eke mine enemy, alas,
That is my lord, steereth with cruelness;

And every oar a thought in readiness
As though that death were light in such a case.
An endless wind doth tear the sail apace
Of forced sighs and trusty fearfulness.
A rain of tears, a cloud of dark disdain
Hath done the wearied cords great hindrance,
Wreathed with error and eke with ignorance.
The stars be hid that led me to this pain.
Drowned is reason that should me comfort
And I remain despairing of the port.

Thomas Wyatt (?1503–1542)

ROY FOSTER   253

Hertford College, Oxford
26 January 1994

Dear Lifelines,

I hope this is in time: sorry for delay. Keep up the good work.
Yours sincerely,
Roy Foster
Carroll Professor of Irish History, Oxford

Favourites change all the time. It would have to be Yeats (though Louis MacNeice's 'Autumn Journal' *runs him close). While I love the grandeur of* 'Byzantium' *and the historical complexity of* 'Meditations in Time Of Civil War', *at the moment I'm very drawn to the deceptive simplicity of his early lyrics and ballads. I would choose* 'The Fiddler Of Dooney' *for the wonderful Yeatsian music of names, and its subversive twist. Also, my mother (who loved Sligo and Yeats) used to recite it to us when we were small, so it appeals on an irrational level too: as Yeats himself said, you can refute Hegel but not the saint or the song of sixpence.*

The Fiddler of Dooney

When I play on my fiddle in Dooney,
Folk dance like a wave of the sea;
My cousin is priest in Kilvarnet,
My brother in Mocharabuiee.

I passed my brother and cousin:
They read in their books of prayer;
I read in my book of songs
I bought at the Sligo fair.

When we come at the end of time
To Peter sitting in state,
He will smile on the three old spirits,
But call me first through the gate;

For the good are always the merry,
Save by an evil chance,
And the merry love the fiddle,
And the merry love to dance:

And when the folk there spy me,
They will all come up to me,
With 'Here is the fiddler of Dooney!'
And dance like a wave of the sea.

W B Yeats (1865–1939)

DEIRDRE MADDEN   254

22 February 1994

Dear Ewan, Áine and Christopher,

Thank you for your letter. I read and enjoyed earlier Lifelines *anthologies, and I'm happy to contribute to the latest issue.*

My favourite poem is 'Vaucluse', by my husband Harry Clifton. It relates to a time before we were married, when I was spending some months in the south of France, and Harry came out to visit me. We went to Aix-En-Provence together, and to Marseilles. It's a marvellous poem, and it means a great deal to me.

Good luck with 'Lifelines'.

All best wishes,
Deirdre Madden

Vaucluse

Cognac, like a gold sun
Blazed in me, turning
The landscape inside out —
I had left the South
An hour ago, and the train
Through Arles, through Avignon,
Fed on electricity
Overhead, and quickened my mind
With infinite platforms, cypress trees,
Stone villages, the granaries
Of Provence, and I saw again
France, like a blue afternoon
Genius makes hay in, and drink improves —
The worked fields, the yellow sheaves
In shockwaves, perceived
And lit from within, by love.

By then, I suppose,
You had made your own connections,
My chance, eventual girl,
And half Marseilles had closed
For the hot hours — the awnings of cafés
With nothingness in their shadows,
And the drink put away
For another day
Not ours . . . .
           I see, I remember
Coldly now, as I see ourselves
And the merchants from Africa, glozening
Liquor on the shelves
Of celebration, everyone dozing
In transmigratory dreams
Of heroin, garlic, and cloves —
And how we got there, you and I,
By trade route or intuition, seems,
Like charts for sale on the Occident streets
As fabulous, as obsolete
As a map of the known world.

But then again, how kind he was,
The dark *patron* . . . and it lasted,
That shot of cognac,
An hour, till the train
Occluded in grey rain
Above Lyons, and the Rhône Valley
Darkened. I would carry
Your books, your winter clothes
Through stations, streets of Paris
To a cold repose
In the North. We would meet again
In months to come, and years,
Exchanging consciousness, reason and tears
Like beggars. Transfigured,
Not yet fallen from grace
I saw us, not as we are
But new in love, in the hallowed place
Of sources, the sacred fountains
Of Petrarch and René Char.

Harry Clifton (b.1952)

BEN BARNES   255

24 January 1994

Dear Mr Gibson, Ms Jackson and Mr Pillow,

Thank you for the invitation to contribute to the new Lifelines. *I enclose a copy of my favourite poem which was written by Patrick Kavanagh and a few lines, as requested, giving the reasons for my choice.*

May I take this opportunity of wishing you the best of luck with this splendid initiative for a deserving cause.

Yours sincerely,
Ben Barnes

Shancoduff

My black hills have never seen the sun rising,
Eternally they look north towards Armagh.
Lot's wife would not be salt if she had been
Incurious as my black hills that are happy
When dawn whitens Glassdrummond chapel.

My hills hoard the bright shillings of March
While the sun searches in every pocket.
They are my Alps and I have climbed the Matterhorn
With a sheaf of hay for three perishing calves
In the field under the Big Forth of Rocksavage.

The sleety winds fondle the rushy beards of Shancoduff
While the cattle-drovers sheltering in the Featherna Bush
Look up and say: 'Who owns them hungry hills
That the water-hen and snipe must have forsaken?
A poet? Then by heavens he must be poor'.
I hear and is my heart not badly shaken?

Patrick Kavanagh (1904–1967)

Solitary boyhood forays in the foothills of the Blackstairs, poor relations to their mighty Wicklow neighbours. Home, the beloved unsung landscape, always conjured by this elegiac descant to the unspectacular. Friend through the glad days. Talisman in troubled times.

Ben Barnes

DAVID MALOUF   256

Sydney
Australia

Dear Ewan Gibson/Áine Jackson/Christopher Pillow

My favourite poem is 'Frost at Midnight' *by Samuel Taylor Coleridge:*

What I love about this poem is the way it contains in a simple incident, a single moment of vision, all the aspects of our human involvement — in nature, in family and domestic life, in the cosmos, so that a special sort of wholeness and balance is achieved, and the way the 'secret ministry' of the creative process in the poet is made one with the processes of the larger world:— and, since this is poetry, the simple nobility of the language Coleridge finds to embody his vision so richly, so memorably.

Hope this is ok!

With all good wishes,
David Malouf

Frost at Midnight

    The Frost performs its secret ministry,
Unhelped by any wind. The owlet's cry
Came loud — and hark, again! loud as before.
The inmates of my cottage, all at rest,
Have left me to that solitude, which suits
Abstruser musings: save that at my side
My cradled infant slumbers peacefully.
'Tis calm indeed! so calm, that it disturbs
And vexes meditation with its strange
And extreme silentness. Sea, hill, and wood,
This populous village! Sea, and hill, and wood,
With all the numberless goings-on of life,
Inaudible as dreams! the thin blue flame
Lies on my low-burnt fire, and quivers not;
Only that film, which fluttered on the grate,
Still flutters there, the sole unquiet thing.
Methinks its motion in this hush of nature
Gives it dim sympathies with me who live,
Making it a companionable form,
Whose puny flaps and freaks the idling Spirit
By its own moods interprets, everywhere
Echo or mirror seeking of itself,
And makes a toy of Thought.

                    But O! how oft,
How oft, at school, with most believing mind,
Presageful, have I gazed upon the bars,

To watch that fluttering *stranger!* and as oft
With unclosed lids, already had I dreamt
Of my sweet birthplace, and the old church tower,
Whose bells, the poor man's only music, rang
From morn to evening, all the hot fair-day,
So sweetly, that they stirred and haunted me
With a wild pleasure, falling on mine ear
Most like articulate sounds of things to come!
So gazed I, till the soothing things, I dreamt,
Lulled me to sleep, and sleep prolonged my dreams!
And so I brooded all the following morn,
Awed by the stern preceptor's face, mine eye
Fixed with mock study on my swimming book:
Save if the door half opened, and I snatched
A hasty glance, and still my heart leaped up,
For still I hoped to see the *stranger's* face,
Townsman, or aunt, or sister more beloved,
My playmate when we both were clothed alike!

Dear Babe, that sleepest cradled by my side,
Whose gentle breathings, heard in this deep calm,
Fill up the interspersèd vacancies
And momentary pauses of the thought!
My babe so beautiful! it thrills my heart
With tender gladness, thus to look at thee,
And think that thou shalt learn far other lore,
And in far other scenes! For I was reared
In the great city, pent 'mid cloisters dim,
And saw nought lovely but the sky and stars.
But *thou*, my babe! shalt wander like a breeze
By lakes and sandy shores, beneath the crags
Of ancient mountain, and beneath the clouds,
Which image in their bulk both lakes and shores
And mountain crags: so shalt thou see and hear
The lovely shapes and sounds intelligible
Of that eternal language, which thy God
Utters, who from eternity doth teach
Himself in all, and all things in himself.
Great universal Teacher! he shall mold
Thy spirit, and by giving make it ask.

Therefore all seasons shall be sweet to thee,
Whether the summer clothe the general earth
With greenness, or the redbreast sit and sing
Betwixt the tufts of snow on the bare branch
Of mossy apple tree, while the nigh thatch
Smokes in the sun-thaw; whether the eave-drops fall
Heard only in the trances of the blast,
Or if the secret ministry of frost
Shall hang them up in silent icicles,
Quietly shining to the quiet Moon.

Samuel Taylor Coleridge (1772–1834)

MICHAEL COLGAN   257

Gate Theatre

Dear Ewan, Áine and Christopher,

Thank you for yours. Apologies for the delay. The poem is from a series of short poems entitled **Light Music** *by Derek Mahon and is entitled 'Absence'. These six lines are so simple and so heart rending that you know that Mahon is a poet of extraordinary ability. It is short but very powerful and very moving.*

Will this do?

Michael Colgan

Absence
from *Light Music*

I wake at night
in a house white
with moonlight.

Somewhere my son,
his vigour, his laughter;
somewhere my daughter.

Derek Mahon (b.1941)

EITHNE STRONG   258

6 January 1994

Dear Ewan Gibson, Áine Jackson, Christopher Pillow

Thank you for your letter and congratulations on your good work on behalf of the Third World. I am very glad to participate in your next project.

My favourite poem is Shakespeare's Sonnet CXVI 'Let me not to the marriage of true minds . . .'

I choose this, in the first place, for its content: its elliptical wisdom expresses what I consider love to be: a durable abiding attitude, proof against fickleness, emotional upheavals, treachery, time. Then I commend it for its excellence of sonnet form — concise, precise.

Every good luck.

Sincerely,
Eithne Strong

CXVI

Let me not to the marriage of true minds
Admit impediments; love is not love
Which alters when it alteration finds,
Or bends with the remover to remove.
O, no, it is an ever-fixèd mark
That looks on tempests and is never shaken;
It is the star to every wand'ring bark,
Whose worth's unknown, although his height be taken.
Love's not Time's fool, though rosy lips and cheeks
Within his bending sickle's compass come;
Love alters not with his brief hours and weeks,
But bears it out even to the edge of doom.
    If this be error and upon me proved,
    I never writ, nor no man ever loved.

William Shakespeare (1564–1616)

ALLEN GINSBERG   259

New York
9 March 1993

Dear Wesley College Editors:

If a favorite poem by another is requested, put Shelley's 'Hymn to Intellectual Beauty' *among elder poets and/or Blake's* 'Auguries of Innocence'.

Or Gregory Corso's 'The Whole Mess . . . Almost' *from his book* Herald of the Autocthonic Spirit. *This represents the present century.*

I thought about the sublime transcendental penetration of Shelley's yearning for permanent beauty, while flying across America yesterday — and realized how much more permanent his vision was than Matthew Arnold's passing disapproval of Shelley's all too human and altogether appropriate Spiritual ambition.

Blake's poem's full of practical and karmic wisdom.

Corso's poem is a condensation of enormous suffering alchemized into pure wisdom in the open space (Sunyata, or natural emptiness) of human mind.

Yours,
Allen Ginsberg

Hymn to Intellectual Beauty

I

The awful shadow of some unseen Power
    Floats, though unseen, among us; visiting
    This various world with as inconstant wing
As summer winds that creep from flower to flower.
Like moonbeams that behind some piny mountain shower,
    It visits with inconstant glance
    Each human heart and countenance;
    Like hues and harmonies of evening,
      Like clouds in starlight widely spread,
      Like memory of music fled,
      Like aught that for its grace may be
Dear, and yet dearer for its mystery.

II

Spirit of BEAUTY, that dost consecrate
    With thine own hues all thou dost shine upon
    Of human thought or form, where art thou gone?
Why dost thou pass away, and leave our state,
This dim vast vale of tears, vacant and desolate? —
    Ask why the sunlight not for ever
    Weaves rainbows o'er yon mountain river;
    Why aught should fail and fade that once is shown
      Why fear and dream and death and birth
      Cast on the daylight of this earth
      Such gloom; why man has such a scope
For love and hate, despondency and hope!

III

No voice from some sublimer world hath ever
    To sage or poet these reponses given:
    Therefore the names of Demon, Ghost, and Heaven,
    Remain the records of their vain endeavour;
Frail spells, whose uttered charm might not avail to sever,
    From all we hear and all we see,
    Doubt, chance, and mutability.
    Thy light alone, like mist o'er mountains driven,
      Or music by the night-wind sent
      Through strings of some still instrument,
      Or moonlight on a midnight stream,
Gives grace and truth to life's unquiet dream.

IV

Love, hope, and self-esteem, like clouds depart
    And come, for some uncertain moments lent.
    Man were immortal and omnipotent,
    Didst thou, unknown and awful as thou art,
Keep with thy glorious train firm state within his heart.
    Thou messenger of sympathies

That wax and wane in lovers' eyes!
Thou that to human thought art nourishment,
    Like darkness to a dying flame!
    Depart not as thy shadow came:
    Depart not, lest the grave should be,
Like life and fear, a dark reality!

V

While yet a boy, I sought for ghosts, and sped
    Through many a listening chamber, cave, and ruin,
    And starlight wood, with fearful steps pursuing
Hopes of high talk with the departed dead.
I called on poisonous names with which our youth is fed.
    I was not heard, I saw them not;
    When, musing deeply on the lot
Of life, at that sweet time when winds are wooing
    All vital things that wake to bring
    News of birds and blossoming,
    Sudden thy shadow fell on me:—
I shrieked, and clasped my hands in ecstasy!

VI

I vowed that I would dedicate my powers
    To thee and thine: have I not kept the vow?
    With beating heart and streaming eyes, even now
I call the phantoms of a thousand hours
Each from his voiceless grave. They have in visioned bowers
    Of studious zeal or love's delight
    Outwatched with me the envious night:
They know that never joy illumed my brow,
    Unlinked with hope that thou wouldst free
    This world from its dark slavery;
    That thou, O awful Loveliness,
Wouldst give whate'er these words cannot express.

VII

The day becomes more solemn and serene
    When noon is past: there is a harmony
    In autumn, and a lustre in its sky,
Which through the summer is not heard nor seen.
As if it could not be, as if it had not been.
    Thus let thy power, which like the truth
    Of Nature on my passive youth
Descended, to my onward life supply
    Its calm, —to one who worships thee,
    And every form containing thee,
    Whom, Spirit fair, thy spells did bind
To fear himself, and love all humankind.

Percy Bysshe Shelley (1792–1822)

Auguries of Innocence

To see a World in a Grain of Sand
And a Heaven in a Wild Flower,
Hold Infinity in the palm of your hand
And Eternity in an hour.

A Robin Red breast in a Cage
Puts all Heaven in a Rage.
A dove house fill'd with doves & Pigeons
Shudders Hell thro' all its regions.
A dog starv'd at his Master's Gate
Predicts the ruin of the State.
A Horse misus'd upon the Road
Calls to Heaven for Human blood.
Each outcry of the hunted Hare
A fibre from the Brain does tear.
A Skylark wounded in the wing,
A Cherubim does cease to sing.
The Game Cock clip'd & arm'd for fight
Does the Rising Sun affright.
Every Wolf's & Lion's howl
Raises from Hell a Human Soul.
The wild deer, wandr'ing here & there,
Keeps the Human Soul from Care.
The Lamb misus'd breeds Public strife
And yet forgives the Butcher's Knife.
The Bat that flits at close of Eve
Has left the Brain that won't Believe.
The Owl that calls upon the Night
Speaks the Unbeliever's fright.
He who shall hurt the little Wren
Shall never be belov'd by Men.
He who the Ox to wrath has mov'd
Shall never be by Woman lov'd.
The wanton Boy that kills the Fly
Shall feel the Spider's enmity.
He who torments the Chafer's sprite
Weaves a Bower in endless Night.
The Catterpiller on the Leaf
Repeats to thee thy Mother's grief.
Kill not the Moth or Butterfly,
For the Last Judgment draweth nigh.
He who shall train the Horse to War
Shall never pass the Polar Bar.
The Begger's Dog & Widow's Cat,
Feed them & thou wilt grow fat.
The Gnat that sings his Summer's song
Poison gets from Slander's tongue.
The poison of the Snake & Newt

Is the sweat of Envy's Foot.
The Poison of the Honey Bee
Is the Artist's Jealousy.
The Prince's Robes & Beggar's Rags
Are Toadstools on the Miser's Bags.
A truth that's told with bad intent
Beats all the Lies you can invent.
It is right it should be so;
Man was made for Joy & Woe;
And when this we rightly know
Thro' the World we safely go.
Joy & Woe are woven fine,
A Clothing for the Soul divine;
Under every grief & pine
Runs a joy with silken twine.
The Babe is more than swadling Bands;
Throughout all these Human Lands
Tools were made, & Born were hands,
Every Farmer Understands.
Every Tear from Every Eye
Becomes a Babe in Eternity;
This is caught by Females bright
And return'd to its own delight.
The Bleat, the Bark, Bellow & Roar
Are Waves that Beat on Heaven's Shore.
The Babe that weeps the Rod beneath
Writes Revenge in realms of death.
The Beggar's Rags, fluttering in Air,
Does to Rags the Heavens tear.
The Soldier, arm'd with Sword & Gun,
Palsied strikes the Summer's Sun.
The poor Man's Farthing is worth more
Than all the Gold on Afric's Shore.
One Mite wrung from the Lab'rer's hands
Shall buy & sell the Miser's Lands:
Or, if protected from on high,
Does that whole Nation sell & buy.
He who mocks the Infant's Faith
Shall be mock'd in Age & Death.
He who shall teach the Child to Doubt
The rotting Grave shall ne'er get out.
He who respects the Infant's faith
Triumphs over Hell & Death.
The Child's Toys & the Old Man's Reasons
Are the Fruits of the Two seasons.
The Questioner, who sits so sly,
Shall never know how to Reply.
He who replies to words of Doubt
Doth put the Light of Knowledge out.

The Strongest Poison ever known
Came from Caesar's Laurel Crown.
Nought can deform the Human Race
Like to the Armour's iron brace.
When Gold & Gems adorn the Plow
To peaceful Arts shall Envy Bow.
A Riddle or the Cricket's Cry
Is to Doubt a fit Reply.
The Emmet's Inch & Eagle's Mile
Make Lame Philosophy to smile.
He who Doubts from what he sees
Will ne'er Believe, do what you Please.
If the Sun & Moon should doubt,
They'd immediately Go out.
To be in a Passion you Good may do,
But no Good if a Passion is in you.
The Whore & Gambler, by the State
Licenc'd, build that Nation's Fate.
The Harlot's cry from Street to Street
Shall weave Old England's winding Sheet.
The Winner's Shout, the Loser's Curse,
Dance before dead England's Hearse.
Every Night & every Morn
Some to Misery are born.
Every Morn & every Night
Some are Born to sweet delight.
Some are Born to sweet delight,
Some are Born to Endless Night.
We are led to Believe a Lie
When we see not Thro' the Eye
Which was Born in a Night to perish in a Night
When the Soul Slept in Beams of Light.
God Appears & God is Light
To those poor Souls who dwell in Night,
But does a Human Form Display
To those who Dwell in Realms of day.

William Blake (1757–1827)

The Whole Mess... Almost

I ran up six flights of stairs
to my small furnished room
opened the window
and began throwing out
those things most important in life

First to go, Truth, squealing like a fink:
'Don't! I'll tell awful things about you!'
'Oh yeah? Well, I've nothing to hide ... OUT!'

Then went God, glowering & whimpering in amazement:
'It's not my fault! I'm not the cause of it all!' 'OUT!'
Then Love, cooing bribes: 'You'll never know impotency!
All the girls on *Vogue* covers, all yours!'
I pushed her fat ass out and screamed:
'You always end up a bummer!'
I picked up Faith Hope Charity
all three clinging together:
'Without us you'll surely die!'
'With you I'm going nuts! Goodbye!'

Then Beauty . . . ah, Beauty —
As I led her to the window
I told her: 'You I loved best in life
. . . but you're a killer; Beauty kills!'
Not really meaning to drop her
I immediately ran downstairs
getting there just in time to catch her
'You saved me!' she cried
I put her down and told her: 'Move on.'

Went back up those six flights
went to the money
there was no money to throw out.
The only thing left in the room was Death
hiding beneath the kitchen sink:
'I'm not real!' It cried
'I'm just a rumor spread by life . . .'
Laughing I threw it out, kitchen sink and all
and suddenly realized Humor
was all that was left —
All I could do with Humor was to say:
'Out the window with the window!'

Gregory Corso (b.1930)

BIBI BASKIN   260

10 January 1994

Dear Wesley Pupils,

*Thank you for your kind invitation to include me in your very
worthwhile project.*

*I can never tear myself away from the war poems of Siegfried Sassoon.
I believe we need a constant reminder of the ugliness and futility of war.
And yes, despite my profession I do think the lovely evocative images of
poetry do a much better job at it than the quick-flash images of television.*

*I have chosen 'Dead Musicians' because through the medium of music,
which is universal, Sassoon has reminded us that all types of music,*

from that of popular culture to classical, have their merits, thus that snobbery is futile. And then inevitably he reminds us at the end of the poem of the horrors of war, as he does so often and so heart-breakingly.

Maybe that's not what this poem is about at all. But that's what it's about for me.

I wish you every success.

Kind regards,
Bibi
Bibi Baskin (TV Presenter and former teacher of the dreaded Irish language and literature in Wesley College!)

Dead Musicians

I
From you, Beethoven, Bach, Mozart,
    The substance of my dreams took fire.
You built cathedrals in my heart,
    And lit my pinnacled desire.
You were the ardour and the bright
    Procession of my thoughts toward prayer.
You were the wrath of storm, the light
    On distant citadels aflare.

II
Great names, I cannot find you now
    In these loud years of youth that strives
Through doom toward peace: upon my brow
    I wear a wreath of banished lives.
You have no part with lads who fought
    And laughed and suffered at my side.
Your fugues and symphonies have brought
    No memory of my friends who died.

III
For when my brain is on their track,
In slangy speech I call them back.
With fox-trot tunes their ghosts I charm.
'Another little drink won't do us any harm.'
    I think of ragtime; a bit of ragtime;
    And see their faces crowding round
    To the sound of the syncopated beat.
    They've got such jolly things to tell,
    Home from hell with a Blighty wound so neat. . .

And so the song breaks off; and I'm alone.
They're dead . . . For God's sake stop that gramophone.

Limerick, 19 January 1918

Siegfried Sassoon (1886–1967)

JAMIE McKENDRICK   261

28 February 1994

Dear Ewan Gibson, Áine Jackson & Christopher Pillow,

Many thanks for your invitation to the new Lifelines *anthology. I feel very honoured, and I'm sorry for the delay in replying. I hope it isn't too late to send in — a small 'eternity' here too.*

The poem I finally settled for is Emily Dickinson's 'Because I could not stop for Death'.

All best wishes for your anthology.

Yours sincerely,
Jamie McKendrick

Because I could not stop for Death —
He kindly stopped for me —
The Carriage held but just Ourselves —
And Immortality.

We slowly drove — He knew no haste
And I had put away
My labor and my leisure too,
For His Civility —

We passed the School, where Children strove
At Recess — in the Ring —
We passed the Fields of Gazing Grain —
We passed the Setting Sun —

Or rather — He passed Us —
The Dews drew quivering and chill —
For only Gossamer, my Gown —
My Tippet — only Tulle —

We paused before a House that seemed
A Swelling of the Ground —
The Roof was scarcely visible —
The Cornice — in the Ground —

Since then — 'tis Centuries — and yet
Feels shorter than the Day
I first surmised the Horses' Heads
Were toward Eternity —

Emily Dickinson (1830–1886)

What I most admire in this poem is its small compass and enormous span — a curve which links the everyday to forever. Dickinson is one of the few poets who can give an abstraction like 'Eternity' a distinct physical presence. Especially here, where the subject is time.

Rhythmically the poem slows down then breathlessly accelerates time, elongates and foreshortens it, until by the final '—' any conventional idea of duration is in shreds.

Jamie McKendrick

JAMES SCANLON   262

24 February 1994

Dear Áine,

Thank you for your letter.

Da Tagte Es

redeem the surrogate goodbyes
the sheet astream in your hand
who have no more for the land
and the glass unmisted above your eyes

Samuel Beckett (1906–89)

When I heard these four lines for the first time they struck at the very core of my being for I knew then that would be how my father would be found.

May God bless your work.

Thank you
James Scanlon

JOHN QUINN   263

RTE

26 January 1994

Dear Ewan, Áine and Christopher,

Thank you for the honour of inviting me to contribute to Lifelines 2. *I enjoy leafing through the first* Lifelines *and commend your predecessors on their initiative. As to my own selection, I initially thought of choosing something by Kavanagh or Hopkins — but then I remembered the enclosed little poem which I like very much. Let me tell you why.*

Twenty years ago, as editor with an educational publishing company, I compiled a series of English anthologies for senior standards in primary schools. As well as including established poets I was anxious to give a platform to the writing of children of that day. Patricia Heeney was then aged twelve and a pupil of Duleek National School Co. Meath. For me, her poem 'Things I Like' has simplicity, a directness and a freshness that time has not withered. There is the reassurance of the familiar, allied to a natural poetic rhythm. (Where are you now, Patricia? I hope you are still writing . . .)

I hope you and your readers will derive as much pleasure from this poem as I do.

Good luck with Lifelines 2.
John Quinn

Things I Like

Bark of our dog to welcome us home,
Croak of a frog on the commons;
Trot of a horse,
Heather and gorse on Bellewstown hill;
Bleat of a lamb,
Gurgling and laughing of Curleys' baby
In her pram.

Patricia Heeney (born c.1962)

LELAND BARDWELL   264

10 January 1994

'Not Waving But Drowning' *by Stevie Smith*

I have chosen this poem because, as in all Stevie Smith's work, there is the duality of absurdity and pain. These twelve lines, therefore, with their beautiful lyrical quality, epitomise the daftness and trip-wire existence of the poet.

With all good wishes for a successful second edition.

Yours sincerely,
Leland Bardwell

Not Waving But Drowning

Nobody heard him, the dead man,
But still he lay moaning:
I was much further out than you thought
And not waving but drowning.

Poor chap, he always loved larking
And now he's dead
It must have been too cold for him his heart gave way,
They said.

Oh, no no no, it was too cold always
(Still the dead one lay moaning)
I was much too far out all my life
And not waving but drowning.

Stevie Smith (1902–1971)

['Not Waving But Drowning' was also chosen by Sara Berkeley and Glenda
Jackson in *Lifelines*.]

BRIAN KEENAN   265

Dear Friends,

*Please excuse this long delay in replying to your request. I have been
travelling much of late and busy with work.*

*Like most people I have many favourite poems and this changes with
each new collection I read. So here it is for what it's worth, 'Spring in
the City' by Pablo Neruda.*

*I have always been a traveller, always part of me an exile. I know the
streets of which Neruda writes. I have been down them one hundred
thousand times. These streets are metaphorical as well as literal. Like a
wonderful impressionist painting they are closely observed and
sensuous. They pose questions. And they are the eternal questions
loosely grasped at, about identity, place, meaning and purpose.*

*Like a fine work of art, Neruda's poems are simple and direct yet they
hold you, and you re-read them again and again.*

*I have always believed all life is a journey. With Neruda one can travel
into many landscapes. The metaphysical, the existential and the simply
exquisite landscape of Chile and South America.*

Yours,
Brian Keenan

La Primavera Urbana

Se gastó el pavimento hasta no ser
sino una red de sucios agujeros
en que la lluvia acumuló sus lágrimas,
luego llegaba el sol como invasor
sobre el gastado piso
de la ciudad sin fin acribillada
de la que huyeron todos los caballos.
Por fin cayeron algunos limones
y algún vestigio rojo de naranjas

la emparentó con árboles y plumas,
le dio un susurro falso de arboleda
que no duraba mucho,
pero probaba que en alguna parte
se desnudaba entre los azahares
la primavera impúdica y plateada.

Era yo de aquel sitio? De la fría
contextura de muro contra muro?
Pertenecía mi alma a la cerveza?
Eso me preguntaron al salir
y al entrar en mí mismo, al acostarme,
eso me preguntaban las paredes,
la pintura, las moscas, los tapices
pisados tantas veces
por otros habitantes parecidos
a mí hasta confundirse:
tenían mi nariz y mis zapatos,
la misma ropa muerta de tristeza,
las mismas uñas pálidas, prolijas,
y un corazón abierto como un mueble
en que se acumularon los racimos,
los amores, los viajes y la arena,
es decir, todo lo que sucediendo
se va y se queda inexorablemente.

Pablo Neruda (1904–1973)

Spring in the City

The sidewalk has been worn till it is only
a network of dirty holes
in which the tears of the rain gathered;
then came the sun, an invader
over the wasted ground
of the endlessly riddled city
from which all the horses fled.
At last, some lemons fell
and a red vestige of oranges
connected it with trees and feathers,
whispered falsely of orchards
which did not last long
but showed that somewhere
the shameless, silvered spring
was undressing among the orange blossoms.

Was I from that place? From the cold
texture of adjoining walls?
Did my spirit have to do with beer?
They asked me that when I went out,
when I entered myself again, when I went to bed,

they were asking me that, the walls,
the paint, the flies, the carpets
trodden so many times
by other inhabitants
who could be confused with me.
They had my nose and my shoes,
the same dead, sorrowing clothes,
the same pale, neat nails,
and a heart as open as a sideboard
in which accumulated bundles,
loves, journeys, and sand.
That's to say, everything in its happening
goes and stays inexorably.

Translated by Alaistair Reid

NANCY WYNNE-JONES   266

1 February 1994

Dear Ewan, Áine, and Christopher,

Thank you very much for asking me to contribute to the new Lifelines.
My copy of the last one is a treasured bedside companion.

*One of my favourite poems is 'The Skellig Way', by Padraic Fallon, a
great and I think still under-appreciated poet. He was also my
father-in-law. I like the close observation in the poem, and the way the
transcendental is found to be made manifest in the huge unstoppable
energy of nature.*

The whole of Spring is in this short poem.

With very best wishes,
Nancy Wynne-Jones

The Skellig Way

The March crow furnishes his twig
In the knowledge that a bigger bird
Above the blow
Is hatching out the whole raw yolk of spring.

There's no Lent in the twitching rookery;
Pair by pair they go,
Feather to feather married;
Easter the nodal point in earth's revolution.

Listen, you dumb stone faces to the West,
You on Skellig Michael,
White hoods of God,
Hermits abounding in the unseen graces,

Matins, and Lauds and Vespers are sung here
In a loud vernacular
Above the trees;
Can you do better down on your knees?
Padraic Fallon (1905–1974)

EMILY O'REILLY   267

30 January 1994

Dear Ewan, Áine and Christopher,

Thanks for your invitation to contribute to the latest Lifelines. *I bought and loved the last one.*

I have lots of favourite poems; I love 'The Green Eye of the Little Yellow God' *and the* 'Tale of Mad Carew' *because they remind me of long car drives with my father as a child when we four in the back seat were held a captive audience to a circular recitation of them both.*

I love 'Raglan Road' *— plain and unsung; I love especially the titles of Paul Durcan's poems as in* 'On Seeing Two Bus Conductors Kissing Each Other in the Middle of the Street' *or,* 'Making Love outside Áras an Uachtaráin'.

But the poem that maybe moves me most is that one by Seamus Heaney when he is evoking the memory of his mother and the time when she and he peeled potatoes together at the kitchen sink. 'Never closer than at that moment' I think he says in the poem which unfortunately I cannot put my hand to but you should be able to find it without too much difficulty.

I remember moments like that with my own mother; I hope my daughter does the same.

Best wishes for another bestseller,
Emily O'Reilly

from *Clearances* —
a sonnet sequence in memoriam MKH, 1911–1984

When all the others were away at Mass
I was all hers as we peeled potatoes.
They broke the silence, let fall one by one
Like solder weeping off the soldering iron:
Cold comforts set between us, things to share
Gleaming in a bucket of clean water.
And again let fall. Little pleasant splashes
From each other's work would bring us to our senses.

So while the parish priest at her bedside
Went hammer and tongs at the prayers for the dying
And some were responding and some crying
I remembered her head bent towards my head,
Her breath in mine, our fluent dipping knives —
Never closer the whole rest of our lives.

Seamus Heaney (b.1939)

[This sonnet was also chosen by Kathleen Watkins in *Lifelines*.]

DICK SPRING   268

Oifig an Tánaiste agus
an Aire Gnóthaí Eachtracha
(Office of the Tánaiste and
Minister for Foreign Affairs)

7 January 1994

Dear Students,

Thank you for your letter concerning your plans to publish a new edition of Lifelines *in order to raise funds for the developing world. I am very pleased to help you with this and I am enclosing therefore a copy of one of my favourite poems, 'Galvin and Vicars' by Gabriel Fitzmaurice, along with a note on the poem.*

Thank you for writing to me. I wish you every success with this venture.

Yours sincerely,
Dick Spring
Tánaiste and Minister for Foreign Affairs

Galvin and Vicars by Gabriel Fitzmaurice, is one of my favourite poems. It has a particular relevance to our efforts to establish peace on this island and to remove violence from politics.

Galvin and Vicars, two individuals who probably have nothing in common are united in Fitzmaurice's lines — reflecting the irony oft present in Anglo-Irish relations.

Galvin and Vicars

i.m. Mick Galvin, killed in action, Kilmorna, Knockanure (in the parish of Newtown Sandes, now Moyvane) on Thursday, 7 April, 1921; Sir Arthur Vicars, shot at Kilmorna House, his residence, on Thursday, 14 April, 1921.

Mick Galvin, Republican,
Arthur Vicars, who knows what? —
Some sort of loyalist,
In Ireland's name were shot —

Vicars by Republicans,
Galvin by the *Tans*,
Both part of my history —
The parish of Newtown Sandes

Named to flatter landlords
(But 'Moyvane' today,
Though some still call it 'Newtown'):
Some things don't go away

Easily. Galvin and Vicars,
I imagine you as one —
Obverse and reverse
Sundered by the gun.

History demands
We admit each other's wrongs:
Galvin and Vicars,
Joined only in this song,

Nonetheless I join you
In the freedom of this state
For art discovers symmetries
Where politics must wait.

Gabriel Fitzmaurice (b.1952)

MAUREEN GAFFNEY   269

2 March 1994

Dear Ewan, Áine and Christopher,

Thank you for inviting me to contribute to your second Lifelines *book.*

Congratulations on your stunning initiative and energy. I hope this volume will be as big a success as the last.

All good wishes,
Maureen Gaffney

'Martial Cadenza'
The poem I have chosen is 'Martial Cadenza' *by Wallace Stevens, one of the great modern American poets. For me, this poem has an indelible association with a very great and beloved friend, Barry Heffernan, from Shanagarry, near Midleton, Co. Cork, who died tragically in November 1979 at the age of 28. We were friends at that time in our lives when we walked and talked with that peculiar and irresistible intensity of youth and it was he who introduced me to the work of Stevens. For me, this poem gives a vivid presence to that lost time. In the critic Helen Vendler's phrase, it provokes 'a sharp and relieving pang', conjuring up again that time of last protests and affirmations of desire. Time flashes again,*

> . . . 'as if evening found us young, still young,
>   Still walking in a present of our own.'

So Barry, wherever you are in that world without time, this is for you, with love.

Martial Cadenza

I
Only this evening I saw again low in the sky
The evening star, at the beginning of winter, the star
That in spring will crown every western horizon,
Again . . . as if it came back, as if life came back,
Not in a later son, a different daughter, another place,
But as if evening found us young, still young,
Still walking in a present of our own.

II
It was like sudden time in a world without time,
This world, this place, the street in which I was,
Without time: as that which is not has no time,
Is not, or is of what there was, is full
Of the silence before the armies, armies without
Either trumpets or drums, the commanders mute, the arms
On the ground, fixed fast in a profound defeat.

III
What had this star to do with the world it lit,
With the blank skies over England, over France
And above the German camps? It looked apart.
Yet it is this that shall maintain — Itself
Is time, apart from any past, apart
From any future, the ever-living and being,
The ever-breathing and moving, the constant fire,

IV
The present close, the present realized,
Not the symbol but that for which the symbol stands,
The vivid thing in the air that never changes,
Though the air change. Only this evening I saw it again,
At the beginning of winter, and I walked and talked
Again, and lived and was again, and breathed again
And moved again and flashed again, time flashed again.

Wallace Stevens (1879–1955)

WENDELL BERRY   270

31 May 1993

I dislike the suggestion that you ought to have a favorite poem, as if a poet's purpose should be to win the world's championship. Blake said that there is no competition among true poets, and I agree. Some poems are better than others, of course, and some are supreme. But there are many supreme poems, and there is plenty of room for more. Why shouldn't you have several 'favorite poems'?

One of my favorite poems is Spenser's 'Epithalamion'. I name it because it seems to me to make a larger, finer, more sustained music than any other English lyric that I know, and as a statement about its subject of marriage it is wonderfully varied and complete.

Wendell Berry

Epithalamion

Ye learned sisters which have oftentimes
Been to me aiding, others to adorn,
Whom ye thought worthy of your graceful rimes,
That even the greatest did not greatly scorn
To hear their names sung in your simple lays,
But joyed in their praise;
And when ye list your own mishaps to mourn,
Which death, or love, or fortune's wreck did raise,
Your string could soon to sadder tenour turn,
And teach the woods and waters to lament
Your doleful dreariment;
Now lay those sorrowful complaints aside,
And having all your heads with garland crowned,
Help me mine own love's praises to resound,
Ne let the same of any be envied:
So Orpheus did for his own bride,
So I unto myself alone will sing;
The woods shall to me answer and my echo ring.

Early before the world's light-giving lamp
His golden beam upon the hills doth spread,
Having dispersed the night's uncheerful damp,
Do ye awake, and with fresh lustihead
Go to the bower of my beloved love,
My truest turtle dove;
Bid her awake; for Hymen is awake,
And long since ready forth his mask to move,
With his bright tead that flames with many a flake,
And many a bachelor to wait on him,

In their fresh garments trim.
Bid her awake therefore and soon her dight,
For lo! the wished day is come at last,
That shall for all the pains and sorrows past
Pay to her usury of long delight;
And whilst she doth her dight,
Do ye to her of joy and solace sing,
That all the woods may answer and your echo ring.

Bring with you all the nymphs that you can hear
Both of the rivers and the forests green,
And of the sea that neighbours to her near,
All with gay garlands goodly well beseen.
And let them also with them bring in hand
Another gay garland
For my fair love of lilies and of roses,
Bound true-love-wise with a blue silk ribband.
And let them make great store of bridal posies,
And let them eke bring store of other flowers
To deck the bridal bowers.
And let the ground whereas her foot shall tread,
For fear the stones her tender foot should wrong,
Be strewed with fragrant flowers all along,
And diapered like the discoloured mead.
Which done, do at her chamber door await,
For she will waken straight,
The whiles do ye this song unto her sing;
The woods shall to you answer and your echo ring.

Ye nymphs of Mulla, which with careful heed
The silver scaly trouts do tend full well,
And greedy pikes which use therein to feed,
(Those trouts and pikes all others do excel)
And ye likewise which keep the rushy lake,
Where none do fishes take,
Bind up the locks the which hang scattered light,
And in his waters, which your mirror make,
Behold your faces as the crystal bright,
That when you come whereas my love doth lie,
No blemish she may spy.
And eke ye lightfoot maids which keep the deer,
That on the hoary mountain use to tower,
And the wild wolves, which seek them to devour,
With your steel darts do chase from coming near,
Be also present here,
To help to deck her and to help to sing,
That all the woods may answer and your echo ring.

Wake now, my love, awake; for it is time.
The rosy morn long since left Tithones bed,
All ready to her silver coach to climb,
And Phoebus 'gins to shew his glorious head.

Hark how the cheerful birds do chant their lays
And carol of love's praise.
The merry lark her matins sings aloft,
The thrush replies, the mavis descant plays,
The ouzel shrills, the ruddock warbles soft,
So goodly all agree with sweet consent,
To this day's merriment.
Ah! my dear love, why do ye sleep thus long,
When meeter were that ye should now awake,
T' await the coming of your joyous make,
And harken to the birds' love-learned song,
The dewy leaves among?
For they of joy and pleasance to you sing,
That all the woods them answer and their echo ring.

My love is now awake out of her dream,
And her fair eyes, like stars that dimmed were
With darksome cloud, now shew their goodly beams
More bright than Hesperus his head doth rear.
Come now ye damsels, daughters of delight,
Help quickly her to dight,
But first come ye, fair hours, which were begot
In love's sweet paradise, of day and night,
Which do the seasons of the year allot,
And all that ever in this world is fair
Do make and still repair.
And ye three handmaids of the Cyprian queen,
The which do still adorn her beauty's pride,
Help to adorn my beautifullest bride;
And as ye her array, still throw between
Some graces to be seen,
And as ye use to Venus, to her sing,
The whiles the woods shall answer and your echo ring.

Now is my love all ready forth to come;
Let all the virgins therefore well await,
And ye fresh boys that tend upon her groom
Prepare yourselves; for he is coming straight.
Set all your things in seemly good array
Fit for so joyful day,
The joyful'st day that ever sun did see.
Fair sun, shew forth thy favourable ray,
And let thy lifeful heat not fervent be,
For fear of burning her sunshiny face,
Her beauty to disgrace.
O fairest Phoebus, father of the Muse,
If ever I did honour thee aright,
Or sing the thing, that mote thy mind delight,
Do not thy servant's simple boon refuse,
But let this day, let this one day, be mine,
Let all the rest be thine.

Then I thy sovereign praises loud will sing,
That all the woods shall answer and their echo ring.

Hark how the minstrels 'gin to shrill aloud
Their merry music that resounds from far,
The pipe, the tabor, and the trembling crowd,
That well agree withouten breach or jar.
But most of all the damsels do delight,
When they their timbrels smite,
And thereunto do dance and carol sweet,
That all the senses they do ravish quite,
The whiles the boys run up and down the street,
Crying aloud with strong confused noise,
As if it were one voice.
Hymen, Io Hymen, Hymen, they do shout,
That even to the heavens their shouting shrill
Doth reach, and all the firmament doth fill,
To which the people standing all about,
As in approvance do thereto applaud
And loud advance her laud,
And evermore they Hymen, Hymen, sing,
That all the woods them answer and their echo ring.

Lo! where she comes along with portly pace
Like Phoebe from her chamber of the east,
Arising forth to run her mighty race,
Clad all in white, that seems a virgin best.
So well it her beseems that ye would ween
Some angel she had been.
Her long loose yellow locks like golden wire,
Sprinkled with pearl, and pearling flowers a-tween,
Do like a golden mantle her attire,
And being crowned with a garland green,
Seem like some maiden queen.
Her modest eyes abashed to behold
So many gazers, as on her do stare,
Upon the lowly ground affixed are.
Ne dare lift up her countenance too bold,
But blush to hear her praises sung so loud,
So far from being proud.
Nathless do ye still loud her praises sing,
That all the woods may answer and your echo ring.

Tell me, ye merchants' daughters, did ye see
So fair a creature in your town before,
So sweet, so lovely, and so mild as she,
Adorned with beauty's grace and virtue's store?
Her goodly eyes like sapphires shining bright,
Her forehead ivory white,
Her cheeks like apples which the sun hath rudded,
Her lips like cherries charming men to bite,
Her breast like to a bowl of cream uncrudded,

Her paps like lilies budded,
Her snowy neck like to a marble tower,
And all her body like a palace fair,
Ascending up with many a stately stair,
To honour's seat and chastity's sweet bower.
Why stand ye still, ye virgins, in amaze,
Upon her so to gaze,
Whiles ye forget your former lay to sing,
To which the woods did answer and your echo ring?

But if ye saw that which no eyes can see,
The inward beauty of her lively spright,
Garnished with heavenly gifts of high degree,
Much more then would ye wonder at that sight,
And stand astonished like to those which read
Medusa's mazeful head.
There dwells sweet love and constant chastity,
Unspotted faith and comely womanhood,
Regard of honour and mild modesty;
There virtue reigns as queen in royal throne,
And giveth laws alone,
The which the base affections do obey,
And yield their services unto her will;
Ne thought of thing uncomely ever may
Thereto approach to tempt her mind to ill.
Had ye once seen these her celestial treasures,
And unrevealed pleasures,
Then would ye wonder and her praises sing,
That all the woods should answer and your echo ring.

Open the temple gates unto my love,
Open them wide that she may enter in,
And all the posts adorn as doth behove,
And all the pillars deck with garlands trim,
For to receive this saint with honour due,
That cometh in to you.
With trembling steps and humble reverence,
She cometh in, before th' Almighty's view.
Of her ye virgins learn obedience,
When so ye come into those holy places,
To humble your proud faces:
Bring her up to th' high altar, that she may
The sacred ceremonies there partake,
The which do endless matrimony make,
And let the roaring organs loudly play
The praises of the Lord in lively notes,
The whiles with hollow throats
The choristers the joyous anthem sing,
That all the woods may answer and their echo ring.

Behold whiles she before the altar stands,
Hearing the holy priest that to her speaks

And blesseth her with his two happy hands,
How the red roses flush up in her cheeks,
And the pure snow with goodly vermeil stain,
Like crimson dyed in grain,
That even th' angels which continually
About the sacred altar do remain,
Forget their service and about her fly,
Oft peeping in her face that seems more fair,
The more they on it stare.
But her sad eyes, still fastened on the ground,
Are governed with goodly modesty,
That suffers not one look to glance awry,
Which may let in a little thought unsound.
Why blush ye, love, to give to me your hand,
The pledge of all our band?
Sing, ye sweet angels, Alleluia sing,
That all the woods may answer and your echo ring.

Now all is done; bring home the bride again,
Bring home the triumph of our victory,
Bring home with you the glory of her gain,
With joyance bring her and with jollity.
Never had man more joyful day than this,
Whom heaven would heap with bliss.
Make feast therefore now all this live-long day,
This day for ever to me holy is;
Pour out the wine without restraint or stay,
Pour not by cups, but by the bellyful,
Pour out to all that wull,
And sprinkle all the posts and walls with wine,
That they may sweat, and drunken be withal.
Crown ye god Bacchus with a coronal,
And Hymen also crown with wreaths of vine,
And let the Graces dance unto the rest;
For they can do it best:
The whiles the maidens do their carol sing,
To which the woods shall answer and their echo ring.

Ring ye the bells, ye young men of the town,
And leave your wonted labours for this day:
This day is holy; do ye write it down,
That ye for ever it remember may.
This day the sun is in his chiefest height,
With Barnaby the bright,
From whence declining daily by degrees,
He somewhat loseth of his heat and light,
When once the Crab behind his back he sees.
But for this time it ill ordained was,
To choose the longest day in all the year,
And shortest night, when longest fitter were:
Yet never day so long, but late would pass.

Ring ye the bells, to make it wear away,
And bonfires make all day,
And dance about them, and about them sing,
That all the woods may answer, and your echo ring.

Ah! when will this long weary day have end,
And lend me leave to come unto my love?
How slowly do the hours their numbers spend!
How slowly does sad Time his feathers move!
Haste thee, O fairest planet, to thy home
Within the western foam;
Thy tired steeds long since have need of rest.
Long though it be, at last I see it gloom,
And the bright evening star with golden crest
Appear out of the east.
Fair child of beauty, glorious lamp of love,
That all the host of heaven in ranks dost lead,
And guidest lovers through the nightes dread,
How cheerfully thou lookest from above,
And seem'st to laugh atween thy twinkling light,
As joying in the sight
Of these glad many which for joy do sing,
That all the woods them answer and their echo ring.

Now cease, ye damsels, your delights forepast;
Enough is it, that all the day was yours.
Now day is done, and night is nighing fast;
Now bring the bride into the bridal bowers.
Now night is come, now soon her disarray,
And in her bed her lay;
Lay her in lilies and in violets,
And silken curtains over her display,
And odoured sheets, and Arras coverlets.
Behold how goodly my fair love does lie
In proud humility;
Like unto Maia, when as Jove her took,
In Tempe, lying on the flowery grass,
'Twixt sleep and wake, after she weary was,
With bathing in the Acidalian brook.
Now it is night, ye damsels may be gone,
And leave my love alone,
And leave likewise your former lay to sing;
The woods no more shall answer, nor your echo ring.

Now welcome, night, thou night so long expected,
That long day's labour dost at last defray,
And all my cares, which cruel love collected,
Hast summed in one, and cancelled for aye:
Spread thy broad wing over my love and me,
That no man may us see,
And in thy sable mantle us enwrap,
From fear of peril and foul horror free.

Let no false treason seek us to entrap,
Nor any dread disquiet once annoy
The safety of our joy:
But let the night be calm and quietsome,
Without tempestuous storms or sad affray;
Like as when Jove with fair Alcmena lay,
When he begot the great Tirynthian groom;
Or like as when he with thyself did lie,
And begot majesty.
And let the maids and young men cease to sing;
Ne let the woods them answer, nor their echo ring.

Let no lamenting cries, nor doleful tears,
Be heard all night within nor yet without;
Ne let false whispers, breeding hidden fears,
Break gentle sleep with misconceived doubt.
Let no deluding dreams nor dreadful sights
Make sudden sad affrights;
Ne let housefires, nor lightning's helpless harms,
Ne let the Puck, nor other evil sprights,
Ne let mischievous witches with their charms,
Ne let hobgoblins, names whose sense we see not,
Fray us with things that be not.
Let not the screech owl, nor the stork be heard;
Nor the night raven that still deadly yells,
Nor damned ghosts called up with mighty spells,
Nor grisly vultures make us once affeared:
Ne let th' unpleasant quire of frogs still croaking
Make us to wish their choking.
Let none of these their dreary accents sing;
Ne let the woods them answer, nor their echo ring.

But let still silence true night watches keep,
That sacred peace may in assurance reign,
And timely sleep, when it is time to sleep,
May pour his limbs forth on your pleasant plain,
The whiles an hundred little winged loves,
Like divers feathered doves,
Shall fly and flutter round about your bed,
And in the secret dark, that none reproves,
Their pretty stealths shall work, and snares shall spread
To filch away sweet snatches of delight,
Concealed through covert night.
Ye sons of Venus, play your sports at will,
For greedy pleasure, careless of your toys,
Thinks more upon her paradise of joys,
Than what ye do, albeit good or ill.
All night therefore attend your merry play,
For it will soon be day:
Now none doth hinder you, that say or sing;
Ne will the woods now answer, nor your echo ring.

Who is the same, which at my window peeps,
Or whose is that fair face, that shines so bright?
Is it not Cynthia, she that never sleeps,
But walks about high heaven all the night?
O fairest goddess, do thou not envy
My love with me to spy;
For thou likewise didst love, though now unthought,
And for a fleece of wool, which privily
The Latmian shepherd once unto thee brought,
His pleasures with thee wrought.
Therefore to us be favourable now;
And sith of women's labours thou hast charge,
And generation goodly dost enlarge,
Incline thy will t'effect our wishful vow,
And the chaste womb inform with timely seed,
That may our comfort breed:
Till which we cease our hopeful hap to sing:
Ne let the woods us answer, nor our echo ring.

And thou great Juno, which with awful might
The laws of wedlock still dost patronize,
And the religion of the faith first plight
With sacred rites hast taught to solemnize,
And eke for comfort often called art
Of women in their smart,
Eternally bind thou this lovely band,
And all thy blessings unto us impart.
And thou glad Genius, in whose gentle hand
The bridal bower and genial bed remain,
Without blemish or stain,
And the sweet pleasures of their love's delight
With secret aid dost succour and supply,
Till they bring forth the fruitful progeny,
Send us the timely fruit of this same night.
And thou fair Hebe, and thou Hymen free,
Grant that it may so be.
Till which we cease your further praise to sing;
Ne any woods shall answer, nor your echo ring.

And ye high heavens, the temple of the gods,
In which a thousand torches flaming bright
Do burn, that to us wretched earthly clods
In dreadful darkness lend desired light;
And all ye powers which in the same remain,
More than we men can feign,
Pour out your blessing on us plenteously,
And happy influence upon us rain,
That we may raise a large posterity,
Which from the earth, which they may long possess,
With lasting happiness,

Up to your haughty palaces may mount,
And for the guerdon of their glorious merit
May heavenly tabernacles there inherit,
Of blessed saints for to increase the count.
So let us rest, sweet love, in hope of this,
And cease till then our timely joys to sing;
The woods no more us answer, nor our echo ring.

Song, made in lieu of many ornaments,
With which my love should duly have been decked,
Which cutting off through hasty accidents,
Ye would not stay your due time to expect,
But promised both to recompense,
Be unto her a goodly ornament,
And for short time an endless monument.

Edmund Spenser (?1552–1599)

BRIAN P KENNEDY   271

The National Gallery of Ireland

22 March 1994

Dear Ewan, Áine and Christopher,

Congratulations on your efforts to continue the success of Lifelines *with another book of poems.*

I have chosen a poem from Paul Durcan's new collection Give Me Your Hand. *It is called 'A Cornfield with Cypresses'.*

Every good wish for a successful publication and thank you for inviting me to participate in it.

Yours sincerely,
Brian Kennedy
Assistant Director

Just as life is always changing, so one's likes and dislikes can change. Therefore, I have chosen my favourite poem of the moment, conscious that it joins a long list of previous 'favourites'. Paul Durcan knows well what Jack Yeats knew: 'All painting to be painting must be poetry and all poetry must be painting'. In his collections Crazy about Women *and* Give Me Your Hand, *Durcan demonstrates his love for paintings and in 'A Cornfield with Cypresses', he offers a salutary lesson to art historians who fail to focus primarily on the act of looking.*

A Cornfield with Cypresses
after van Gogh

Let me make no bones about 'A Cornfield with Cypresses' —
Make clear straightaway who I am.
I am the painter's mother.
I am old, frail, quivering on my pins,
My trees almost leafless
Being stripped into senility.
But I have still got enough leaves to be able to see
My son's picture for what it is —
The serenest canvas I have ever seen.
(That's saying something
Because my son painted a great many
Serene canvases.)

So why am I so hot under the bra?
(Yes, the bra, I still wear bras
For old times' sake. I am old fashioned.)
I am sore and vexed because the art historian says
That Vincent's 'A Cornfield with Cypresses'
Is evidence of an unbalanced mind.
Poppycock.
Oh I am sure that the art historian
Is a nice little man somewhere
In the lobes of Hampstead
Tending his own poppies, tending his own cocks.
But I do wish that he would look at my son's picture.
Is that too much to ask?
That the art historian might—might—might—might—might
Look at the picture?

I am Vincent's mother
Come to heal the wounds of art history
So smile a little and let me touch you
And as you gaze into the cornfield
You will find yourself
At the heart of the megalotropolis of London
Sitting still and being calm and seeing
In the skies — as my son saw in the skies —
The soul of tiger.
If you look long enough you might even hear a fieldmouse
Piping: Nought sad about death.

Paul Durcan (b.1944)

PENELOPE LEACH   272

7 February 1994

Dear Mr Gibson,

Thank you for writing to me and for giving me the opportunity to contribute to Lifelines.

The Poem I choose is 'Ash Wednesday' *by T S Eliot.*

> Because I know that time is always time
> And place is always and only place
> And what is actual is actual only for one time
> And only for one place
> I rejoice that things are as they are. . .

Apart from being a poem I love, 'Ash Wednesday' *seems to me to speak directly to cross-cultural research and work with children. It is a salutary reminder that however hard we try, we can never hope to understand other times, places or people but only to respect them.*

Best wishes for the project.

Yours sincerely,
Penelope Leach
PhD, C Psychol, FBPsS

Ash Wednesday

I
Because I do not hope to turn again
Because I do not hope
Because I do not hope to turn
Desiring this man's gift and that man's scope
I no longer strive to strive towards such things
(Why should the agèd eagle stretch its wings?)
Why should I mourn
The vanished power of the usual reign?

Because I do not hope to know again
The infirm glory of the positive hour
Because I do not think
Because I know I shall not know
The one veritable transitory power
Because I cannot drink
There, where trees flower, and springs flow, for there is
    nothing again

Because I know that time is always time
And place is always and only place

And what is actual is actual only for one time
And only for one place
I rejoice that things are as they are and
I renounce the blessèd face
And renounce the voice
Because I cannot hope to turn again
Consequently I rejoice, having to construct something
Upon which to rejoice

And pray to God to have mercy upon us
And I pray that I may forget
These matters that with myself I too much discuss
Too much explain
Because I do not hope to turn again
Let these words answer
For what is done, not to be done again
May the judgement not be too heavy upon us

Because these wings are no longer wings to fly
But merely vans to beat the air
The air which is now thoroughly small and dry
Smaller and dryer than the will
Teach us to care and not to care
Teach us to sit still.

Pray for us sinners now and at the hour of our death
Pray for us now and at the hour of our death.

II
Lady, three white leopards sat under a juniper-tree
In the cool of the day, having fed to satiety
On my legs my heart my liver and that which had been
        contained
In the hollow round of my skull. And God said
Shall these bones live? shall these
Bones live? And that which had been contained
In the bones (which were already dry) said chirping:
Because of the goodness of this Lady
And because of her loveliness, and because
She honours the Virgin in meditation,
We shine with brightness. And I who am here dissembled
Proffer my deeds to oblivion, and my love
To the posterity of the desert and the fruit of the gourd.
It is this which recovers
My guts the strings of my eyes and the indigestible portions
Which the leopards reject. The Lady is withdrawn
In a white gown, to contemplation, in a white gown.
Let the whiteness of bones atone to forgetfulness.
There is no life in them. As I am forgotten
And would be forgotten, so I would forget
Thus devoted, concentrated in purpose. And God said

Prophesy to the wind, to the wind only for only
The wind will listen. And the bones sang chirping
With the burden of the grasshopper, saying

Lady of silences
Calm and distressed
Torn and most whole
Rose of memory
Rose of forgetfulness
Exhausted and life-giving
Worried reposeful
The single Rose
Is now the Garden
Where all loves end
Terminate torment
Of love unsatisfied
The greater torment
Of love satisfied
End of the endless
Journey to no end
Conclusion of all that
Is inconclusible
Speech without word and
Word of no speech
Grace to the Mother
For the Garden
Where all love ends.

Under a juniper-tree the bones sang, scattered and shining
We are glad to be scattered, we did little good to each other,
Under a tree in the cool of the day, with the blessing of sand,
Forgetting themselves and each other, united
In the quiet of the desert. This is the land which ye
Shall divide by lot. And neither division nor unity
Matters. This is the land. We have our inheritance.

III
At the first turning of the second stair
I turned and saw below
The same shape twisted on the banister
Under the vapour in the fetid air
Struggling with the devil of the stairs who wears
The deceitful face of hope and of despair.

At the second turning of the second stair
I left them twisting, turning below;
There were no more faces and the stair was dark,
Damp, jaggèd, like an old man's mouth drivelling, beyond
     repair,
Or the toothed gullet of an agèd shark.

At the first turning of the third stair
Was a slotted window bellied like the fig's fruit

And beyond the hawthorn blossom and a pasture scene
The broadbacked figure drest in blue and green
Enchanted the maytime with an antique flute.
Blown hair is sweet, brown hair over the mouth blown,
Lilac and brown hair;
Distraction, music of the flute, stops and steps of the mind over
    the third stair,
Fading, fading; strength beyond hope and despair
Climbing the third stair.

Lord, I am not worthy
Lord, I am not worthy
        but speak the word only.

IV
Who walked between the violet and the violet
Who walked between
The various ranks of varied green
Going in white and blue, in Mary's colour,
Talking of trivial things
In ignorance and in knowledge of eternal dolour
Who moved among the others as they walked,
Who then made strong the fountains and made fresh the
    springs

Made cool the dry rock and made firm the sand
In blue of larkspur, blue of Mary's colour,
Sovegna vos

Here are the years that walk between, bearing
Away the fiddles and the flutes, restoring
One who moves in the time between sleep and waking,
    wearing

White light folded, sheathed about her, folded.
The new years walk, restoring
Through a bright cloud of tears, the years, restoring
With a new verse the ancient rhyme. Redeem
The time. Redeem
The unread vision in the higher dream
While jewelled unicorns draw by the gilded hearse.

The silent sister veiled in white and blue
Between the yews, behind the garden god,
Whose flute is breathless, bent her head and signed but spoke
    no word

But the fountain sprang up and the bird sang down
Redeem the time, redeem the dream
The token of the word unheard, unspoken

Till the wind shake a thousand whispers from the yew

And after this our exile

V

If the lost word is lost, if the spent word is spent
If the unheard, unspoken
Word is unspoken, unheard;
Still is the unspoken word, the Word unheard,
The Word without a word, the Word within
The world and for the world;
And the light shone in darkness and
Against the Word the unstilled world still whirled
About the centre of the silent Word.

    O my people, what have I done unto thee.

Where shall the word be found, where will the word
Resound? Not here, there is not enough silence
Not on the sea or on the islands, not
On the mainland, in the desert or the rain land,
For those who walk in darkness
Both in the day time and in the night time
The right time and the right place are not here
No place of grace for those who avoid the face
No time to rejoice for those who walk among noise and deny
    the voice

Will the veiled sister pray for
Those who walk in darkness, who chose thee and oppose thee,
Those who are torn on the horn between season and season,
    time and time, between
Hour and hour, word and word, power and power, those who
    wait
In darkness? Will the veiled sister pray
For children at the gate
Who will not go away and cannot pray:
Pray for those who chose and oppose

    O my people, what have I done unto thee.

Will the veiled sister between the slender
Yew trees pray for those who offend her
And are terrified and cannot surrender
And affirm before the world and deny between the rocks
In the last desert between the last blue rocks
The desert in the garden the garden in the desert
Of drouth, spitting from the mouth the withered apple-seed.

    O my people.

VI

Although I do not hope to turn again
Although I do not hope
Although I do not hope to turn

Wavering between the profit and the loss
In this brief transit where the dreams cross

The dreamcrossed twilight between birth and dying
(Bless me father) though I do not wish to wish these things
From the wide window towards the granite shore
The white sails still fly seaward, seaward flying
Unbroken wings

And the lost heart stiffens and rejoices
In the lost lilac and the lost sea voices
And the weak spirit quickens to rebel
For the bent golden-rod and the lost sea smell
Quickens to recover
The cry of quail and the whirling plover
And the blind eye creates
The empty forms between the ivory gates
And smell renews the salt savour of the sandy earth

This is the time of tension between dying and birth
The place of solitude where three dreams cross
Between blue rocks
But when the voices shaken from the yew-tree drift away
Let the other yew be shaken and reply.
Blessèd sister, holy mother, spirit of the fountain, spirit of the
    garden,
Suffer us not to mock ourselves with falsehood
Teach us to care and not to care
Teach us to sit still
Even among these rocks,
Our peace in His will

And even among these rocks
Sister, mother
And spirit of the river, spirit of the sea,
Suffer me not to be separated

And let my cry come unto Thee.
T S Eliot (1888–1965)

BRENDAN O'REILLY   273

RTE Sport

7 February 1994

Dear Áine, Christopher and Ewan,

Thank you for inviting me to submit my favourite poem to Lifelines *in aid of your Third World project. Unfortunately your request comes at a time when I'm between houses and all my books are in storage, so, I'll select from the two poems that remain longest and most accurately in my memory, the two which, I suppose, adhere most readily to my own particular psyche — Yeats's 'The Second Coming' and Wordsworth's*

'The World is Too Much with Us', *and since Yeats has already been selected in the first book I give you Wordsworth:*

The World is Too Much with Us

The world is too much with us; late and soon,
Getting and spending, we lay waste our powers:
Little we see in Nature that is ours;
We have given our hearts away, a sordid boon!
This Sea that bares her bosom to the moon;
The winds that will be howling at all hours,
And are up-gathered now like sleeping flowers;
For this, for everything, we are out of tune;
It moves us not.—Great God! I'd rather be
A Pagan suckled in a creed outworn;
So might I, standing on this pleasant lea,
Have glimpses that would make me less forlorn;
Have sight of Proteus rising from the sea;
Or hear old Triton blow his wreathèd horn.

William Wordsworth (1770–1850)

Good luck with the project.

Yours sincerely,
Brendan O'Reilly

KEVIN BARRY   274

Department of English
University College Galway

10 January 1994

Dear Ewan, Áine and Christopher,

Thank you for your note. I wish your new anthology all the best. The poem I have selected is 'A Disused Shed in County Wexford' by Derek Mahon. Born in Belfast in 1941 Mahon has become one of Ireland's most respected poets of the 20th century. I choose 'A Disused Shed in County Wexford' because of its objective beauty. The poem has extraordinary scope. Its title remembers a shed which had first been imagined in J. G. Farrell's comic colonial novel, Troubles. *Its rhythms remember W H Auden's* 'In Memory of Sigmund Freud'. *Its narrative remembers the innumerable and, therefore, the unnameable dead. The poem is about being almost forgotten. The resources of hope are asserted in its first lines with scepticism. Its last lines do not let us, its anonymous readers, off the hook.*

Best Wishes,
Kevin
Professor Kevin Barry

A Disused Shed in Co. Wexford

Let them not forget us, the weak souls among the asphodels.
— Seferis, *Mythistorema*

For J G Farrell

Even now there are places where a thought might grow—
Peruvian mines, worked out and abandoned
To a slow clock of condensation,
An echo trapped for ever, and a flutter
Of wild-flowers in the lift-shaft,
Indian compounds where the wind dances
And a door bangs with diminished confidence,
Lime crevices behind rippling rain-barrels,
Dog corners for bone burials;
And in a disused shed in Co. Wexford,

Deep in the grounds of a burnt-out hotel,
Among the bathtubs and the washbasins
A thousand mushrooms crowd to a keyhole.
This is the one star in their firmament
Or frames a star within a star.
What should they do there but desire?
So many days beyond the rhododendrons
With the world waltzing in its bowl of cloud,
They have learnt patience and silence
Listening to the rooks querulous in the high wood.

They have been waiting for us in a foetor
Of vegetable sweat since civil war days,
Since the gravel-crunching, interminable departure
Of the expropriated mycologist.
He never came back, and light since then
Is a keyhole rusting gently after rain.
Spiders have spun, flies dusted to mildew
And once a day, perhaps, they have heard something —
A trickle of masonry, a shout from the blue
Or a lorry changing gear at the end of the lane.

There have been deaths, the pale flesh flaking
Into the earth that nourished it;
And nightmares, born of these and the grim
Dominion of stale air and rank moisture.
Those nearest the door grow strong —
'Elbow room! Elbow room!'
The rest, dim in a twilight of crumbling
Utensils and broken pitchers, groaning
For their deliverance, have been so long
Expectant that there is left only the posture.

A half century, without visitors, in the dark —
Poor preparation for the cracking lock
And creak of hinges. Magi, moonmen,
Powdery prisoners of the old regime,
Web-throated, stalked like triffids, racked by drought
And insomnia, only the ghost of a scream
At the flash-bulb firing-squad we wake them with
Shows there is life yet in their feverish forms.
Grown beyond nature now, soft food for worms,
They lift frail heads in gravity and good faith.

They are begging us, you see, in their wordless way,
To do something, to speak on their behalf
Or at least not to close the door again.
Lost people of Treblinka and Pompeii!
'Save us, save us,' they seem to say,
'Let the god not abandon us
Who have come so far in darkness and in pain.
We too had our lives to live.
You with your light meter and relaxed itinerary,
Let not our naive labours have been in vain!'

Derek Mahon (b.1941)

['A Disused Shed in Co. Wexford' was also chosen by
Seamus Deane in *Lifelines*.]

JAMES HANLEY   275

1 February 1994

Dear Ewan, Áine and Christopher,

*Many thanks for your kind invitation to nominate my favourite poem
for your forthcoming publication. I am delighted to accept your offer,
and I congratulate your efforts for such an interesting project and
towards such a worthwhile end.*

*I have many favourite poems and it was difficult to select one that would
be of real interest to a reader of the collection. Many of the poems I
considered would be too well known, or at least the poets involved would
be too well known.*

*I decided therefore to select a poem by Oliver Dunne, a young poet and
friend of mine. We went to University together and since then Oliver
has pursued post-graduate work, written reviews and published his own
poetry. His unique style and quirky black humour appeals to me, and is
not unlike a thread of humour that runs through my own work.*

I wish you all the best of luck with Lifelines *and hope that it will be a
success.*

Yours sincerely,
James Hanley

Uh-Oh

(The last words spoken by the captain of the spaceship Challenger)

uh-oh
he said

they were
at
the pinnacle
of human
achievement

they wore
white space-suits

he had talked
to
the president
on the
telephone
the day before

little boys
played with
models
of their
spaceship

they were headed
straight up

he had kissed
his girl-friend
the night before

tired his mind
on other things

she touched
his tense muscles

'it's just a job
to those guys'

his mother couldn't
think of what
to give him

settled on
home-made jam
for his wife

it was a life
he hadn't
really chosen

he had just
over-achieved

what had the
president
said?

his wife asked

oh, i don't know

it wasn't like
they were going
to the moon

that had been
done
already

good luck, i suppose

good luck
yes
that was probably it

that was probably
what the president
had said

words to that effect

and now the little
meter
had gone red
all of a sudden
and there was
nothing he could do

no split-second
decision

taken out
of his hands

just a little
surprised

that the routine
should be
interrupted
like that

Oliver Dunne (b.1961)

I like this poem because knowing Oliver I can relate to his quirky vision
of life. It is not dissimilar to a thread of black humour that is in my own
painting. The simplicity of the language and its easy flow mocks the

grandeur of the event without offending the victims. The arrogance so often close to achievement is exposed as pure folly. The flight had become routine. All that sophistication could not compensate for human error. The banality of the President's words, for me, sums up the feeling that tragedy is soon forgotten. Myths collapse. It's yesterday's news. Life goes on.

James Hanley

SIOBHÁN CLEARY   276

Dear Ewan, Áine, and Christopher,

Thank you for asking me to choose my favourite poem. I hope this is in time for your deadline, and that the book is a great success for you, for those who will benefit from the proceeds, and for everyone who reads it.

Some years ago I interviewed Roger McGough on television and really enjoyed meeting him. 'Conservation Piece' was one of the poems he read on the programme. It appeals to me for lots of reasons. I think it's clever, funny, direct, unpretentious, honest.

As a devoted fan of the great indoors, I can relate to every word of every line. I wish I had written this poem.

With best wishes,
Siobhán Cleary

Conservation Piece

The countryside must be preserved!
(Preferably miles away from me.)
Neat hectares of the stuff reserved
For those in need of flower or tree.

I'll make do with landscape painting
Film documentaries on TV
And when I need to escape, panting,
Then open-mouthed I'll head for the sea.

Let others stroll and take their leisure,
In grasses wade up to their knees,
For I derive no earthly pleasure
From the green green rash that makes me sneeze.

Roger McGough (b.1937)

TED HUGHES   277

Dear Lifelines,

Since I let my mail grow in a corner, like a mutant mushroom that I daren't eat, often I don't see for a long time what comes when I'm away. Forgive me for this delay in answering your letter.

I expect I'm too late. Maybe not.

My favourite poem is 'Donal Og' in Lady Gregory's translation. Why is this my favourite? I think no short poem has ever hit me so hard, or stayed with me so closely.

There's my reason why.

All my best to you.
Ted Hughes

Donal Og

It is late last night the dog was speaking of you;
the snipe was speaking of you in her deep marsh.
It is you are the lonely bird through the woods;
and that you may be without a mate until you find me.

You promised me, and you said a lie to me,
that you would be before me where the sheep are flocked;
I gave a whistle and three hundred cries to you,
and I found nothing there but a bleating lamb.

You promised me a thing that was hard for you,
a ship of gold under a silver mast;
twelve towns with a market in all of them,
and a fine white court by the side of the sea.

You promised me a thing that is not possible,
that you would give me gloves of the skin of a fish;
that you would give me shoes of the skin of a bird;
and a suit of the dearest silk in Ireland.

When I go by myself to the Well of Loneliness,
I sit down and I go through my trouble;
when I see the world and do not see my boy,
he that has an amber shade in his hair.

It was on that Sunday I gave my love to you;
the Sunday that is last before Easter Sunday.
And myself on my knees reading the Passion;
and my two eyes giving love to you for ever.

My mother said to me not to be talking with you today,
or tomorrow, or on the Sunday;
it was a bad time she took for telling me that;
it was shutting the door after the house was robbed.

My heart is as black as the blackness of the sloe,
or as the black coal that is on the smith's forge;
or as the sole of a shoe left in white halls;
it was you put that darkness over my life.

You have taken the east from me; you have taken the west from
    me;
you have taken what is before me and what is behind me;
you have taken the moon, you have taken the sun from me;
and my fear is great that you have taken God from me!

Anonymous
From the Irish (translated by Lady Augusta Gregory)

ROBERT PINSKY   278

10 March 1993

Dear Ewan Gibson, Áine Jackson and Christopher Pillow:

*Thanks for your letter about your planned anthology. Good luck to you
in this excellent project.*

Sincerely,
Robert Pinsky

On 'Sailing to Byzantium'

*Difficult though it is for me to choose one poem as a favourite, my choice
seems clear:* 'Sailing to Byzantium' *by William Butler Yeats.*

*It is a great poem, but many of my reasons for choosing it are personal,
even coincidental. It happens to be the first poem of its caliber that I
recognized with an inner conviction, and the first that I got by heart.
Also, when I ask myself about the poem's central place for me, it seems
obvious that I must have been attracted by the way it implies a definition
of my vocation, the study and pursuit of poetry. The poem associates the
art of poetry not only with music, the art I strove to master before I made
a lifework of poetry, but also with certain arts of the hand:
mosaic-making and a kind of jeweler's tinkering, efforts to make
something beautiful by hammering and assembling many different
pieces, a kind of undertaking that I think has had some kind of special
appeal for me. I think that the poem's idea of poetry as musical, historical,
and involving a kind of improvisatory skill — the inventive fitting
together of disparate pieces to create something that has pattern or
animation — appeals to me quite apart from any glorification of poetry.*

*But I do have to admit that the glorification has appealed to me, too: the
heroic and possibly extravagant terms in which Yeats beseeches the help
of his singing masters — 'Consume my heart away; sick with
desire/And fastened to a dying animal/It knows not what it is' —*

continue to move me, continue to express a tremendous reality. These lines present the glory of struggle, however: of effort rooted in desperate yearning. The poem's title denotes a process.

It occurs to me that a still more personal reason for my particular attachment to this poem, out of so many that I revere, may be that unlike other profound works by, for instance, George Herbert, John Donne or Gerard Manley Hopkins, 'Sailing to Byzantium' stands somewhat apart from or beyond Christianity: reading it, I need not feel any sharpening of my sense that the poems I love best, and the language to which I devote my life, are somehow divided from me, or less mine to love, simply because they are Christian, while I — a pagan humanist raised as an Orthodox Jew — am not Christian. Perhaps Yeats's 'holy city,' being at least half pagan, has represented for me a kind of holiness to which I have felt intuitively welcome. Byzantium represents a spiritual force not as secular as that in great poems by Keats or Stevens. In Yeats's words and images I sensed at once, before I learned anything about his ideas — some of them perhaps foolish in themselves — the vision of a spiritual reality that includes historical religion, but reaches beyond it. That inclusion, and that reaching, continue to have a powerful significance for me.

When I was seventeen I typed out the words of 'Sailing to Byzantium' and stuck the page on my kitchen wall, above the toaster. Now many years later my thoughts about poetry still return often to such phrases as 'the artifice of eternity,' or 'Whatever is begotten, born, and dies' or that other triad, 'Of what is past, or passing, or to come.' And in such thoughts, or on a more mundane level whenever I think about my profession of teaching writing and literature, I come inevitably to the words 'Nor is there singing school but studying/Monuments of its own magnificence.' The principle in these lines — that one learns by paying close attention to the most magnificent, enduring models to be found — is endlessly humbling and inspiring.

Robert Pinsky

Sailing to Byzantium

I
That is no country for old men. The young
In one another's arms, birds in the trees,
— Those dying generations — at their song,
The salmon-falls, the mackerel-crowded seas,
Fish, flesh, or fowl, commend all summer long
Whatever is begotten, born, and dies.
Caught in that sensual music all neglect
Monuments of unageing intellect.

II
An aged man is but a paltry thing,
A tattered coat upon a stick, unless
Soul clap its hands and sing, and louder sing
For every tatter in its mortal dress,
Nor is there singing school but studying
Monuments of its own magnificence;
And therefore I have sailed the seas and come
To the holy city of Byzantium.

III
O sages standing in God's holy fire
As in the gold mosaic of a wall,
Come from the holy fire, perne in a gyre,
And be the singing-masters of my soul.
Consume my heart away; sick with desire
And fastened to a dying animal
It knows not what it is; and gather me
Into the artifice of eternity.

IV
Once out of nature I shall never take
My bodily form from any natural thing,
But such a form as Grecian goldsmiths make
Of hammered gold and gold enamelling
To keep a drowsy Emperor awake;
Or set upon a golden bough to sing
To lords and ladies of Byzantium
Of what is past, or passing, or to come.

William Butler Yeats (1865–1939)

['Sailing to Byzantium' was also chosen by John Montague in *Lifelines*.]

MADELEINE KEANE   279

Dear Ewan, Áine and Christopher,

One of my favourite poems is Raymond Carver's 'Late Fragment'.

I love it because for me, it encapsulates what people search for all their lives, namely the secret of life.

And for me the secret of life is loving and being loved, something your wonderful and worthwhile project is all about.

Yours sincerely,
Madeleine Keane

JO SLADE   280

8 February 1994

Dear Áine, Ewan and Christopher,

I am delighted to send you a copy of my favourite poem as requested. I have had many favourite poems at different times of my life. At this particular time this short poem by Raymond Carver called 'Late Fragment' seems to express one common desire of all people, to be loved.

Thank you for asking me to contribute to Lifelines *and good luck with your very worthy project.*

Kind regards,
Jo Slade

Late Fragment

And did you get what
you wanted from this life, even so?
I did.
And what did you want?
To call myself beloved, to feel myself
beloved on the earth.

Raymond Carver (1939–1988)

ART SPIEGELMAN   281

New York

25 April 1993

Dear Lifelines,

I've always been a sucker for Edgar Allan Poe and have had a lifelong fondness for 'Bells,' the poem that Max Eastman, in Enjoyment of Laughter *described as 'so patently artificial as serious poetry that a question has arisen whether Poe himself was not fooling . . . Taken seriously it is bad. But playfully it might be very good.'*

I dunno if the distinction between Poe's seriousness and playfulness is that important; I know that the clanging repetitions ('Keeping time, time, time/In a sort of Runic rhyme') have bonged their way deep into my brain. And the word 'tintinnabulation' was seemingly built expressly for this poem. Maybe 'Bells' is a cartoon of a poem, going right for the rhythmic essence of what a poem really is, a kind of synesthesic word music.

I remember, back in 1978, sitting on a broken down couch in
Shakespeare's bookshop, in Paris, reading this poem to Françoise shortly
after I met her, when her command of English was still wobbly, and her
delight in the sounds. Not too long after that we hooked up for life, to
the jingling and tinkling of wedding bells, bells, bells, bells, bells, bells,
bells — to the rhyming and the chiming of the bells.

All the best with your project.
art spiegelman

The Bells

I
    Hear the sledges with the bells —
        Silver bells!
What a world of merriment their melody foretells!
    How they tinkle, tinkle, tinkle,
      In the icy air of night!
    While the stars that oversprinkle
    All the heavens seem to twinkle
        With a crystalline delight;
    Keeping time, time, time,
    In a sort of Runic rhyme,
To the tintinnabulation that so musically wells
    From the bells, bells, bells, bells,
        Bells, bells, bells —
From the jingling and the tinkling of the bells.

II
    Hear the mellow wedding bells,
      Golden bells!
What a world of happiness their harmony foretells!
    Through the balmy air of night
    How they ring out their delight!
      From the molten-golden notes,
        And all in tune,
      What a liquid ditty floats
To the turtle-dove that listens, while she gloats
        On the moon!
    Oh, from out the sounding cells
What a gush of euphony voluminously wells!
        How it swells!
        How it dwells
      On the Future! how it tells
      Of the rapture that impels
    To the swinging and the ringing
      Of the bells, bells, bells,
    Of the bells, bells, bells, bells,
        Bells, bells, bells —
To the rhyming and the chiming of the bells!

III
> Hear the loud alarum bells —
>> Brazen bells!
> What a tale of terror, now, their turbulency tells!
>> In the startled ear of night
>> How they scream out their affright!
>>> Too much horrified to speak,
>>> They can only shriek, shriek,
>>>> Out of tune,
> In a clamorous appealing to the mercy of the fire,
> In a mad expostulation with the deaf and frantic fire,
>>> Leaping higher, higher, higher,
>>> With a desperate desire,
>> And a resolute endeavor
>> Now—now to sit, or never,
> By the side of the pale-faced moon.
>> Oh, the bells, bells, bells!
>> What a tale their terror tells
>>> Of despair!
>> How they clang, and clash, and roar!
>> What a horror they outpour
> On the bosom of the palpitating air!
>> Yet the ear it fully knows,
>>> By the twanging,
>>> And the clanging,
>> How the danger ebbs and flows;
> Yet the ear distinctly tells,
>>> In the jangling,
>>> And the wrangling,
>> How the danger sinks and swells,
> By the sinking or the swelling in the anger of the bells—
>>> Of the bells—
>> Of the bells, bells, bells, bells,
>>> Bells, bells, bells—
> In the clamor and the clangor of the bells!

IV
> Hear the tolling of the bells—
>> Iron bells!
> What a world of solemn thought their melody compels!
>> In the silence of the night,
>> How we shiver with affright
> At the melancholy menace of their tone!
>> For every sound that floats
>> From the rust within their throats
>>> Is a groan.
>> And the people—ah, the people—
>> They that dwell up in the steeple,
>>> All alone,
>> And who tolling, tolling, tolling,

In that muffled monotone,
Feel a glory in so rolling
   On the human heart a stone—
They are neither man nor woman—
They are neither brute nor human—
   They are Ghouls:
And their king it is who tolls;
And he rolls, rolls, rolls,
      Rolls
   A pæan from the bells!
And his merry bosom swells
   With the pæan of the bells!
And he dances, and he yells;
Keeping time, time, time,
In a sort of Runic rhyme,
   To the pæan of the bells—
      Of the bells:
Keeping time, time, time,
In a sort of Runic rhyme,
   To the throbbing of the bells—
Of the bells, bells, bells—
   To the sobbing of the bells;
Keeping time, time, time,
   As he knells, knells, knells,
In a happy Runic rhyme,
   To the rolling of the bells—
Of the bells, bells, bells —
   To the tolling of the bells,
Of the bells, bells, bells, bells—
     Bells, bells, bells—
To the moaning and the groaning of the bells.

Edgar Allan Poe (1809–1849)

LIZ McMANUS   282

Dáil Éireann
28 January 1994

Dear Ewan, Áine and Christopher,

I chose the poem 'Prayer' by Carol Ann Duffy because it is written about moments that we all experience in daily life. These moments are hard to define. They touch our memory and our imagination and remind us of our universal humanity. I often read this poem. Like the moments themselves, Prayer *is powerful enough to stop me in my tracks.*

I wish you all the very best with your anthology Lifelines. *It is a wonderful project and I hope that you are as successful as you were the last time.*

Good luck with the project.

Yours sincerely,
Liz
Cllr Liz McManus, TD
Democratic Left

Prayer

Some days, although we cannot pray, a prayer
utters itself. So, a woman will lift
her head from the sieve of her hands and stare
at the minims sung by a tree, a sudden gift.

Some nights, although we are faithless, the truth
enters our hearts, that small familiar pain;
then a man will stand stock-still, hearing his youth
in the distant Latin chanting of a train.

Pray for us now. Grade I piano scales
console the lodger looking out across
a Midlands town. Then dusk, and someone calls
a child's name as though they named their loss.

Darkness outside. Inside, the radio's prayer —
Rockall. Malin. Dogger. Finisterre.

Carol Ann Duffy (b.1955)

BRIAN D'ARCY 283

8 February 1994

Dear Ewan, Áine and Christopher,

Thank you very much indeed for the kind invitation to contribute to the next edition of Lifelines.

I think it's a wonderful idea and may I congratulate you on your past successes. I think it is excellent that you have raised so much for such a worthy charity. Well done.

I have chosen an unusual poem, it's called 'Over The Hollow Land'. It's by Edna St Vincent Millay.

I love this poem because of its simplicity, the tangible images it evokes, the beauty of nature, the need for tender stewardship of natural resources and how Love is in all things beautiful.

It's one of those poems which has to be read aloud to capture its stillness. I hope this is suitable.

God bless for now.

Yours sincerely,
Brian D'Arcy
Fr Brian D'Arcy, CP

Over the Hollow Land
from *To Elinor Wylie*

VI
Over the hollow land the nightingale
Sang out in the full moonlight.
'Immortal bird,'
We said, who heard;
'What rapture, what serene despair';
And paused between a question and reply
To hear his varied song across the tulip-scented air.

But I thought of the small brown bird among the
    rhododendrons at the garden's end,
Crouching close to the bough,
Pale cheek wherefrom the black magnificent eye obliquely
    stared,
The great song boiling in the narrow throat
And the beak near splitting,
A small bird hunched and frail,
Whom the divine uncompromising note that brought the
    world to its window
Shook from head to tail.

Close to the branch, I thought, he cowers now,
Lest his own passion shake him from the bough.

Thinking of him, I thought of you . . .
Shaken from the bough, and the pure song half-way through.
Edna St Vincent Millay (1892–1950)

ÉAMON de BUITLÉAR   284

19 March 1994

Dear Ewan, Áine and Christopher,

Congratulations on deciding to publish another edition of Lifelines. *Not
alone are you helping a very worthy cause in gathering money for the
Third World, you are also going to learn a great deal about poetry. I am
sure that the skills gained in putting the project together for publication
will also be a very worthwhile experience.*

The Poem I have chosen is from Tom Kinsella's A Selected Life.
*Although it contains only nine lines, it is a very graphic description of
the late Seán Ó Riada playing the bodhrán. During the very early sixties,
Ó Riada formed his own folk-orchestra Ceoltóirí Chualann and this was
to change forever the style of music being played by traditional groups
in Ireland. It was from this group that the Chieftains were later to
emerge.*

I was a founder member of Ceoltóirí Chualann and I remember Tom Kinsella sitting in on many of those early rehearsals in Seán Ó Riada's house in Galloping Green, Co. Dublin. Little did I realize that years later some of those sessions would come to life in Kinsella's poetry. Where the poet says, — 'He stared to one side towards the others', *he is referring to Seán directing the musicians while at the same time playing the bodhrán. Every time I read this poem I can see and hear Seán Ó Riada!*

I am sending you also 'An Droighneán Donn', *The Dark Thorn Tree. In Seán Ó Tuama's* Poems of the Dispossessed *it is listed as folk poetry and I have heard it sung to a number of airs in different Gaeltachts. Seán Ó Riada gave a very fine Munster version of this piece of music to Ceoltóirí Chualann.*

Very sincerely,
Éamon de Buitléar

Galloping Green: May 1962
from *A Selected Life*

He clutched the shallow drum
and crouched forward, thin
as a beast of prey. The shirt
stretched at his waist. He stared
to one side, toward the others,
and struck the skin cruelly
with his nails. Sharp
as the answering arid bark
his head quivered, counting.

Thomas Kinsella (b.1928)

An Droighneán Donn

Shílfeadh aon fhear gur dil dó féin mé nuair a luíonn dom
    mionn
's go dtéann dhá dtrian síos díom nuair a smaoiním ar do
    chomhrá liom —
sneachta síobtha 's é á shíorchur faoi Shliabh Uí Fhloinn;
's go bhfuil mo ghrá-sa mar bhláth na n-airní atá ar an
    droighneán donn.

Shíl mé féin nach ag ceasacht spré orm a rachadh grá mo
    chroí
's nach bhfágfadh sé ina dhiaidh mé mar gheall ar
    mhaoin;
fa-raoir géar nach bhfuilim féin 's an fear a chráigh mo
    chroí
i ngleanntán sléibhe i bhfad ó éinneach 's an drúcht 'na
    luí

Tá féirín le mo chéadsearc i mo phóca thíos
is fearaibh Éireann ní leigheasfaidís mo bhrón
       fa-raoir;
nuair a smaoinímse ar a chúrsaí 's a chúl breá donn
bím ag géarghol os íseal 's ag osnaíl go trom.

Go bhfaighe mé féirín lá an aonaigh ó mo bhuachaill
       deas,
is comhrá séimhí 'na dhéidh sin ó phlúr na bhfear;
fa-raoir géar nach bhfuileam féin is an sagart 'nár
       gcionn
go ndúblaímis ár gcúrsaí sul fá dtéid sé anonn.

Pé 'narbh olc leis é, molfaidh mise grá mo chroí,
is pé 'narbh olc leis é, suífidh mé lena thaoibh,
is pé 'narbh olc leis é, míle arraing trí lár a chroí;
's a réalta an tsolais i mbéal an phobail, is tú a bhreoigh
       mo chroí.

'S a Dhia dhílis, céard a dhéanfas mé má imíonn tú uaim?—
níl eolas chun do thí agam, chun do thine ná do chlúid;
tá mo mháithrín faoi leatrom is m'athair san uaigh,
tá mo mhuintir go mór i bhfeirg liom is mo ghrá i bhfad
       uaim.

Tá smúid ar mo shúile 's níor chodail mé néal
ach ag smaoineamh ortsa, a chéadghrá, má b'fhada an
       oíche aréir.
Faoi do chúrsaí do dhiúltaigh mé an domhan go léir,
's a chraobh chumhra cad as a dtabharfá do leabhar i
       mbréig?

Is fear gan chéill a bheadh ag dréim leis an gclaí a bhíonn
       ard,
is claí beag íseal lena thaoibh sin ar a leagfadh sé a lámh;
cé gur ard an crann cárthainn bíonn sé searbh 'na bharr
's go bhfásann sméara is sú craobh ar an gcrann is ísle
       bláth.

Dhá chéad slán is duit a bhéarfainn, a mhíle grá;
's ó lucht na mbréag ní maith fhéadaim do thaobhacht
       d'fháil;
níl coite agam a chuirfinn i do dhiaidh ná bád
's go bhfuil an fharraige ina lán mara romham is nach eol
       dom snámh.

The Dark Thorn Tree

A man imagines that I'm devoted when he swears his vow;
two parts in three die when I remember your talk with me
— the driven snow for ever falling on Sliabh Uí Fhloinn.
O my beloved is like sloe-blossom on the dark thorn tree!

I thought my heart's love would not go whining about a
    dowry
and would not leave me forsaken ever on account of wealth,
It is bitter pity that I'm not with him who has vexed my heart,
in a mountain valley, away from everyone, and the dew lying.

Down in my pocket I have a present from my first-beloved:
no man in Ireland can ever remedy my grief, alas.
When I remember his way of going and his fine brown hair
bitterly I cry, and quietly, and heave a sigh.

Next market day I would like a present from my lovely boy,
and gentle converse to follow after with my flower of men.
It is bitter pity we are not together with the priest before us
to join together our double fortune ere he goes abroad.

Who'er condemn it, I'll utter praise of my heart's love.
Who'er condemn it, myself I'll settle down by his side.
Who'er condemn it, a thousand arrows through his heart's
    core!
O star of knowledge among these people, you have seared my
    heart.

And O dear God what will I do if you go and leave me?
I do not know the way to your home or your hearth or bed.
My mother dear, she is afflicted, and my father's in the grave.
Much angered at me are all my people, and my love far off.

Upon my eyes there is a shadow, and I have not slept
for thinking of you, my first-beloved, all last night long.
On your account I have rejected the world entire:
my fragrant branch, o what possessed you to swear untruly?

A foolish man will take to climbing the higher ditch
when there beside him is a little low ditch to rest his hand on.
The mountain ash is a lofty tree but its fruit is bitter:
while blackberries and raspberries grow on the bush of the
    lowliest blossom.

Two hundred farewells I would bid you, love thousandfold!
I cannot well, with these lying gossips, depend upon you.
I have no skiff to chase you in, nor any boat,
the sea is full-tide and runs against me, and I cannot swim.

Translated by Thomas Kinsella

GWEN O'DOWD   285

30 March 1994

Dear Ewan, Áine and Christopher,

I am sending this poem 'Chicory, Chicory Dock' *written by my father for inclusion in* Lifelines. *One of many he wrote during his life-time for the various literary competitions he entered in the* Irish Times, Dublin Opinion *and many other publications over the years. I certainly think it's a very entertaining piece and sound advice for any perplexed gardeners. The best of luck with your project, I hope you get a very healthy response.*

Best wishes,
Gwen O'Dowd

Chicory Chicory Dock

I am an expert on all kinds of weeds
From common types to more exotic breeds,
Because my garden's full of every sort
From nettles to plantain and swallow-wort.
A creeping thing called bindweed chokes my plants
And even fruit trees if it gets the chance —
Its proper name's *convolvulus arvensis*
And it's a thing would drive you from your senses.
I dig and pull and spray and hoe
But still the damn things thrive and grow.

On television I see lawns being laid
And manicured to each obedient blade
With never once a single weed in sight
And so I'm left with thinking I'm not right.
My lawn is hardly what you'd call first-class —
It's mostly weeds with an odd patch of grass.
Although I conscientiously comply
With what the seedsman's packets specify,
And listen to the best of counsel,
I end up with a load of groundsel.

Goutweed, goosegrass, dock and thistles spread
Where I should have fine fruit and flowers instead
And where asparagus and peas I nourish,
It's only dandelions and spurge that flourish.
I once tried sowing seeds the wrong way up,
And got a crop of creeping buttercup.
My wife came out and looked at this and said
'That comes from standing Nature on its head.'

She said she'd like some cherry trees,
But then she's very hard to please.

Take berries (rasp or straw or even goose) —
I plant them and protect them from abuse,
But creepy greeny things with long tap roots
Come up in Spring and smother all the shoots.
And every year I fight an endless battle
With charlock, melilot and yellow rattle.
But now I've got a plot, that is to say,
A plan that came to me the other day.
This brilliant thought to me occurred,
Though you may think it quite absurd.

It seemed to me, or so at least I reasoned,
That nobody could keep a garden decent
By sowing, hoeing, spraying every Spring,
When there before my eyes, the very thing
Was at my feet and underneath my nose:
The thing, no matter what, that always grows.
Weeds never wither, wilt nor even wane
Though bruised and battered time and time again.
And so my weeds I'll cultivate
And grow to love the things I hate.

I'll root out all the dahlias and clematis
And give the lowly weed a higher status.
Out go potatoes, cabbages and peas
And in come dock and others as I please.
With vigour I'll uproot herbaceous borders
And fill the space with twitch till further orders.
I'll cut down apple trees without remorse,
And maybe plant a bush or two of gorse.
And very happy we will be,
My wife, my weedery and me.

'Come see my garden, Maud,' I'll proudly say,
(Maud's not her name but that is by the way.)
'Here's shepherd's purse and coltsfoot and some twitch
And buttonweed transplanted from a ditch.
And see the moss — it's full of scores and scores
Of very busy hard to get at spores,
And over here we've chickweed and fat hen,
(I think we'll call this part the Poultry Pen.)
And here's a thing I grew from seed,
It is a very weedy weed.'

So never more I'll need to hoe and mow,
But merely stand and watch my garden grow,
With just the odd dig at my scutch and such,
But I won't have to labour over much.
And people from all parts will come to see

What can be done with weedy husbandry.
But if I find that too much cultivation
Breeds in my weeds ideas above their station
And leaves them free to grow or not,
I'll concrete in the whole damn lot.

Frank O'Dowd (1921–1991)

BRIAN BOYDELL   286

24 January 1994

Dear Ewan, Áine and Christopher,

When asked to name my favourite poem, musical composition or composer, I find it impossible to give a simple reply. My taste changes with the passing of time, and with changes of mood. I cannot therefore name 'my favourite poem'. The answer might well be different tomorrow, or next year, or from what I might have named a decade ago.

The poetry of W B Yeats has however remained very special for me for as long as sixty years. It evokes the timeless magic of the Irish landscape which has inspired so much of my music.

The three early poems of Yeats which have constantly held a special place in my mind have all been firmly implanted through musical settings: the first I have set myself, the other two are included in Peter Warlock's wonderfully moving song-cycle entitled 'The Curlew'.

With best wishes,
Brian Boydell

He Wishes for the Cloths of Heaven

Had I the heavens' embroidered cloths,
Enwrought with golden and silver light,
The blue and the dim and the dark cloths
Of night and light and the half-light,
I would spread the cloths under your feet:
But I, being poor, have only my dreams;
I have spread my dreams under your feet;
Tread softly because you tread on my dreams.

He Reproves the Curlew

O Curlew, cry no more in the air,
Or only to the water in the West;
Because your crying brings to my mind
Passion-dimmed eyes and long heavy hair
That was shaken out over my breast:
There is enough evil in the crying of wind.

The Withering of the Boughs

I cried when the moon was murmuring to the birds:
'Let peewit call and curlew cry where they will,
I long for your merry and tender and pitiful words,
For the roads are unending, and there is no place to my
    mind.'
The honey-pale moon lay low on the sleepy hill,
And I fell asleep upon lonely Echtge of streams.
No boughs have withered because of the wintry wind;
The boughs have withered because I have told them my dreams.

I know of the leafy paths that the witches take
Who come with their crowns of pearl and their spindles
    of wool,
And their secret smile, out of the depths of the lake;
I know where a dim moon drifts, where the Danaan
    kind
Wind and unwind their dances when the light grows
    cool
On the island lawns, their feet where the pale foam
    gleams.
No boughs have withered because of the wintry wind;
The boughs have withered because I have told them my dreams.

I know of the sleepy country, where swans fly round
Coupled with golden chains, and sing as they fly.
A king and a queen are wandering there, and the sound
Has made them so happy and hopeless, so deaf and so
    blind
With wisdom, they wander till all the years have gone
    by;
I know, and the curlew and peewit on Echtge of
    streams.
No boughs have withered because of the wintry wind;
The boughs have withered because I have told them my dreams.

W B Yeats (1865–1939)

DENIS BROWN   287

10 February 1994

My favourite poem?

Well, first I looked to Tennyson, whose sheer drama of sound and poetic craftsmanship, I thought, more than compensate any disinclination of his to push beyond the accepted values of his day. I surprised myself with this thought, as in visual art (my own and that of others) I look for some broader significance beyond the aesthetic — some message which at its best will change our way of looking at/thinking about something. In this respect Tennyson loses marks. For while he wrapped ideas in a cloak of the most magnificent cloth, the ideas themselves were accepted and understood before Tennyson's superb re-packaging.

Notwithstanding, Tennyson's poems maintain a power and integrity which speak to me. However, in the end I decided to choose some Shakespeare: King Lear, Act III, Scene ii, ll.1-9 and 14-24.

I have sketched the first line in calligraphy for you. If you wish, you are welcome to publish it in 'Lifelines'.

Denis Brown,
Calligrapher, Artist

from *King Lear*

Act III

Scene (ii) *Another part of the Heath. Storm still.*
Enter Lear and Fool.

Lear. Blow, winds, and crack your cheeks! rage! blow!
    You cataracts and hurricanoes, spout
Till you have drench'd our steeples, drown'd the cocks!
You sulph'rous and thought-executing fires,
Vaunt-couriers of oak-cleaving thunderbolts,
Singe my white head! And thou, all-shaking thunder,
Strike flat the thick rotundity o'th'world!
Crack Nature's moulds, all germens spill at once
That makes ingrateful man! . . .

Rumble thy bellyful! Spit, fire! spout, rain!
Nor rain, wind, thunder, fire, are my daughters:
I tax you not, you elements, with unkindness;
I never gave you kingdom, call'd you children,
You owe me no subscription: then let fall
Your horrible pleasure; here I stand, your slave,
A poor, infirm, weak, and despis'd old man.
But yet I call you servile ministers,
That will with two pernicious daughters join
Your high-engender'd battles 'gainst a head
So old and white as this. O, ho! 'tis foul.

King Lear, Act III, sc ii, ll 1-9; 14-24
William Shakespeare (1564–1616)

SEAN HUGHES   288

Dear Ewan, Áine and Christopher,

Good luck with the new venture. I am well aware of your books and have the last one. I will give you a choice of three poems in case some have been used by others.

1. 'Night Air' — Brendan Kennelly, for tackling a sensitive area with mastery and conviction. I wish more poets would dare to plunge with such courage. A beautiful tender poem about a moment we would rather erase from our mind.

Night Air
from The Book of Judas

'My friend Rebecca returned from a party,
Glad of the peace of home, sat in
Her living-room listening to music.
After a while she decided to check the children,
Softly upstairs towards Jonathan's bedroom.
He was twelve, her favourite. She found him
Lying in bed, naked, asleep, his penis
Erect in the light thrown from the landing.
Before she knew it she was at the bedside,
Wanting the boy's penis inside her. Breathing
'Jonathan! Jonathan!' she leaned towards him, then realising
Herself, turned, closed the door, rushed downstairs, out
Into the garden, gulped the night air, her shocked mind shivering.'

Brendan Kennelly (b.1936)

2. 'Felicity in Turin' — Paul Durcan from Daddy Daddy, *within this small poem he manages to look at the complexity of relationships and shows how close and wide the mind and body are. A pathetic moment captured well.*

Felicity in Turin

We met in the Valentino in Turin
And travelled down through Italy by train,
Sleeping together.
I do not mean having sex.
I mean sleeping together.
Of which sexuality is,
And is not, a part.

It is this sleeping together
That is sacred to me.
This yawning together.
You can have sex with anyone
But with whom can you sleep?

I hate you
Because having slept with me
You left me.

Paul Durcan (b.1944)

3. 'Clearances' — *Seamus Heaney from* The Haw Lantern, *my favourite poem of all time. I read it at least four times a year and each time it says more and more. I envy his touch, I envy the moments he remembers, I envy his love of life and this of course leaves me with the utter need to express my love for my mother before her time comes. A rich, soft, beautiful poem.*

Love,
Sean Hughes

Clearances
in memoriam MKH, 1911–1984

She taught me what her uncle once taught her:
How easily the biggest coal block split
If you got the grain and hammer angled right.

The sound of that relaxed alluring blow,
Its co-opted and obliterated echo,
Taught me to hit, taught me to loosen,

Taught me between the hammer and the block
To face the music. Teach me now to listen,
To strike it rich behind the linear black.

1
A cobble thrown a hundred years ago
Keeps coming at me, the first stone
Aimed at a great-grandmother's turncoat brow.
The pony jerks and the riot's on.
She's crouched low in the trap
Running the gauntlet that first Sunday
Down the brae to Mass at a panicked gallop.
He whips on through the town to cries of 'Lundy!'

Call her 'The Convert'. 'The Exogamous Bride'.
Anyhow, it is a genre piece

Inherited on my mother's side
And mine to dispose with now she's gone.
Instead of silver and Victorian lace,
The exonerating, exonerated stone.

2

Polished linoleum shone there. Brass taps shone.
The china cups were very white and big —
An unchipped set with sugar bowl and jug.
The kettle whistled. Sandwich and teascone
Were present and correct. In case it run,
The butter must be kept out of the sun.
And don't be dropping crumbs. Don't tilt your chair.
Don't reach. Don't point. Don't make noise when your stir.

It is Number 5, New Row, Land of the Dead,
Where grandfather is rising from his place
With spectacles pushed back on a clean bald head
To welcome a bewildered homing daughter
Before she even knocks. 'What's this? What's this?'
And they sit down in the shining room together.

3

When all the others were away at Mass
I was all hers as we peeled potatoes.
They broke the silence, let fall one by one
Like solder weeping off the soldering iron:
Cold comforts set between us, things to share
Gleaming in a bucket of clean water.
And again let fall. Little pleasant splashes
From each other's work would bring us to our senses.

So while the parish priest at her bedside
Went hammer and tongs at the prayers for the dying
And some were responding and some crying
I remembered her head bent towards my head,
Her breath in mine, our fluent dipping knives —
Never closer the whole rest of our lives.

4

Fear of affectation made her affect
Inadequacy whenever it came to
Pronouncing words 'beyond her'. *Bertold Brek*.
She'd manage something hampered and askew
Every time, as if she might betray
The hampered and inadequate by too
Well-adjusted a vocabulary.
With more challenge than pride, she'd tell me, 'You
Know all them things.' So I governed my tongue
In front of her, a genuinely well-
adjusted adequate betrayal

Of what I knew better. I'd *naw* and *aye*
And decently relapse into the wrong
Grammar which kept us allied and at bay.

5
The cool that came off sheets just off the line
Made me think the damp must still be in them
But when I took my corners of the linen
And pulled against her, first straight down the hem
And then diagonally, then flapped and shook
The fabric like a sail in a cross-wind,
They made a dried-out undulating thwack.
So we'd stretch and fold and end up hand to hand
For a split second as if nothing had happened
For nothing had that had not always happened
Beforehand, day by day, just touch and go,
Coming close again by holding back
In moves where I was x and she was o
Inscribed in sheets she'd sewn from ripped-out flour sacks.

6
In the first flush of the Easter holidays
The ceremonies during Holy Week
Were highpoints of our *Sons and Lovers* phase.
The midnight fire. The paschal candlestick.
Elbow to elbow, glad to be kneeling next
To each other up there near the front
Of the packed church, we would follow the text
And rubrics for the blessing of the font.
As the hind longs for the streams, so my soul . . .
Dippings. Towellings. The water breathed on.
The water mixed with chrism and with oil.
Cruet tinkle. Formal incensation
And the psalmist's outcry taken up with pride:
Day and night my tears have been my bread.

7
In the last minutes he said more to her
Almost than in all their life together.
'You'll be in New Row on Monday night
And I'll come up for you and you'll be glad
When I walk in the door . . . Isn't that right?'
His head was bent down to her propped-up head.
She could not hear but we were overjoyed.
He called her good and girl. Then she was dead,
The searching for a pulsebeat was abandoned
And we all knew one thing by being there.
The space we stood around had been emptied
Into us to keep, it penetrated
Clearances that suddenly stood open.
High cries were felled and a pure change happened.

8

I thought of walking round and round a space
Utterly empty, utterly a source
Where the decked chestnut tree had lost its place
In our front hedge above the wallflowers.
The white chips jumped and jumped and skited high.
I heard the hatchet's differentiated
Accurate cut, the crack, the sigh
And collapse of what luxuriated
Through the shocked tips and wreckage of it all.
Deep planted and long gone, my coeval
Chestnut from a jam jar in a hole,
Its heft and hush become a bright nowhere,
A soul ramifying and forever
Silent, beyond silence listened for.

Seamus Heaney (b.1939)

[Sonnet 3 from 'Clearances' was chosen by Kathleen Watkins in *Lifelines*. Felim Egan chose Sonnet 8.]

DOLORES WALSHE   289

7 February 1994

Dear Ewan, Áine and Christopher,

Thank you for inviting me to participate in your new Lifelines *anthology. I'm delighted to be part of your project which will raise money to help children in the Third World.*

The poem I've chosen is 'Surprised by Joy', by William Wordsworth. For me, this poem perfectly expresses the poet's passionate grief at the loss of someone he loved, and it gave me great solace to read it again and again after the death of someone I loved dearly.

The very best of luck with your endeavour.

Kindest regards,
Dolores Walshe

Surprised by Joy — Impatient as the Wind

Surprised by joy—impatient as the Wind
I turned to share the transport—Oh! with whom
But Thee, deep buried in the silent tomb,
That spot which no vicissitude can find?
Love, faithful love, recalled thee to my mind—
But how could I forget thee? Through what power,
Even for the least division of an hour,
Have I been so beguiled as to be blind
To my most grievous loss!—That thought's return

Was the worst pang that sorrow ever bore,
Save one, one only, when I stood forlorn,
Knowing my heart's best treasure was no more;
That neither present time, nor years unborn
Could to my sight that heavenly face restore.

William Wordsworth (1770–1850)

JOE DUFFY   290

RTE

23 January 1994

Dear Ewan, Áine and Christopher,

Enclosed please find my choice of poetry — 'The Windhover' by Gerard Manley Hopkins.

I always come back to the 'Windhover' mainly because it was the first poem to cast a sheltering shadow over my life. Up to encountering Hopkins's masterpiece for my Leaving Certificate in 1976 I don't think I understood the power, grace, release and deep kaleidoscope that is good poetry.

Every word seems carefully hewn from wood, stonily chiselled from granite, and unleashed from the farrier's grasp to soar, inspire and thrill.

The imaginative power of language alliterating its way through the onomatopoeia of carefully chosen words and phrases is but a gateway to the wide world — a world I can thankfully say I recently returned to asking myself all the while, where I'd been all those years. It is also a reminder that good poetry contains deep understandings that maybe are not of this world.

Yours sincerely,
Joe Duffy

The Windhover

To Christ our Lord

I caught this morning morning's minion, kingdom of daylight's
        dauphin, dapple-dawn-drawn Falcon, in his riding
    Of the rolling level underneath him steady air, and striding
High there, how he rung upon the rein of a wimpling wing
In his ecstasy! then off, off forth on swing,
    As a skate's heel sweeps smooth on a bow-bend: the hurl and
        gliding
    Rebuffed the big wind. My heart in hiding
Stirred for a bird, —the achieve of, the mastery of the thing!

Brute beauty and valour and act, oh, air, pride, plume, here
    Buckle! AND the fire that breaks from thee then, a billion
Times told lovelier, more dangerous, O my chevalier!

No wonder of it: shéer plód makes plough down sillion
Shine, and blue-bleak embers, ah my dear,
    Fall, gall themselves, and gash gold-vermilion.

Gerard Manley Hopkins (1844–1889)

LILIAN ROBERTS FINLAY   291

16 February 1994

Dear Ewan, Áine and Christopher,

Greetings, and congratulations on your fundraising for the Third World. If my efforts are of interest to your cause, here is my contribution. The delay in replying is accounted for by the fact that I have been in New York since the end of November. (One of my sons teaches in NYU.)

I have been writing short stories for fifty years and completing full length novels since the eighties. When an idea forms (or haunts?) which is not big enough for a story, it ends up in verse. Down through the years, there have been many such verses which I could not honestly claim to be poetry so I have never submitted any for publication.

Herewith are two pieces, hopefully in contrast but perhaps the same voice is discernible? If you wish to use either or both, they are yours.

If you prefer to use your own established format of a favourite poem with a 'Why' note, I have included one also. The best of luck to a great idea.

Sincerely yours,
Lilian Roberts Finlay

I hope we are in agreement that, with the exception of Manley Hopkins, verse must be read aloud? Oh, good.

Bon Voyage, Mon Capitaine!

You say you never make an atmosphere
Inimical to others?
You are sensitive to such, and clear
That you deplore the mothers,
And the wives, who create for their families
Gyves so galling and rows so appalling
That husbands, and sons too, depart
To pubs and clubs, and even start
With a new tart a more-rewarding
Affair of the heart.

I wish you would, my dove!
And take with you all the sporty dirt
Of sock and underwear and shirt
For her to wash with love!

I'll help you pack,
Help you off the torture-rack,
Lift my flail from your weak hind
And send you off to find that enigmatic beauty
You imagine waiting with silver tongue
For you to come . . .

And where was she when you were young?

Lilian Roberts Finlay (b.1915)

The First-Born

I nudged you awake at dawn: It's happening, I said.
You leaped out of bed, still asleep you hit the floor,
And I began to laugh.
I remember how you swore, you dropped your watch,
The more you panicked, the more I laughed:
I lay there laughing in between the minutes
That betokened pain . . . softly, gently laughing as
You rushed to phone, you brought me tea, you spilled the cup,
I laughed again.
You kissed me, your eyes wondering if it was right to joke
When such a solemn morning broke upon our lives.
I'll be a Dad, you muttered and then the laughter spluttered
As we rocked together on the bed.
No taxi came. You picked up the case and we set off
To face the great day when the race
Of nations would be added to by us . . .we saw ourselves
As people of security, beamed and blushed at our maturity.
Does it hurt? I scarcely know. Should we hurry?
Please go slow. Will he stay? Or will they ban?
Course not! Family man!
And all the laughter that began our day
Trembled in and out of pain that ebbed and flowed
And ebbed again.

They told you I was low, might go. Oh, would that it
Had been so. I would have drowned in waves of laughter
And you would have mourned me ever after, remembered
My beauty and my grace as people do when the face
Of the beloved has joined the dead,
And not grown old instead.

Lilian Roberts Finlay (b.1915)

XXX

When to the sessions of sweet silent thought
I summon up remembrance of things past,
I sigh the lack of many a thing I sought,
And with old woes new wail my dear time's waste:
Then can I drown an eye, unused to flow,
For precious friends hid in death's dateless night,
And weep afresh love's long since cancelled woe
And moan the expense of many a vanish'd sight:
Then can I grieve at grievances foregone,
And heavily from woe to woe tell o'er
The sad account of fore-bemoaned moan,
Which I new pay as if not paid before.
    But if the while I think on thee, dear friend
    All losses are restored and sorrows end.

William Shakespeare (1564–1616)

When I was young, this would not have been a favoured poem, although I had been taught that in the Sonnets there would always be recompense. Now, when life is surely drawing to a close, these words have become very precious, and very expressive. Memory is heart-breakingly sad with loss, and marvellously sweet with experience. Shakespeare is still, after all the centuries of writing, the Master.

Lilian Roberts Finlay

PÁDRAIG J DALY   292

24 January 1994

Dear Ewan, Áine and Christopher,

I am very sorry for not getting back to you sooner. There seemed to be so much stuff to get through in the after-Christmas period. Good luck for your venture.

It is an honour and a pleasure to be associated with it.

Sincerely,
Pádraig J Daly

When trying to choose a favourite poem, I found myself swamped by the possibilities.

I thought of the bleak, 'H'M' by R S Thomas; of John F Deane's heartbreaking 'On a Dark Night'; and of Pearse Hutchinson's superbly sensuous 'Malaga'.

Finally however I settled on 'Swineherd', a poem by Eileán Ní Chuilleanáin. It is a poem that creates its own world. It offers us an intact and complete imaginative experience. It leads us into the mysterious, perhaps fairytale, time and place of swineherds and Portuguese lay sisters.

I love the poem above all for its breathtaking evocation of quiet and silence:

> I want to lie awake at night
> Listening to cream crawling to the top of the jug
> And the water lying soft in the cistern.

They are lines to kill for. Writing about them now reminds me of how I first came across Eileán Ní Chuilleanáin's poems in newspapers and magazines; and of how imaginatively liberating they were for me then; and they still are.

Pádraig J Daly

Swineherd

'When all this is over', said the swineherd,
'I mean to retire, where
Nobody will have heard about my special skills
And conversation is mainly about the weather.

I intend to learn how to make coffee, at least as well
As the Portuguese lay-sister in the kitchen
And polish the brass fenders every day.
I want to lie awake at night
Listening to cream crawling to the top of the jug
And the water lying soft in the cistern.

I want to see an orchard where the trees grow in straight
        lines
And the yellow fox finds shelter between the navy-blue
        trunks,
Where it gets dark early in summer
And the apple-blossom is allowed to wither on the bough.'

Eiléan Ní Chuilleanáin (b.1942)

CAROL RUMENS   293

2 February 1994

Dear Ewan, Áine and Christopher,

I hope I'm not too late to offer a favourite poem for Lifelines. *It's called* 'Epilogue' *and it's a late poem by the American poet, Robert Lowell, from his collection* Day by Day.

I hope you don't have this one already. Let me know if you do, for I have many 'favourite poems'!

All best wishes,
Carol Rumens

Epilogue

Those blessèd structures, plot and rhyme—
why are they no help to me now
I want to make
something imagined, not recalled?
I hear the noise of my own voice:
The painter's vision is not a lens,
it trembles to caress the light.
But sometimes everything I write
with the threadbare art of my eye
seems a snapshot,
lurid, rapid, garish, grouped,
heightened from life,
yet paralyzed by fact.
All's misalliance.
Yet why not say what happened?
Pray for the grace of accuracy
Vermeer gave to the sun's illumination
stealing like the tide across a map
to his girl solid with yearning.
We are poor passing facts,
warned by that to give
each figure in the photograph
his living name.

Robert Lowell (1917–1977)

This is a small hesitant impressionistic poem, but I feel it is a major one. How such confident and memorable statements can add up to such a sense of anguish and uncertainty is its central mystery. Any poet or artist will recognise the dilemma between veracity to the thing described and to the self that is describing, the awful tensions between humility and egotism, public and personal, etc. But it is not simply a poem about artists or poets. Any one of us who, as 'poor passing facts' has tried to make one moment that will outlive us or recapture a lost time knows that dilemma and its pathos. The poem bows down to the living name of each of us.

Carol Rumens

PATRICK McCABE   294

Dear Ewan Gibson et al,

In response to your query, my favourite poem is 'The Man from God-Knows-Where' by Florence M Wilson, because it is eerie and spooky, lyrical, with a powerful narrative drive in the tradition of the great ballads.

All the best,
Pat McCabe

The Man from God-Knows-Where
A County Down telling of the winter time of 1795 and the autumn of 1803

Into our townlan', on a night of snow,
Rode a man from God-knows-where;
None of us bade him stay or go,
Nor deemed him friend, nor damned him foe,
But we stabled his big roan mare:
For in our townlan' we're a decent folk,
And if he didn't speak, why none of us spoke,
And we sat till the fire burned low.

We're a civil sort in our wee place,
So we made the circle wide
Round Andy Lemon's cheerful blaze,
And wished the man his lenth o' days,
And a good end to his ride.
He smiled in under his slouchy hat—
Says he, 'There's a bit of a joke in that,
For we ride different ways.'

The whiles we smoked we watched him stare,
From his seat fornenst the glow.
I nudged Joe Moore, 'You wouldn't dare
To ask him, who he's for meetin' there,
And how far he has got to go.'
But Joe wouldn't dare, nor Wully Scott,
And he took no drink—neither cold nor hot—
This man from God-knows-where.

It was closin' time, an' late forbye,
When us ones braved the air—
I never saw worse (may I live or die)
Than the sleet that night, an' I says, says I,
'You'll find he's for stoppin' there.'
But at screek o' day, through the gable pane,
I watched him spur in the peltin' rain,
And I juked from his rovin' eye.

Two winters more, then the Trouble Year
When the best that a man could feel
Was the pike he kept in hidlin's near,
Till the blood o' hate an' the blood o' fear
Would be redder nor rust on the steel.
Us ones quet from mindin' the farms,
Let them take what we gave wi' the weight o' our arms,
From Saintfield to Kilkeel.

In the time o' the Hurry we had no lead—
We all of us fought with the rest—
An' if e'er a one shook like a tremblin' reed,
None of us gave neither hint nor heed,
Nor ever even'd we'd guessed.
We, men of the North, had a word to say,
An' we said it then in our own dour way,
An' we spoke as we thought was best.

All Ulster over, the weemen cried
For the stan'in' crops on the lan'—
Many's the sweetheart an' many's the bride
Would liefer ha' gone till where *he* died,
And ha' murned her lone by her man.
But us ones weathered the thick of it,
And we used to dander along, and sit
In Andy's side by side.

What with discoorse goin' to and fro,
The night would be wearin' thin,
Yet never so late when we rose to go
But someone would say: 'Do ye min' thon snow,
An' the man what came wanderin' in?'
And we be to fall to the talk again,
If by any chance he was *one o' them*—
The man who went like the win'.

Well 'twas gettin' on past the heat o' the year
When I rode to Newtown fair:
I sold as I could (the dealers were near—
Only three pound-eight for the Innish steer,
An' nothin' at all for the mare!)
I met M'Kee in the throng o' the street,
Says he, 'The grass has grown under our feet
Since they hanged young Warwick here.'

And he told that Boney had promised help
To a man in Dublin town.
Says he, 'If ye've laid the pike on the shelf,
Ye'd better go home hot-fut by yerself,
An' polish the old girl down.'
So by Comber road I trotted the gray,
And never cut corn until Killyleagh
Stood plain on the risin' groun'.

For a wheen o' days we sat waitin' the word
To rise and go at it like men.
But no French ships sailed into Cloughey Bay,
And we heard the black news on a harvest day
That the cause was lost again;
And Joey and me, and Wully Boy Scott,
We agreed to ourselves we'd as lief as not
Ha' been found in the thick o' the slain.

By Downpatrick gaol I was bound to fare
On a day I'll remember, feth;
For when I came to the prison square
The people were waitin' in hundreds there,
An' you wouldn't hear stir nor breath!
For the sodgers were standing, grim an' tall,
Round a scaffold built there fornent the wall,
An' a man stepped out for death!

I was brave an' near to the edge of the throng,
Yet I knowed the face again,
An' I knowed the set, an' I knowed the walk,
An' the sound of his strange up-country talk,
For he spoke out right an' plain.
Then he bowed his head to the swinging rope,
Whiles I said, 'Please God' to his dying hope,
And 'Amen' to his dying prayer,
That the Wrong would cease, and the Right prevail,
For the man that they hanged at Downpatrick jail
Was the Man from God-Knows-Where!

Florence M Wilson

[The 'man' of this ballad was Thomas Russell, who organised Co. Down, but
was in prison and unable to lead in '98. He returned in 1803 to try and rally the
North simultaneously with Emmet's Dublin rising, failed in his effort, and died
on the scaffold at Downpatrick. At the opening of the poem, where he visits
the inn, in the depth of winter, '95, we will suppose he does not make his name
or mission known in mixed company, or maybe does not suspect the
possibilities underlying the dour reticence of the group of countrymen, though
they afterwards gave a good account of themselves. 'Warwick', alluded to by
M'Kee, was a young Presbyterian minister hanged at Newtownards as was
Rev. James Porter, at Grey Abbey, some miles away.]

MACDARA Ó FÁTHARTA　　　295

7 February 1994

October

O leafy yellowness you create for me
A world that was and now is poised above time,
I do not need to puzzle out Eternity
As I walk this arboreal street on the edge of a town.
The breeze too, even the temperature
And pattern of movement is precisely the same
As broke my heart for youth passing. Now I am sure
Of something. Something will be mine wherever I am.
I want to throw myself on the public street without caring
For anything but the prayering that the earth offers.
It is October over all my life and the light is staring
As it caught me once in a plantation by the fox coverts.
A man is ploughing ground for winter wheat
And my nineteen years weigh heavily on my feet.

Patrick Kavanagh (1904–1967)

When travelling by Dart which I do twice a day, I always — or nearly always — sit opposite this lovely lyrical sonnet. It's a constant reminder of my rural roots.

Na Blátha Craige

A dúirt mé leis na blátha:
'Nach suarach an áit a fuair sibh
Le bheith ag déanamh aeir,
Teannta suas anseo le bruach na haille,
Gan fúibh ach an chloch ghlas
Agus salachar na n-éan,
Áit bhradach, lán le ceo
Agus farraige cháite,
Ní scairteann grian anseo
Ó Luan go Satharn
Le gliondar a chur oraibh.'

A dúirt na blátha craige:
' Is cuma linn, a stór,
Táimid faoi dhraíocht
Ag ceol na farraige.'

Liam Ó Flaitheartaigh

I met the author of this poem on a few occasions and once, he explained to me how he came to write the poem and what he meant by it.

Good luck with your latest collection.

Macdara Ó Fátharta

SEÁN LYSAGHT   296

7 January 1994

Dear Ewan Gibson, Áine Jackson, and Christopher Pillow,

John Keats's 'To Autumn' has stayed with me since I first read it about twenty years ago, at the age of fifteen. The poem embodies a truth that I have only lately realised for myself: that the poet does not have to parade his/her own private emotions to write effectively. At this late stage in his career, with the knowledge that he is soon going to die, Keats transcends the psychological drama of the Odes by writing a poem descriptive of the dying year. His art achieves great serenity here; at the same time, it communicates the full pathos of his personal situation.

With best wishes for a laudable project,

Seán Lysaght

To Autumn

I
Season of mists and mellow fruitfulness,
    Close bosom friend of the maturing sun,
Conspiring with him how to load and bless
    With fruit the vines that round the thatch-eves run:
To bend with apples the mossed cottage-trees,
    And fill all fruit with ripeness to the core;
        To swell the gourd, and plump the hazel shells
    With a sweet kernel; to set budding more,
And still more, later flowers for the bees,
Until they think warm days will never cease,
        For summer has o'er-brimmed their clammy
        cells.

II
Who hath not seen thee oft amid thy store?
    Sometimes whoever seeks abroad may find
Thee sitting careless on a granary floor,
    Thy hair soft-lifted by the winnowing wind;
Or on a half-reaped furrow sound asleep,
    Drowsed with the fume of poppies, while thy hook
        Spares the next swath and all its twinèd flowers;

And sometimes like a gleaner thou dost keep
    Steady thy laden head across a brook;
    Or by a cyder-press, with patient look,
        Thou watchest the last oozings hours by hours.

III
Where are the songs of spring? Aye, where are they?
    Think not of them, thou hast thy music too—
While barrèd clouds bloom the soft-dying day,
    And touch the stubble-plains with rosy hue.
Then in a wailful choir the small gnats mourn
    Among the river sallows, borne aloft
        Or sinking as the light wind lives or dies;
And full-grown lambs loud bleat from hilly bourn;
    Hedge-crickets sing; and now with treble soft
    The red-breast whistles from a garden-croft;
        And gathering swallows twitter in the skies.

John Keats (1795–1821)

E ANNIE PROULX   297

7 February 1994

Dear Ewan Gibson, Áine Jackson and Christopher Pillow,

Your letter asking for my favorite poem for your forthcoming edition of
Lifelines *arrived a few days ago. I am not very comfortable with the
idea of a favorite anything, especially books, authors, poems. One's
tastes change with knowledge and experience — think of what you might
have replied if someone had asked you what your favorite books were
when you were five years old; I doubt you would name the same books
today. And I seem to have new favorites every week. Casting about in
my mind for a poem I could call a 'favorite' created a fizz of shorted-out
neurons and a sensation of imprisonment.*

*Yet there is a poem, 'Upon a Wasp Child with Cold,' by Edward
Taylor (b. 1642?, d.1729) I have liked a great deal for many years, and
while it is not pinned up over my bed nor whipped out on every possible
occasion as my guiding light through life, nor do I refer to it for solace
or philosophy, yet I continue to take delight in it. I am charmed by
Taylor's imagery, his taste for conceits, his mental agility in fitting a
macrocosmic view into a microcosmic observation, and his sharp eye for
the workings of the natural world.*

*Who was Edward Taylor? He was born in England, came to America
in 1668 and for most of his life was a Congregational minister in
Westfield, Massachusetts. His chief biographer, Donald Stanford,
describes him as the epitome of a puritan. 'He was learned, grave, severe,
stubborn, and stiff-necked. He was very, very pious. But his piety was
sincere.' He was also a marvelous and secret poet whose work was not*

discovered until this century. I have little taste for piety or religion, but the Reverend Taylor's poems still gleam fresh for me.

Best regards,
E Annie Proulx

P.S. In the title of the poem the word 'child' does not mean a youthful creature, but is a curious spelling of the adjective 'chilled'.

Upon a Wasp Child with Cold

The Bare that breaths the Northern blast
Did numb, Torpedo like, a Wasp
Whose stiffend limbs encrampt, lay bathing
In Sol's warm breath and shine as saving,
Which with her hands she chafes and stands
Rubbing her Legs, Shanks, Thighs, and hands.
Her petty toes, and fingers ends
Nipt with this breath, she out extends
Unto the Sun, in greate desire
To warm her digits at that fire.
Doth hold her Temples in this state
Where pulse doth beate, and head doth ake.
Doth turn, and stretch her body small,
Doth Comb her velvet Capitall.
As if her little brain pan were
A Volume of Choice precepts cleare.
As if her sattin jacket hot
Contained Apothecaries Shop
Of Natures recepts, that prevails
To remedy all her sad ailes,
As if her velvet helmet high
Did turret rationality.
She fans her wing up to the Winde
As if her Pettycoate were lin'de,
With reasons fleece, and hoises sails
And hu'ming flies in thankfull gails
Unto her dun Curld palace Hall
Her warm thanks offering for all.
    Lord cleare my misted sight that I
May hence view thy Divinity.
Some sparkes whereof thou up dost hasp
Within this little downy Wasp
In whose small Corporation wee
A school and a schoolmaster see
Where we may learn, and easily finde
A nimble Spirit bravely minde
Her worke in e'ry limb: and lace
It up neate with a vitall grace,
Acting each part though ne'er so small

Here of this Fustian animall.
Till I enravisht Climb into
The Godhead on this Lather doe.
Where all my pipes inspir'de upraise
An Heavenly musick furrd with praise.

Edward Taylor (?1642–1729)

EAMON KELLY   298

*In Co. Kerry when I was a child a Gárda came once a year to take down
the stock and tillage census. He stood his bicycle outside our door. He
sat at our kitchen table writing in his ledger, while his peaked cap rested
on the newel post of the stairs. I admired the silver buttons of his uniform
and the case by his left hip which held his baton. Unlike Seamus
Heaney's constable he had no gun.*

*Once, when rain and darkness threatened, we guessed the number of
cocks, hens, pigs, dry heifers and cultivated acres in a distant farm and
saved him the bother of peddling up a long boreen.*

Eamon Kelly

A Constable Calls
from *Singing School*

His bicycle stood at the window-sill,
The rubber cowl of a mud-splasher
Skirting the front mudguard,
Its fat black handlegrips

Heating in sunlight, the 'spud'
Of the dynamo gleaming and cocked back,
The pedal treads hanging relieved
Of the boot of the law.

His cap was upside down
On the floor, next his chair.
The line of its pressure ran like a bevel
In his slightly sweating hair.

He had unstrapped
The heavy ledger, and my father
Was making tillage returns
In acres, roods, and perches.

Arithmetic and fear.
I sat staring at the polished holster
With its buttoned flap, the braid cord
Looped into the revolver butt.

'Any other root crops?
Mangolds? Marrowstems? Anything like that?'
'No.' But was there not a line
Of turnips where the seed ran out

In the potato field? I assumed
Small guilts and sat
Imagining the black hole in the barracks.
He stood up, shifted the baton-case

Further round on his belt,
Closed the domesday book,
Fitted his cap back with two hands,
And looked at me as he said goodbye.

A shadow bobbed in the window.
He was snapping the carrier spring
Over the ledger. His boot pushed off
And the bicycle ticked, ticked, ticked.

Seamus Heaney (b.1939)

CIANA CAMPBELL   299

20 February 1994

Dear Ewan, Áine and Christopher,

Thank you very much for your invitation to contribute to the next
Lifelines. *It is a real joy to be involved with a project that is not alone worthwhile but that also provides so much pleasure to so many.*

I bought numerous copies of Lifelines *last Christmas and they made very welcome presents. One copy remains beside my bed and I dip into it regularly.*

Making a choice of one favourite poem is terribly hard, in fact, it is impossible. I certainly enjoy Paul Durcan and Rita Ann Higgins for their wicked humour and their celebration of my native West of Ireland. 'Between Them' by Rita Ann is one I particularly like. I'm sure it will raise a smile and a stab of recognition.

Congratulations to you and to your teachers for the terrific work you do.

All the best,
Ciana Campbell

Between Them

You only see
good-looking couples
out driving
on a Sunday afternoon.

His hair is blonde,
her eyes are blue.

Between them
they have no broken veins
stretch marks
Guinness guts
fat necks
barrel chests
or swollen ankles.

Between them
they never curse.
His give-away sign
is the way he holds the steering wheel
in the twenty-to-two position.

Her give-away sign
is the sweep of the perfume
she leaves lingering at the traffic lights
where the pedestrians often turn green.

Between them
they never eat fries
red or brown sauce
shanks of anybody
mackerel from the basin.
Putrid, they say, putrid.

Between them
they have no cholesterol in the blood
no coal in the shed,
everything is centrally heated,
it's easier that way
cuts out the middle man
and the mess.
Sometimes
when they are not out
looking good-looking,

between them
you could fit:
two McInerney Homes
three Berlin Walls
Martha Glynn's fantasies
four empty factories (I.D.A)

seventeen rocket couriers (slightly overweight)
forty-eight good quality reconditioned colour T.Vs
incalculable curriculum Vs
cat fights
frog fights
bull fights
dog fights
broken hearts
hearts in jars
lost wars
lost teeth
teeth in jars
Pope's intentions
sexist free Bibles
Ceaucescu's wealth
Bush's blushes
tea-leaf prophecy classes
sole-of-the-feet prophecy classes
black-eye prophecy classes
white-of-the-eye prophecy classes
moveable feasts
grow your own cameras
poster poems
dirty water
and murder mysteries.

Rita Ann Higgins (b.1955)

CARL TIGHE   300

1 February 1994

Dear Ewan Gibson, Áine Jackson and Christopher Pillow,

Many thanks for your letter. I'm sorry the reply has taken so long, but it took more than two weeks for your letter to struggle across the Irish Sea. I think the post office has gone back to using carrier pigeons.

My area is prose. I'm not much of a poet and it takes me a very long time to get to grips with a poet. My favourite poets are Zbigniew Herbert, Seamus Heaney, John Cooper Clarke, Nigel Jenkins, Czeslaw Milosz and W B Yeats. So what to choose . . . let me give you a couple of possibles.

1. Czeslaw Milosz, 'Campo Dei Fiori', from Ocalenie *(Salvation, Warsaw, 1945), included in* Collected Poems 1931-87, *Viking, London, 1988. The poem, dated 1943, the time of the Warsaw ghetto uprising, is from a collection of Milosz's wartime poetry, one of the first post-war publications to appear. It was also the only collection of his verse to appear in Poland until 1980. I love the vividness of the fruit and fish, the startling connection with Giordano Bruno: the leap to Warsaw, the carousel, the burning ghetto: incredible economy. Does it matter whether it really happened? Can we shrug and say 'Well, life goes on'? Pain and death are intensely lonely experiences. We are alone when we suffer, alone when we die. The death of Bruno, the deaths of the ghetto, they are incomprehensible to those thronging the taverns or riding the carousel. It is hard to take an interest if it is not your pain, your death — and if it is your pain, your death, there is nothing anyone can do to relieve you. There is no language, not even that of the poet, adequate to the task. And even if there, the crowds, having paused for a moment, are back at the tavern, riding the carousel. Pain and dying are a separate language. They leave us behind, we speak a language lost to those who went before. It is permanently lost. The past is another language. A lost language. Is that a matter for morality? The poet only makes this clear, points this out. The rage of the last line is at the recognition and frustration that this is so, that this is how we are, at the poet for daring to say so.*

Campo Dei Fiori

In Rome on the Campo dei Fiori
baskets of olives and lemons,
cobbles spattered with wine
and the wreckage of flowers.
Vendors cover the trestles
with rose-pink fish;
armfuls of dark grapes
heaped on peach-down.

On this same square
they burned Giordano Bruno.
Henchmen kindled the pyre
close-pressed by the mob.
Before the flames had died
the taverns were full again,
baskets of olives and lemons
again on the vendors' shoulders.

I thought of the Campo dei Fiori
in Warsaw by the sky-carousel
one clear spring evening
to the strains of a carnival tune.
The bright melody drowned
the salvos from the ghetto wall,
and couples were flying
high in the cloudless sky.

At times wind from the burning
would drift dark kites along
and riders on the carousel
caught petals in midair.

That same hot wind
blew open the skirts of the girls
and the crowds were laughing
on that beautiful Warsaw Sunday.

Someone will read as moral
that the people of Rome or Warsaw
haggle, laugh, make love
as they pass by martyrs' pyres.
Someone else will read
of the passing of things human,
of the oblivion
born before the flames have died.

But that day I thought only
of the loneliness of the dying,
of how, when Giordano
climbed to his burning
he could not find
in any human tongue
words for mankind,
mankind who live on.

Already they were back at their wine
or peddled their white starfish,
baskets of olives and lemons
they had shouldered to the fair,
and he already distanced
as if centuries had passed
while they paused just a moment
for his flying in the fire.

Those dying here, the lonely
forgotten by the world,
our tongue becomes for them
the language of an ancient planet.
Until, when all is legend
and many years have passed,
on a new Campo dei Fiori
rage will kindle at a poet's word.

Warsaw, 1943

Czeslaw Milosz (b.1911)
Translated by Louis Iribarne and David Brooks

2. John Cooper Clarke, 'a distant relation' from Ten Years in an
Open Necked Shirt. *Cooper Clarke is a performer — you might catch
a glimpse of his elongated razor thin frame, hung with a skin tight black
suit, dark glasses and fuzz of hair, in a TV ad, playing opposite the
Honey Monster. It is a rare family where affairs are not in a state of
permanent tension. You can choose your friends, but not your family.*

But relations are always intense. You reach an age when family photo albums suddenly become very interesting, for what they reveal as much as what they leave out: and suddenly you are interpreting these fuzzy, wobbly pictures of the back of people's heads, of handstands on the beach, of mysterious uncles and god-mothers that no-one has seen for thirty years. Pore over the pictures in the belief that somehow you are in them, that a secret will make everything clear, that you will learn who you are before it is too late. And suddenly you realise: that's it, your elders have gone. It is too late to ask them. You are the family memory, you are the walking repository of knowledge about who was who, of secrets and skeletons. The 'permanent fixtures' were not so permanent. You are senior. You are next. The fascination of who we are remains.

a distant relation

a family affair
look at this picture
we're in there somewhere
permanent fixtures
people who care
stranger beware
this is a family affair

all of our yesterdays
familiar rings
i have to get away
it's breaking my heart strings
we have a drink
it's a special occasion
it makes me think
about a distant relation

a family affair
always a mixture
of people in chairs
permanent fixtures
bring pressure to bear
and problems to share
this is a family affair

holiday snapshots
of you and myself
acting like crackpots
like everyone else
the bermuda shorts
and the summer creations
bringing thoughts
of that distant relation

a family affair
we break ornaments
and get them repaired
we bring up past events

that hang in the air
stranger beware
this is a family affair

all of our yesterdays
familiar rings
i have to get away
from certain surroundings
weddings and funerals
and special occasions
and all the usual
distant relations

a family affair
look at this picture
we're in there look there
permanent fixtures
people who care
whisper who dares
this is a family affair

John Cooper Clarke (b.1948)

3. *Nigel Jenkins*, 'To Ms Evans, with thanks' *from* Acts of Union *(Gomer, Llandysul Dyfed, 1990). Nigel is a fine and distinctive poet whose work conjures the landscape and scenic rhythms of South Wales, particularly the area around Swansea and the Gower peninsula. He has a fine ear for the nuances of language and is an acute observer of the steady inroads that English (and its accompanying mental world map) has made into Wales and into Welsh language culture. His poetry is often on a wide variety of public and political themes, and so strong are his beliefs that he has been to prison for civil disobedience. In Nigel's poetry the dissidents' cagoules swish, beards drip in the gentle Welsh rain, women are honoured for the gifts they bring, the pinball culture is lashed and the slow death of a Wales governed from London is manifest at every turn: his landscape is a very un-romantic Celtic twilight. This poem has a special feel: it is rare that a poet displays a delicate, private feeling so publicly, but the private is often the public, and vice versa. Often we do not find a gift, a gift finds us: and a gift of love, like the gift of flowers, can be made but not possessed. A poem like this urges us to think again about the way we have ordered our priorities.*

To Ms Evans, with thanks

we'd been both out walking

me in the poisoned mud
of Swansea Bay
& you where no insecticides, the
bouldered headland
of Dewi Sant.

slurried flats at tide-fall dis-
graced mussels
the turnstones turning stones when
madreperla! I
find, am found by
this cup of slippery light
that here I give you

a shone translucence
no words can tender.

early morning there you picked for me
                    bluebells
                    campions
                    sea-pinks
                    ox-eyes
                    one guilty cowslip
                    'from the hundreds, the thousands'

& there out west
—your dash for the train—
the bunch got left, locked
all weekend
in an office in Milford.

I give,
      you name
your giving:

though I'll never see them
exchange is made
& of no possession
I am in receipt

your wild flowers
                    their dawn.

Nigel Jenkins

I hope this is what you had in mind. Best wishes and good luck with the publication. I am flattered that you asked me to take part and I thank you for it.

Yours sincerely,
Carl Tighe

HELEN DUNMORE   301

14 January 1994

Dear Ewan Gibson, Áine Jackson and Christopher Pillow,

Thank you for your letter about your Lifelines *anthology. I'm glad you've had so much success in raising money for Third World causes — congratulations. Very hard to choose a favourite poem, but this is one of my favourites: 'Buffalo Bill's' by E E Cummings. I like it because it's funny and moving and uses the word 'defunct' quite brilliantly. It has made a permanent home in my imagination. It has to be read aloud, and I like poems to be read aloud.*

All best wishes,
Helen Dunmore

Buffalo Bill's
defunct
          who used to
          ride a watersmooth-silver
                                        stallion
and break onetwothreefourfive pigeonsjustlikethat
                                        Jesus
he was a handsome man
                    and what i want to know is
how do you like your blueeyed boy
Mister Death

E E Cummings (1894–1962)

EUGENE McCABE   302

28 January 1994

Twenty years ago I wrote a pageant for St Mary's Cathedral in Limerick. In the course of agreeable research I came across a poem called 'St Columcille leaves for Iona' or 'St Columcille's Farewell'. I am almost certain it's a translation from the Irish but have no idea who wrote the original, who translated it or where I came across it. And why choose it? Why has it persisted? It deals with a heart ache too well known to every family in this island, the awful sadness of leavetaking, of breaking the umbilical cord that ties us to childhood, to growing up here, to place, to family, to a sense of belonging. It contains images and details so highly charged with love of place and people, a voice so heart breaking that it never fails to move me.

Eugene McCabe

Columcille's Farewell

How quickly my coracle speeds on,
The salt spray blinds my gaze,
I grieve on the trackless sea,
Sailing from Ireland to Alba of the Ravens.

The Cliffs grow small,
As through a mist of death my eyes look back,

I shall never see again,
The wives of Ireland or their men.

Gael, Gael, oh precious name,
Broken is my heart within my breast;

Should sudden death overtake me,
It is for my great love of the Gael.

Beloved are Durrow and Derry,
Beloved is Raphoe in purity,
Beloved Drumhone of rich fruits,
Beloved are Swords and Kells.

Beloved to my heart is the West,
Drumcliff and Culcinne Strand,
Their sad mains on which seagulls cry,
The bareness of their rocks and shores.

How cruelly my coracle speeds on,
Wrenching from my gaze the earth I love.

Oh God the bitter sea is teeming on my face,
Sailing from Ireland to Alba of the Ravens.

Anonymous

ADI ROCHE   303

CND
Irish Campaign for Nuclear Disarmament
5 March 1994

Dear Friends,

Many thanks for your letter of invitation to participate in this very special publication. Congratulations on your work. It is both an example to your own generation and to mine that you have chosen such a creative way to show your compassion, love and care of humanity.

It is very difficult to choose one poem above another but my most 'constant' poem is by a young Cork poet, Greg Delanty, now living and working in the US. Greg is a great friend of mine and shares a common vision for a Nuclear Free World.

The poem gives me renewed hope and encouragement when I'm feeling weary particularly when I think of the plight of the Chernobyl children.

I love the image of the swan raising its lovely neck and then soaring into the sky — it lifts me up too with its strong and powerful wings.

Greg told me he got the idea when he saw a peace lantern ceremony on the River Lee for a Hiroshima Day Commemoration. As he looked he saw a group of swans swim further upstream and then take to the air. Thus the idea for this poem came to him.

I love the idea of a poem dedicated to me and to all my friends in Irish CND. The poem has so much to offer. It is a well loved companion of mine now at this stage and it continues to be a spring of hope for me.

I hope your readers will enjoy it.

Yours in Peace,
Adi Roche
National Sec ICND
Director Chernobyl Children's Project

The Fable of Swans
to Adi Roche & CND

I can't quite recall
how my dream went.
You're floating lanterns
down the Lee.
I stop to see,
& realize you're giving
some sort of gift.
A swan sails by,
its neck a question mark.
Someone asks is it freedom
from the dread
of something shaped
like a common fungus
blooming
in some general's head?
As you nod,
the swan unfurls its neck
& takes off
down the river's runway,
clearing other swans
with heads
ostrich-buried
in murky water.

Greg Delanty (b.1958)

CIARAN CARSON   304

17 January 1994

Dear Ewan Gibson, Áine Jackson and Christopher Pillow,

Thank you for giving me the opportunity to contribute to your Lifelines *anthology.*

My favourite poem is 'After Apple-Picking' by Robert Frost, which I have loved ever since I came across it in a school anthology. It's a beautifully subtle piece of work, in which the craft is almost invisible. As my old English teacher, Brother Hickey told us at the time, 'Every line in the poem rhymes with another one, though you'd hardly know it when you read it out'.

After some thirty years of reading it off and on, I'm not entirely clear what's it's all about, though the ordinary speech rhythms lull you into thinking that you know. The last lines are especially mysterious. Memory, anticipation, art, time . . . the big themes are all in there: emotion recollected in tranquility. I've just read it again, and it gets better every time.

Ciaran Carson

After Apple-Picking

My long two-pointed ladder's sticking through a tree
Toward heaven still,
And there's a barrel that I didn't fill
Beside it, and there may be two or three
Apples I didn't pick upon some bough.
But I am done with apple-picking now.
Essence of winter sleep is on the night,
The scent of apples: I am drowsing off.
I cannot rub the strangeness from my sight
I got from looking through a pane of glass
I skimmed this morning from the drinking trough
And held against the world of hoary grass.
It melted, and I let it fall and break.
But I was well
Upon my way to sleep before it fell,
And I could tell
What form my dreaming was about to take.
Magnified apples appear and disappear,
Stem end and blossom end,
And every fleck of russet showing clear.
My instep arch not only keeps the ache,
It keeps the pressure of a ladder-round.

I feel the ladder sway as the boughs bend.
And I keep hearing from the cellar bin
The rumbling sound
Of load on load of apples coming in.
For I have had too much
Of apple-picking: I am overtired
Of the great harvest I myself desired.
There were ten thousand thousand fruit to touch,
Cherish in hand, lift down, and not let fall.
For all
That struck the earth,
No matter if not bruised or spiked with stubble,
Went surely to the cider-apple heap
As of no worth.
One can see what will trouble
This sleep of mine, whatever sleep it is.
Were he not gone,
The woodchuck could say whether it's like his
Long sleep, as I describe its coming on,
Or just some human sleep.

Robert Frost (1874–1963)

EILÍS DILLON   305

Dear Ewan Gibson, Áine Jackson, Christopher Pillow,

Thank you for asking me to contribute to your poetry anthology, which I have admired for the last few years. The poem I have chosen is a great favourite, called 'Bredon Hill' (pronounced Breedon). The poet is A E Housman and is one from A Shropshire Lad, one of the gentlest collections of poems in the English language, celebrating a dearly loved place.

Bredon Hill
from *A Shropshire Lad*

XXI
In summertime on Bredon
    The bells they sound so clear;
Round both the shires they ring them
    In steeples far and near,
    A happy noise to hear.

Here of a Sunday morning
    My love and I would lie,
And see the coloured counties,
    And hear the larks so high
    About us in the sky.

The bells would ring to call her
   In valleys miles away:
'Come all to church, good people;
   Good people, come and pray.'
   But here my love would stay.

And I would turn and answer
   Among the springing thyme,
'Oh, peal upon our wedding,
   And we will hear the chime,
   And come to church in time.'

But when the snows at Christmas
   On Bredon top were strown,
My love rose up so early
   And stole out unbeknown
   And went to church alone.

They tolled the one bell only,
   Groom there was none to see,
The mourners followed after,
   And so to church went she,
   And would not wait for me.

The bells they sound on Bredon,
   And still the steeples hum,
'Come all to church, good people' —
   Oh, noisy bells, be dumb;
   I hear you, I will come.

A E Housman (1859–1936)

Housman himself told how that wonderful 'coloured', came to him in a dream, first as 'painted', then as 'coloured', a completely satisfactory adjective. The other delightful aspect of this poem is the sense of certainty that one gets in a ballad.

Music to this was written by Vaughan Williams. I have heard it sung by Sidney MacEwan.

Eilís Dillon

['Bredon Hill' was also chosen by Sir John Gielgud in *Lifelines*.]

GABRIEL ROSENSTOCK   306

13 January 1994

Dear Lifeliners,

The poem I have chosen is 'Clann-Nighean an Sgadain'/'The Herring Girls' *by Ruaraidh Mac Thòmais/Derick Thomson, from* Creachadh na Clàrsaich/Plundering the Harp.

Reason: 'I like this moving poem for its artistry, its power to communicate, the vividness and importance of the setting, the eloquence of the Scots-Gaelic original, the history and the humanity it enshrines.

I could have chosen a poem by Li Po, Rumi, Kabir or Basho, but here we have a poet who writes in a language that is closest to our own ancestral tongue yet little or nothing of the significance of Scots-Gaelic literature is brought to the attention of Irish school-children; so, in this small way, I offer a lifeline that might help to redress the imbalance.

Gabriel Rosenstock

Clann-Nighean an Sgadain

An gàire mar chraiteachan salainn
ga fhroiseadh bho 'm beul,
an sàl 's am picil air an teanga,
's na miaran cruinne, goirid a dheanadh giullachd,
no a thogadh leanabh gu socair, cuimir,
seasgair, fallain,
gun mhearachd,
's na sùilean cho domhainn ri fèath.

B'e bun-os-cionn na h-eachdraidh a dh' fhàg iad
'nan tràillean aig ciùrairean cutach,
thall 's a-bhos air Galldachd 's an Sasainn.
Bu shaillte an duais a thàrr iad
ás na mìltean bharaillean ud,
gaoth na mara geur air an craiceann,
is eallach a' bhochdainn 'nan ciste,
is mara b'e an gàire
shaoileadh tu gu robh an teud briste.

Ach bha craiteachan uaille air an cridhe,
ga chumail fallain,
is bheireadh cutag an teanga
slisinn á fanaid nan Gall—
agus bha obair rompa fhathast
nuair gheibheadh iad dhachaigh,
ged nach biodh maoin ac':

air oidhche robach gheamhraidh,
ma bha siud an dàn dhaibh,
dheanadh iad daoine.

Ruaraidh Mac Thòmais

The Herring Girls

Their laughter like a sprinkling of salt
showered from their lips,
brine and pickle on their tongues,
and the stubby short fingers that could handle fish,
or lift a child gently, neatly,
safely, wholesomely,
unerringly,
and the eyes that were as deep as a calm.

The topsy-turvy of history had made them
slaves to short-arsed curers,
here and there in the Lowlands, in England.
Salt the reward they won
from those thousands of barrels,
the sea-wind sharp on their skins,
and the burden of poverty in their kists,
and were it not for their laughter
you might think the harp-string was broken.

But there was a sprinkling of pride on their hearts,
keeping them sound,
and their tongues' gutting-knife
would tear a strip from the Lowlanders' mockery—
and there was work awaiting them
when they got home,
though they had no wealth:
on a wild winter's night,
if that were their lot,
they would make men.

Derick Thomson

JOHN WATERS   307

Irish Times
Dublin

9 February 1994

Dear Ewan, Áine and Christopher,

Thank you for the invitation to nominate a poem for the new edition of Lifelines. *Hope I'm in time.*

I'd like to nominate 'The Force that Through the Green Fuse Drives the Flower', *by Dylan Thomas.*

Why? Because it puts an end to politics and ideology in 22 lines.

Best wishes,
John Waters

The Force that Through the Green Fuse Drives the Flower

The force that through the green fuse drives the flower
Drives my green age; that blasts the roots of trees
Is my destroyer.
And I am dumb to tell the crooked rose
My youth is bent by the same wintry fever.

The force that drives the water through the rocks
Drives my red blood; that dries the mouthing streams
Turns mine to wax.
And I am dumb to mouth unto my veins
How at the mountain spring the same mouth sucks.

The hand that whirls the water in the pool
Stirs the quicksand; that ropes the blowing wind
Hauls my shroud sail.
And I am dumb to tell the hanging man
How of my clay is made the hangman's lime.

The lips of time leech to the fountain head;
Love drips and gathers, but the fallen blood
Shall calm her sores.
And I am dumb to tell a weather's wind
How time has ticked a heaven round the stars.

And I am dumb to tell the lover's tomb
How at my sheet goes the same crooked worm.

Dylan Thomas (1914–1953)

BRIAN DOBSON   308

11 January 1993

Dear Ewan, Áine and Christopher,

Thank you for your invitation to contribute to the new edition of
Lifelines. *I have heard a good deal about the project and I am delighted
to have been asked to nominate a poem.*

I have chosen Richard Murphy's poem 'Sailing to an Island' *which
recounts a difficult and dangerous journey to the island of Inishbofin in
County Galway. Inishbofin has one of the finest natural harbours along
that stretch of the west coast.*

*The poem describes how the crew take refuge there after their boat has
been damaged in a storm. It is a poem about the sea; about those who
live by the sea; and those who earn their living from the sea. Other poets
have written on the same theme, I believe few have done so as effectively
as Richard Murphy.*

Best wishes for your project.

Yours sincerely,
Brian Dobson

Sailing to an Island

The boom above my knees lifts, and the boat
Drops, and the surge departs, departs, my cheek
Kissed and rejected, kissed, as the gaff sways
A tangent, cuts the infinite sky to red
Maps, and the mast draws eight and eight across
Measureless blue, the boatmen sing or sleep.

We point all day for our chosen island,
Clare, with its crags purpled by legend:
There under castles the hot O'Malleys,
Daughters of Granuaile, the pirate queen
Who boarded a Turk with a blunderbuss,
Comb red hair and assemble cattle.
Across the shelved Atlantic groundswell
Plumbed by the sun's kingfisher rod,
We sail to locate in sea, earth and stone
The myth of a shrewd and brutal swordswoman
Who piously endowed an abbey.
Seven hours we try against the wind and tide,
Tack and return, making no headway.
The north wind sticks like a gag in our teeth.

Encased in a mirage, steam on the water,
Loosely we coast where hideous rocks jag

An acropolis of cormorants, an extinct
Volcano where spiders spin, a purgatory
Guarded by hags and bristled with breakers.

The breeze as we plunge slowly stiffens:
There are hills of sea between us and land,
Between our hopes and the island harbour.
A child vomits. The boat veers and bucks

There is no refuge on the gannet's cliff.
We are far, far out: the hull is rotten,
The spars are splitting, the rigging is frayed,
And our helmsman laughs uncautiously.
What of those who must earn their living
On the ribald face of a mad mistress?
We in holiday fashion know
This is the boat that belched its crew
Dead on the shingle in the Cleggan disaster.

Now she dips and the sail hits the water.
She luffs to a squall; is struck; and shudders.
Someone is shouting. The boom, weak as scissors,
Has snapped. The boatman is praying.
Orders thunder and canvas cannonades.
She smothers in spray. We still have a mast;
The oar makes a boom. I am told to cut
Cords out of fishing-lines, fasten the jib.
Ropes lash my cheeks. Ease! Ease at last:
She swings to leeward, we can safely run.
Washed over rails our Clare Island dreams,
With storm behind us we straddle the wakeful
Waters that draw us headfast to Inishbofin.

The bows rock as she overtakes the surge.
We neither sleep nor sing nor talk,
But look to the land where the men are mowing.
What will the islanders think of our folly?

The whispering spontaneous reception committee
Nods and smokes by the calm jetty.
Am I jealous of these courteous fishermen
Who hand us ashore, for knowing the sea
Intimately, for respecting the storm
That took nine of their men on one bad night
And five from Rossadillisk in this very boat?
Their harbour is sheltered. They are slow to tell
The story again. There is local pride
In their home-built ships.
We are advised to return next day by the mail.

But tonight we stay, drinking with people
Happy in the monotony of boats,
Bringing the catch to the Cleggan market,

Cultivating fields, or retiring from America
With enough to soak till morning or old age.

The bench below my knees lifts, and the floor
Drops, and the words depart, depart, with faces
Blurred by the smoke. An old man grips my arm,
His shot eyes twitch, quietly dissatisfied.
He has lost his watch, an American gold
From Boston gas-works. He treats the company
To the secretive surge, the sea of his sadness.
I slip outside, fall among stones and nettles,
Crackling dry twigs on an elder tree,
While an accordion drones above the hill.

Later, I reach a room, where the moon stares
Cob-webbed through the window. The tide has ebbed,
Boats are careened in the harbour. Here is a bed.

Richard Murphy (b.1927)

CHARLES BRADY   309

3 February 1994

Dear Ewan,

Thank you for writing to me for Lifelines. *I enclose a favorite poem by Louis MacNeice, 'Dublin'.*

Sincerely,
Charles Brady

Dublin
from *The Closing Album*

Grey brick upon brick,
Declamatory bronze
On sombre pedestals—
O'Connell, Grattan, Moore—
And the brewery tugs and the swans
On the balustraded stream
And the bare bones of a fanlight
Over a hungry door
And the air soft on the cheek
And porter running from the taps
With a head of yellow cream
And Nelson on his pillar
Watching his world collapse.

This was never my town,
I was not born nor bred
Nor schooled here and she will not

Have me alive or dead
But yet she holds my mind
With her seedy elegance,
With her gentle veils of rain
And all her ghosts that walk
And all that hide behind
Her Georgian façades—
The catcalls and the pain,
The glamour of her squalor,
The bravado of her talk.

The lights jig in the river
With a concertina movement
And the sun comes up in the morning
Like barley-sugar on the water
And the mist on the Wicklow hills
Is close, as close
As the peasantry were to the landlord,
As the Irish to the Anglo-Irish,
As the killer is close one moment
To the man he kills,
Or as the moment itself
Is close to the next moment.

She is not an Irish town
And she is not English,
Historic with guns and vermin
And the cold renown
Of a fragment of Church latin,
Of an oratorical phrase.
But oh the days are soft,
Soft enough to forget
The lesson better learnt,
The bullet on the wet
Streets, the crooked deal,
The steel behind the laugh,
The Four Courts burnt.

Fort of the Dane,
Garrison of the Saxon,
Augustan capital
Of a Gaelic nation,
Appropriating all
The alien brought,
You give me time for thought
And by a juggler's trick
You poise the toppling hour—
O greyness run to flower,
Grey stone, grey water,
And brick upon grey brick.

Louis MacNeice (1907–1963)

I often think of this poem and the first days I got to meet Baggot Street, on damp autumn evenings in 1956 when I first arrived in Ireland from New York. Much in the poem seems autobiographical to me: i.e. worried feelings of never being accepted in Dublin, yet even then this area of the city gave me an inner warmth.

On the evening of the day President Kennedy visited Dublin my wife and I were introduced to Louis MacNeice by another poet, Anthony Cronin. It was a brief encounter but I'll never forget it.

Charles Brady

MAEVE KELLY   310

Dear Áine,

Thank you and your fellow pupils for inviting me to select my favourite poem. This is a wonderful idea and I wish it continued success.

With best wishes,

Yours sincerely,
Maeve Kelly

'Certain Octobers' *from* In Fields I hear them Sing, *by Jo Slade.*

This elegiac poem was written after the death of the poet's young nephew. The tone of the poem, its dignified, measured pace, the imaginative use of metaphor and simile bring to mind the immensity of loss suffered after the death of a child. I find it particularly moving because, although I have written poems of grief after the death of my own daughter, this poem seems to me to catch, in a subtle and powerful way, the sense of alienation and loss experienced by a grieving mother.

Maeve Kelly

Certain Octobers
for Peter Christopher Donnelly

I
The sky's winter primrose swells . . .
What lives murmur inside these
Wet impressions of boots?

Is life not all a kind of base survival?
Every day as light exonerates,
Spiffs its mucal froth

I am reminded of my dead child's face
Swamped in a pure marble;
And the void and the music

And where to put all this and what
To do with it now it's done.
I am old as all our childhood recollections.

I have buried him where dogs can dig,
Where insects turn in cuckoo-spit.
I have walked for years a space fenced

But with no limit, for my journey was
Ever upward and so no time nor cause
Would impose law or a biding of time

And now it seems as farcical to me
As the birds would feel, if all their
Trees were felled and I were left

Alone to know as much of knowing
Or be compelled to split the
Wood of infinity.

II
Already the solar fires burn . . .
My insanity thirsts a darkness
I belong to no-one, except within

The great planetary move, this timetide
Of emersion; or after your visit,
Black stars patterned global

Pictures on tea-stained cups
And I was there when Cygnus
Formed its cross.

And again the void and the music
And the trees tall erection.
The quiet sun has dropped inside

The wood and now the gentle song
Thrush moves away. In the distance
I could hear thunder;

The world spun upon its axis.

III
Is it all caught in a single drop?
This rain that pours continuously
Down, a soft mist rising

And descending, the mountain's damp
Amorphous frost. I did not see
Winter's white funeral pass

Nor hear the rosary of purple sloes
Perish on his lips; he left quietly
As a mouse, how secretly

The great door clicks and only me
Left inside the utter black,
Swirling in the black hole

The woman of the mountains,
The woman of the stars, the childless
Woman of the trees, of copper coloured

Moon, of charcoal burnt in shadow
And fallen husks of useless seed.

IV
But the dead come back,
Even minute life returns,
Little-veined memories, transparent

Paper wings outstretched,
A catechism of centuries;
His rib, my bone, gone to the purple earth

And to the sky, pure white of winter's
Drift. October swallows the pointed
Earth green leaves, and now I start

My long procession and I could not
Have foreseen all this.

Jo Slade (b.1952)

RICHARD W RILEY   311

Washington DC

23 April 1993

Dear Friends,

Thank you so much for your letter and for giving me the opportunity to include a poem in the Lifelines *anthology.*

My favorite poem is entitled 'Duty was Joy', *and was written by an Indian poet named Tagore. It gives me great pleasure to share it with you:*

Duty was Joy

I slept and dreamt
That life was joy—
I awoke and found
That life was duty—
I acted and behold
Duty was joy.

Rabindranath Tagore (1861–1941)

Very simply, it is meaningful to me because it ties responsibility and action to happiness in life. I share this view, and find that my duties and responsibilities give me great joy.

I, personally, appreciate your expression of interest. I wish you the best with your noble cause.

Yours sincerely,
Dick Riley

Richard W Riley
Fmr Governor
(South Carolina)

EMMA COOKE   312

8 January 1994

Dear Ewan, Áine and Christopher,

Thank you for your letter and congratulations on planning another volume of Lifelines, *and for asking me to suggest a favourite poem.*

I enclose a copy of 'The Chess Board' *by Edward Robert Bulwer-Lytton (1831–1891), and also a few lines giving my reasons for choosing it.*

Wishing you every success,
Emma Cooke

The Chess-Board

Irene, do you yet remember
Ere we were grown so sadly wise,
Those evenings in the bleak December,
Curtained warm from the snowy weather,
When you and I played chess together,
    Checkmated by each other's eyes?
    Ah, still I see your soft white hand
Hovering warm o'er Queen and Knight,
    Brave Pawns in valiant battle stand:
The double Castles guard the wings:
The Bishop, bent on distant things,
Moves, sidling, through the fight,
    Our fingers touch; our glances meet,
    And falter; falls your golden hair
    Against my cheek; your bosom sweet
Is heaving. Down the field, your Queen
Rides slow her soldiery all between,
    And checks me unaware.
    Ah me! the little battle's done,
Disperst is all its chivalry;
Full many a move, since then, have we
'Mid Life's perplexing chequers made,
And many a game with Fortune play'd,—

What is it we have won?
This, this at least—if this alone;—
That never, never, never more,
As in those old still nights of yore,
   (Ere we were grown so sadly wise)
   Can you and I shut out the skies,
Shut out the world, and wintry weather,
And, eyes exchanging warmth with eyes,
Play chess, as then we played, together!

Edward Robert Bulwer-Lytton (1831–1891)

'The Chess Board' *by Edward Bulwer-Lytton*

I chose this poem firstly because I think it is a good poem. It is also a Victorian poem as were a lot of books and poems lying around the house when I was growing up in the 1930s and forties. It records a relationship by using the game of chess as a metaphor and it also gives a very vivid impression of the forces at work when the game itself is being played. John and I have been playing chess against each other as well as having been married for the past thirty-eight years. This says a lot of it for both of us.

Emma Cooke

AGNES BERNELLE   313

24 January 1994

Dear Ewan, Áine and Christopher,

I am enclosing one of my favourite poems which is by Louis MacNeice.

I am finding it difficult to give the reason why I like it particularly as it is really contained in the poem itself. Unlike more lyrical pieces it does rather speak for itself.

All I can think of saying is that it is so very apt for our century where man's inhumanity to man is not only apparent in acts of violence and mass torture but also runs insidiously through our daily lives, where ordinary citizens cause suffering to peoples in countries far away and are even putting our planet at risk through their greed and selfishness.

The piece encompasses all that is most deplorable in the world to-day in the unborn being's fears, yet it also admits the possibility that he or she will grow into a worthwhile human being whatever environment he or she will be born into and gives us all hope that the human condition may not after all be entirely evil.

I don't know if this makes any sense?

I wish you much success with your next publication and feel very flattered that you have asked me to be part of it.

Yours sincerely,
Agnes Bernelle

Prayer Before Birth

I am not yet born; O hear me.
Let not the bloodsucking bat or the rat or the stoat or the
    club-footed ghoul come near me.

I am not yet born, console me.
I fear that the human race may with tall walls wall me,
    with strong drugs dope me, with wise lies lure me,
        on black racks rack me, in blood-baths roll me.

I am not yet born; provide me
With water to dandle me, grass to grow for me, trees to talk
    to me, sky to sing to me, birds and a white light
        in the back of my mind to guide me.

I am not yet born; forgive me
For the sins that in me the world shall commit, my words
    when they speak me, my thoughts when they think me,
        my treason engendered by traitors beyond me,
            my life when they murder by means of my
                hands, my death when they live me.

I am not yet born; rehearse me
In the parts I must play and the cues I must take when
    old men lecture me, bureaucrats hector me, mountains
        frown at me, lovers laugh at me, the white
            waves call me to folly and the desert calls
                me to doom and the beggar refuses
                    my gift and my children curse me.

I am not yet born; O hear me,
Let not the man who is beast or who thinks he is God
    come near me.

I am not yet born; O fill me
With strength against those who would freeze my
    humanity, would dragoon me into a lethal automaton,
        would make me a cog in a machine, a thing with
            one face, a thing, and against all those
                who would dissipate my entirety, would
                    blow me like thistledown hither and
                      thither or hither and thither
                        like water held in the
                          hands would spill me.

Let them not make me a stone and let them not spill me.
Otherwise kill me.

Louis MacNeice (1907–1963)

JEAN VALENTINE   314

8 April 1993

Dear Ewan, Áine and Christopher,

Thank you for your letter, and thank you deeply for Lifelines.

I have chosen 'Stings' by Sylvia Plath. With Emily Dickinson I think she marks a turning point for women writers, and I always think of her with gratitude.

With best wishes,
Jean Valentine

Stings

Bare-handed, I hand the combs.
The man in white smiles, bare-handed,
Our cheesecloth gauntlets neat and sweet,
The throats of our wrists brave lilies.
He and I

Have a thousand clean cells between us,
Eight combs of yellow cups,
And the hive itself a teacup,
White with pink flowers on it,
With excessive love I enameled it

Thinking 'Sweetness, sweetness'.
Brood cells gray as the fossils of shells
Terrify me, they seem so old.
What am I buying, wormy mahogany?
Is there any queen at all in it?

If there is, she is old,
Her wings torn shawls, her long body
Rubbed of its plush—
Poor and bare and unqueenly and even shameful.
I stand in a column

Of winged, unmiraculous women,
Honey-drudgers.
I am no drudge
Though for years I have eaten dust
And dried plates with my dense hair.

And seen my strangeness evaporate,
Blue dew from dangerous skin.
Will they hate me,
These women who only scurry,
Whose news is the open cherry, the open clover?

It is almost over.
I am in control.
Here is my honey-machine,
It will work without thinking,
Opening, in spring, like an industrious virgin

To scour the creaming crests
As the moon, for its ivory powders, scours the sea.
A third person is watching.
He has nothing to do with the bee-seller or with me.
Now he is gone

In eight great bounds, a great scapegoat.
Here is his slipper, here is another,
And here the square of white linen
He wore instead of a hat.
He was sweet,

The sweat of his efforts a rain
Tugging the world to fruit.
The bees found him out,
Molding onto his lips like lies,
Complicating his features.

They thought death was worth it, but I
Have a self to recover, a queen.
Is she dead, is she sleeping?
Where has she been,
With her lion-red body, her wings of glass?

Now she is flying
More terrible than she ever was, red
Scar in the sky, red comet
Over the engine that killed her—
The mausoleum, the wax house.

Sylvia Plath (1932–1963)

SEAN DUNNE   315

Cork Examiner
Academy Street
Cork

10 January 1994

Dear Ewan, Áine and Christopher,

Trying to name a favourite poem is as difficult as having to name my favourite among my children, and as impossible. At different times, certain poems have loomed large in my life and have been a kind of sustenance. Such poems include 'Four Quartets' by T S Eliot; 'Filling Station' by Elizabeth Bishop; 'Heart's Needle' by W D Snodgrass; 'Requiem' by Anna Akhmatova (whose poems and person I love); 'The

Journey' *by Eavan Boland;* 'The Unquiet Grave' *(an old ballad by an unknown writer); the Psalms;* 'Sunday Morning' *by Wallace Stevens;* 'Briggflats' *by Basil Bunting; the love poems of Paul Eluard; just about anything by Derek Mahon.*

Just at the moment, I'm carrying around a poem in my head the way you might carry around an old song. It's been lodged there firmly for days like a piece of shrapnel. It might be gone by next week but just now it's top of the list. It was written by Edward Thomas and it's called 'Cock-Crow'.

Every good wish,
Sean Dunne

Cock-Crow

Out of the wood of thoughts that grows by night
To be cut down by the sharp axe of light,—
Out of the night, two cocks together crow,
Cleaving the darkness with a silver blow:
And bright before my eyes twin trumpeters stand,
Heralds of splendour, one at either hand,
Each facing each as in a coat of arms:
The milkers lace their boots up at the farms.

Edward Thomas (1878–1917)

LEONARD MICHAELS   316

A slumber did my spirit seal

A slumber did my spirit seal;
    I had no human fears:
    She seemed a thing that could not feel
        The touch of earthly years.

No motion has she now, no force;
    She neither hears nor sees;
    Rolled round in earth's diurnal course,
        With rocks, and stones, and trees.

William Wordsworth (1770–1850)

My favorite poem is 'A Slumber Did My Spirit Seal'. *I like the way Wordsworth's very plain statement becomes melancholy and exhilarating at once. He says he didn't imagine the woman could die, and he remembers that he thought of her as a* 'thing'. *Now she is dead, and she is indeed a thing, like* 'rocks and stones and trees'. *But despite the final, chilling desolation of her burial in the insentient earth, the woman's death suggests something about human life that death cannot annihilate. It is that our existence is in and for one another. This isn't said, but the poem is wonderful for much that isn't said. In its simplicity, we feel the fierce power and mystery of its truth.*

Leonard Michaels

AVRIL DOYLE   317

Dáil Éireann
Baile Átha Cliath 2
Dublin 2

The enclosed is forwarded for your information with the best wishes and compliments of Avril Doyle, TD

Children

If children live with criticism
    they learn to condemn

If children live with hostility
    they learn to fight

If children live with ridicule
    they learn to be shy

If children live with shame
    they learn to feel guilty

If children live with tolerance
    they learn to be patient

If children live with encouragement
    they learn confidence

If children live with praise
    they learn to appreciate

If children live with fairness
    they learn justice

If children live with security
    they learn to have faith

If children live with approval
    they learn to like themselves

If children live with acceptance and friendship
    they learn to find love in the world

Anonymous

CIARÁN BENSON   318

The Arts Council
16 February 1994

Dear Ewan, Áine and Christopher,

My apologies for not writing sooner but I have been in America and am just back for these few days. The poem I chose is one by Theodore Roethke called 'The Waking'.

My accompanying lines are these:

It can be a hard realisation that life is not always as you think it is, that the world is not divided into simple opposites such as love or hate, thinking or feeling, waking or sleeping. We learn this by living and not by some given inborn knowledge. What we learn is that paradoxes, apparent contradictions, are the colours of life; and more often than not we come to know this when we are humbled and in distress.

This is why I came to like and admire Roethke's 'The Waking' *so much. A good poem is itself a reconciliation of apparent opposites, a synthesis of the highest form often in the simplest language. It speaks to you but always more than you can ever say about it.* 'The Waking' *is in this league. I especially like the wonderful opening line which recurs like a consoling mantra but also like a tantalising Zen riddle: 'I wake to sleep, and take my waking slow'. 'This shaking keeps me steady' is a line of reassurance from a poet who knows and a link of sympathy to those who might.*

Every success with your book.

Yours sincerely,
Ciarán Benson
Chairman

The Waking

I wake to sleep, and take my waking slow.
I feel my fate in what I cannot fear.
I learn by going where I have to go.

We think by feeling. What is there to know?
I hear my being dance from ear to ear.
I wake to sleep, and take my waking slow.

Of those so close beside me, which are you?
God bless the Ground! I shall walk softly there,
And learn by going where I have to go.

Light takes the Tree; but who can tell us how?
The lowly worm climbs up a winding stair;
I wake to sleep, and take my waking slow.

Great Nature has another thing to do
To you and me; so take the lively air,
And, lovely, learn by going where to go.

This shaking keeps me steady. I should know.
What falls away is always. And is near.
I wake to sleep, and take my waking slow.
I learn by going where I have to go.

Theodore Roethke (1908–1963)

HAROLD BLOOM   319

Whitney Humanities Center
Yale University
6 April 1993

Dear Mr Gibson et al:

My favorite poem is Walt Whitman's elegy for Lincoln, 'When Lilacs Last in the Dooryard Bloom'd'. It seems to me the finest poem yet written by an American, and fully comparable to the 'Lycidas' of Milton. Truly it is an elegy for the self, the poet's self and all our selves. In nuance, and in subtle minglings of celebration and lament, it marks the close of Whitman's major phase.

Harold Bloom
Sterling Professor of the Humanities, Yale

When Lilacs Last in the Dooryard Bloom'd

I
When lilacs last in the dooryard bloom'd,
And the great star early droop'd in the western sky in the
    night,
I mourn'd, and yet shall mourn with ever-returning spring.

Ever-returning spring, trinity sure to me you bring,
Lilac blooming perennial and drooping star in the west,
And thought of him I love.
II
O powerful western fallen star!
O shades of night — O moody, tearful night!
O great star disappear'd — O the black murk that hides the star!
O cruel hands that hold me powerless — O helpless soul of me!
O harsh surrounding cloud that will not free my soul.

III

In the dooryard fronting an old farm-house near the white-
    wash'd palings,
Stands the lilac-bush tall-growing with heart-shaped leaves
    of rich green,
With many a pointed blossom rising delicate, with the per-
    fume strong I love,
With every leaf a miracle—and from this bush in the door-
    yard,
With delicate-color'd blossoms and heart-shaped leaves of
    rich green,
A sprig with its flower I break.

IV

In the swamp in secluded recesses,
A shy and hidden bird is warbling a song.

Solitary the thrush,
The hermit withdrawn to himself, avoiding the settlements,
Sings by himself a song.

Song of the bleeding throat,
Death's outlet song of life, (for well dear brother I know,
If thou wast not granted to sing thou would'st surely die.)

V

Over the breast of the spring, the land, amid cities,
Amid lanes and through old woods, where lately the violets
    peep'd from the ground, spotting the gray debris,
Amid the grass in the fields each side of the lanes, passing the
    endless grass,
Passing the yellow-spear'd wheat, every grain from its shroud
    in the dark-brown fields uprisen,
Passing the apple-tree blows of white and pink in the or-
    chards,
Carrying a corpse to where it shall rest in the grave,
Night and day journeys a coffin.

VI

Coffin that passes through lanes and streets,
Through day and night with the great cloud darkening the
    land,
With the pomp of the inloop'd flags with the cities draped in
    black,
With the show of the States themselves as of crape-veil'd
    women standing,
With processions long and winding and the flambeaus of the
    night,
With the countless torches lit, with the silent sea of faces and
    the unbared heads,
With the waiting depot, the arriving coffin, and the sombre
    faces,

With dirges through the night, with the thousand voices
    rising strong and solemn,
With all the mournful voices of the dirges pour'd around the
    coffin,
The dim-lit churches and the shuddering organs—where
    amid these you journey,
With the tolling tolling bells' perpetual clang,
Here, coffin that slowly passes,
I give you my sprig of lilac.

VII
(Nor for you, for one alone,
Blossoms and branches green to coffins all I bring,
For fresh as the morning, thus would I chant a song for you
    O sane and sacred death.

All over bouquets of roses,
O death, I cover you over with roses and early lilies,
But mostly and now the lilac that blooms the first,
Copious I break, I break the sprigs from the bushes,
With loaded arms I come, pouring for you,
For you and the coffins all of you O death.)

VIII
O western orb sailing the heaven,
Now I know what you must have meant as a month since I
    walk'd,
As I walk'd in silence the transparent shadowy night,
As I saw you had something to tell as you bent to me night
    after night,
As you droop'd from the sky low down as if to my side,
    (while the other stars all look'd on,)
As we wander'd together the solemn night, (for something I
    know not what kept me from sleep,)
As the night advanced, and I saw on the rim of the west how
    full you were of woe,
As I stood on the rising ground in the breeze in the cool
    transparent night,
As I watch'd where you pass'd and was lost in the nether-
    ward black of the night,

As my soul in its trouble dissatisfied sank, as where you sad
    orb,
Concluded, dropt in the night, and was gone.

IX
Sing on there in the swamp,
O singer bashful and tender, I hear your notes, I hear your
    call,
I hear, I come presently, I understand you,
But a moment I linger, for the lustrous star has detain'd me,
The star my departing comrade holds and detains me.

X
O how shall I warble myself for the dead one there I loved?
And how shall I deck my song for the large sweet soul that
    has gone?
And what shall my perfume be for the grave of him I love?

Sea-winds blown from east and west,
Blown from the Eastern sea and blown from the Western
    sea, till there on the prairies meeting,
These and with these and the breath of my chant,
I'll perfume the grave of him I love.

XI
O what shall I hang on the chamber walls?
And what shall the pictures be that I hang on the walls,
To adorn the burial-house of him I love?

Pictures of growing spring and farms and homes,
With the Fourth-month eve at sundown, and the gray smoke
    lucid and bright,
With floods of the yellow gold of the gorgeous, indolent,
    sinking sun, burning, expanding the air,
With the fresh sweet herbage under foot, and the pale green
    leaves of the trees prolific,
In the distance the flowing glaze, the breast of the river, with
    a wind-dapple here and there,
With ranging hills on the banks, with many a line against the
    sky, and shadows,

And the city at hand with dwellings so dense, and stacks of
    chimneys,
And all the scenes of life and the workshops, and the work-
    men homeward returning.

XII
Lo, body and soul—this land,
My own Manhattan with spires, and the sparkling and
    hurrying tides, and the ships,
The varied and ample land, the South and the North in the
    light, Ohio's shores and flashing Missouri,
And ever the far-spreading prairies cover'd with grass and
    corn.

Lo, the most excellent sun so calm and haughty,
The violet and purple morn with just-felt breezes,
The gentle soft-born measureless light,
The miracle spreading bathing all, the fulfill'd noon,
The coming eve delicious, the welcome night and the stars,
Over my cities shining all, enveloping man and land.

XIII
Sing on, sing on you gray-brown bird,
Sing from the swamps, the recesses, pour your chant from
    the bushes,
Limitless out of the dusk, out of the cedars and pines.

Sing on dearest brother, warble your reedy song,
Loud human song, with voice of uttermost woe.

O liquid and free and tender!
O wild and loose to my soul—O wondrous singer!
You only I hear—yet the star holds me, (but will soon
    depart,)
Yet the lilac with mastering odor holds me.

XIV
Now while I sat in the day and look'd forth,
In the close of the day with its light and the fields of spring,
    and the farmers preparing their crops,
In the large unconscious scenery of my land with its lakes
    and forests,

In the heavenly aerial beauty, (after the perturb'd winds and
    the storms,)
Under the arching heavens of the afternoon swift passing,
    and the voices of children and women,
The many-moving sea-tides, and I saw the ships how they
    sail'd,
And the summer approaching with richness, and the fields all
    busy with labor,
And the infinite separate houses, how they all went on, each
    with its meals and minutia of daily usages,
And the streets how their throbbings throbb'd, and the cities
    pent—lo, then and there,
Falling upon them all and among them all, enveloping me
    with the rest,
Appear'd the cloud, appear'd the long black trail,
And I knew death, its thought, and the sacred knowledge of
    death.

Then with the knowledge of death as walking one side of me,
And the thought of death close-walking the other side of me,
And I in the middle as with companions, and as holding the
    hands of companions,
I fled forth to the hiding receiving night that talks not,
Down to the shores of the water, the path by the swamp in
    the dimness,
To the solemn shadowy cedars and ghostly pines so still.

And the singer so shy to the rest receiv'd me,
The gray-brown bird I know receiv'd us comrades three,
And he sang the carol of death, and a verse for him I love.

From deep secluded recesses,
From the fragrant cedars and the ghostly pines so still,
Came the carol of the bird.

And the charm of the carol rapt me,
As I held as if by their hands my comrades in the night,
And the voice of my spirit tallied the song of the bird.

Come lovely and soothing death,
Undulate round the world, serenely arriving, arriving,
In the day, in the night, to all, to each,
Sooner or later delicate death

Prais'd be the fathomless universe,
For life and joy, and for objects and knowledge curious,
And for love, sweet love—but praise! praise! praise!
For the sure-enwinding arms of cool-enfolding death.

Dark mother always gliding near with soft feet,
Have none chanted for thee a chant of fullest welcome?
Then I chant it for thee, I glorify thee above all,
I bring thee a song that when thou must indeed come, come
    unfalteringly.

Approach strong deliveress,
When it is so, when thou hast taken them I joyously sing the
    dead,
Lost in the loving floating ocean of thee,
Laved in the flood of thy bliss O death.

From me to thee glad serenades,
Dances for thee I propose saluting thee, adornments and feast-
    ings for thee,
And the sights of the open landscape and the high-spread sky
    are fitting,
And life and the fields, and the huge and thoughtful night.

The night in silence under many a star,
The ocean shore and the husky whispering wave whose voice I
    know,
And the soul turning to thee O vast and well-veil'd death,
And the body gratefully nestling close to thee.

Over the tree-tops I float thee a song,
Over the rising and sinking waves, over the myriad fields and
    the prairies wide,
Over the dense-pack'd cities all and the teeming wharves and
    ways,
I float this carol with joy, with joy to thee O death.

XV
To the tally of my soul,
Loud and strong kept up the gray-brown bird,
With pure deliberate notes spreading filling the night.

Loud in the pines and cedars dim,
Clear in the freshness moist and the swamp-perfume,
And I with my comrades there in the night.

While my sight that was bound in my eyes unclosed,
As to long panoramas of visions.

And I saw askant the armies,
I saw as in noiseless dreams hundreds of battle-flags,
Borne through the smoke of the battles and pierc'd with
    missiles I saw them,
And carried hither and yon through the smoke, and torn and
    bloody,
And at last but a few shreds left on the staffs, (and all in
    silence,)
And the staffs all splinter'd and broken.

I saw battle-corpses, myriads of them,
And the white skeletons of young men, I saw them,
I saw the debris and debris of all the slain soldiers of the war,
But I saw they were not as was thought,
They themselves were fully at rest, they suffer'd not,
The living remain'd and suffer'd, the mother suffer'd,
And the wife and the child and the musing comrade suffer'd,
And the armies that remain'd suffer'd.

XVI
Passing the visions, passing the night,
Passing, unloosing the hold of my comrades' hands,
Passing the song of the hermit bird and the tallying song of
    my soul,
Victorious song, death's outlet song, yet varying ever-altering
    song,
As low and wailing, yet clear the notes, rising and falling,
    flooding the night,
Sadly sinking and fainting, as warning and warning, and yet
    again bursting with joy,
Covering the earth and filling the spread of the heaven,
As that powerful psalm in the night I heard from recesses,
Passing, I leave thee lilac with heart-shaped leaves,
I leave thee there in the dooryard, blooming, returning with
    spring.

I cease from my song for thee,
From my gaze on thee in the west, fronting the west, com-
    muning with thee,
O comrade lustrous with silver face in the night.

Yet each to keep and all, retrievements out of the night,
The song, the wondrous chant of the gray-brown bird,
And the tallying chant, the echo arous'd in my soul,
With the lustrous and drooping star with the countenance
    full of woe,

With the holders holding my hand nearing the call of the bird,
Comrades mine and I in the midst, and their memory ever to
    keep, for the dead I loved so well,
For the sweetest, wisest soul of all my days and lands—and
    this for his dear sake,
Lilac and star and bird twined with the chant of the soul,
There in the fragrant pines and the cedars dusk and dim.

Walt Whitman (1819–1892)

MOY McCRORY   320

10 January 1994

Your letter has been forwarded to me and I shall either fax or mail this reply at the first chance. I am actually away from home working in deepest Devon, where even the simplest act of buying a stamp becomes protracted. I hope to catch the postman and see if he'll send this off.

A favourite poem is always one of those nightmare questions because whatever I choose I will be missing out thousands that I love equally.

However, a significant poem for me has to be 'Pangur Bán'. (I'm thinking of the Robin Flower translation.)

This has been a favourite, since childhood. Its simple lyric quality and its clearness, gives it a childlike simplicity which is deceptive. You can't hear it without being whisked back in time, the listener shares the scriptorium with the frozen scribe, who finds his mind wandering late in the night, watching his white Pangur chase mice. And that final irreverent gesture, to scribble it down the side of St Paul's Epistle, makes it both profane, vernacular and sacred.

I think this is a writer's poem, comparing the hunting of words to Pangur's hunting. As such it serves as a hymn for anyone who has sat up late trying to get the exact phrase, that word which always eludes.

Yours sincerely and with poor typing (I'm away from my computer and can't do any correcting).

Moy McCrory

Pangur Bán

I and Pangur Bán my cat,
'Tis a like task we are at:
Hunting mice is his delight,
Hunting words I sit all night.

Better far than praise of men
'Tis to sit with book and pen;
Pangur bears me no ill will,
He too plies his simple skill.

'Tis a merry thing to see
At our tasks how glad are we,
When at home we sit and find
Entertainment to our mind.

Oftentimes a mouse will stray
In the hero Pangur's way;
Oftentimes my keen thought set
Takes a meaning in its net.

'Gainst the wall he sets his eye
Full and fierce and sharp and sly;
'Gainst the wall of knowledge I
All my little wisdom try.

When a mouse darts from its den
O how glad is Pangur then!
O what gladness do I prove
When I solve the doubts I love!

So in peace our tasks we ply,
Pangur Bán, my cat, and I;
In our arts we find our bliss,
I have mine and he has his.

Practice every day has made
Pangur perfect in his trade;
I get wisdom day and night
Turning darkness into light.

Anonymous (eighth or early ninth century)
Translated by Robin Flower

[This poem, in a version based on translations by Whitley Stokes, John
Strachan and Kuno Meyer, was also chosen by Cardinal Tomás Ó Fiaich in
Lifelines.]

VINCENT BANVILLE   321

13 January 1994

Dear Ewan, Áine and Christopher,

*Thank you very much for your letter asking me to contribute to your
anthology of favourite poems.*

I've chosen the poem that introduces Through the Looking-Glass and
What Alice Found There *as my piece, mainly because it harks back to
childhood and to the innocence and sense of wonder that the young mind
possesses before the cares and sorrows of a naughty world wheel in to
sweep them away.*

I hope you'll find it appropriate.

Yours,
Vincent Banville

from *Through the Looking-Glass and What Alice Found There*

Child of the pure unclouded brow
    And dreaming eyes of wonder!
Though time be fleet, and I and thou
    Are half a life asunder,
Thy loving smile will surely hail
The love-gift of a fairy-tale.

I have not seen thy sunny face,
    Nor heard thy silver laughter;
No thought of me shall find a place
    In thy young life's hereafter—
Enough that now thou wilt not fail
To listen to my fairy-tale.

A tale begun in other days,
    When summer suns were glowing—
A simple chime, that served to time
    The rhythm of our rowing—
Whose echoes live in memory yet,
Though envious years would say 'forget'.

Come, hearken then, ere voice of dread,
    With bitter tidings laden,
Shall summon to unwelcome bed
    A melancholy maiden!
We are but older children, dear,
Who fret to find our bedtime near.

Without, the frost, the blinding snow,
    The storm-wind's moody madness—
Within, the firelight's ruddy glow,
    And childhood's nest of gladness.
The magic words shall hold thee fast;
Thou shalt not heed the raving blast.

And, though the shadow of a sigh
    May tremble through the story,
For 'happy summer days' gone by
    And vanish'd summer glory—
It shall not touch, with breath of bale,
The pleasance of our fairy-tale.

Lewis Carroll (1832–1898)

JIMMY MURPHY   322

Peacock Theatre,
Lwr Abbey St, Dublin 1
17 January 1994

Thank you for your invitation and I would be delighted to help.

I suppose if I was to have a favourite poem it would be a poem that would stir up in me a fond memory that was lost in where ever memories lose themselves. Yeats's 'He wishes for the cloths of heaven' *is one and, if I was to choose a favourite, then Kavanagh's* 'Raglan Road' *is it.*

I don't know what he intended but it's a poem of unrequited love to me. And whether we're ready or not one day we will all trip lightly along the ledge of our own 'quiet street . . .'.

Best wishes,
Jimmy Murphy

On Raglan Road

On Raglan Road on an autumn day I met her first and knew
That her dark hair would weave a snare that I might one day
    rue;
I saw the danger, yet I walked along the enchanted way,
And I said, let grief be a fallen leaf at the dawning of the day.

On Grafton Street in November we tripped lightly along the
    ledge
Of the deep ravine where can be seen the worth of passion's
    pledge,
The Queen of Hearts still making tarts and I not making hay—
O I loved too much and by such by such is happiness thrown
    away.

I gave her gifts of the mind I gave her the secret sign that's
    known
To the artists who have known the true gods of sound and
    stone
And word and tint. I did not stint for I gave her poems to say.
With her own name there and her own dark hair like clouds
    over fields of May.

On a quiet street where old ghosts meet I see her walking now
Away from me so hurriedly my reason must allow
That I had wooed not as I should a creature made of clay—
When the angel woos the clay he'd lose his wings at the dawn
    of day.

Patrick Kavanagh (1904–1967)

[This poem was also chosen by Ken Bourke in *Lifelines*.]

CATHERINE PHIL MacCARTHY   323

20 January 1994

Dear Ewan, Áine and Chris,

Thanks for inviting me to participate in your wonderful project for hunger relief. I am full of admiration for Lifelines *and hope you make a fortune with your next book.*

My favourite poem is 'The Pomegranate' *by Eavan Boland. I love it for the beauty and intimacy of the private world it reveals — the sleeping child, her can of Coke, the uncut fruit, her mother's resolve to say nothing. It makes instant and magical changes always from legend to life, in a voice that is never less than exhilarating for its urgency and ability to surprise. At the heart of the poem is love and loss, at once ritualized and totally formless.*

Good luck with your work.

Yours sincerely,
Catherine Phil MacCarthy

The Pomegranate

The only legend I have ever loved is
the story of a daughter lost in hell.
And found and rescued there.
Love and blackmail are the gist of it.
Ceres and Persephone the names.
And the best thing about the legend is
I can enter it anywhere. And have.
As a child in exile in
a city of fogs and strange consonants,
I read it first and at first I was
an exiled child in the crackling dusk of
the underworld, the stars blighted. Later
I walked out in a summer twilight
searching for my daughter at bed-time.
When she came running I was ready
to make any bargain to keep her.
I carried her back past whitebeams
and wasps and honey-scented buddleias.
But I was Ceres then and I knew
winter was in store for every leaf
on every tree on that road.
Was inescapable for each one we passed.
And for me.

It is winter
and the stars are hidden.
I climb the stairs and stand where I can see
my child asleep beside her teen magazines,
her can of Coke, her plate of uncut fruit.
The pomegranate! How did I forget it?
She could have come home and been safe
and ended the story and all
our heart-broken searching but she reached
out a hand and plucked a pomegranate.
She put out her hand and pulled down
the French sound for apple and
the noise of stone and the proof
that even in the place of death,
at the heart of legend, in the midst
of rocks full of unshed tears
ready to be diamonds by the time
the story was told, a child can be
hungry. I could warn her. There is still a chance.
The rain is cold. The road is flint-coloured.
The suburb has cars and cable television.
The veiled stars are above ground.
It is another world. But what else
can a mother give her daughter but such
beautiful rifts in time?
If I defer the grief I will diminish the gift.
The legend will be hers as well as mine.
She will enter it. As I have.
She will wake up. She will hold
the papery flushed skin in her hand.
And to her lips. I will say nothing.

Eavan Boland (b.1944)

EVELYN CONLON   324

10 January 1994

Dear Ewan, Áine and Christopher,

*I want to cheat because it's not possible to have one favourite poem,
however I won't. Grace Paley is known as a surprising and satisfying
short story writer. Her poetry could never be as good, only because it
becomes the blueprint for something more marvellous; stories that tell
an entire history in two pages, tragically but with wipe-the-floor wit.
Born in 1922 she has always been politically active in feminist and
anti-war causes. She once described herself as a co-operative anarchist
and a combative pacifist; this poem is an illustration of the latter stance.
Hope you enjoy it and good luck with your book.*

Evelyn

I Gave Away That Kid

I gave away that kidlike he was an old button
   Here old button get off of me
   I don't need you anymore
   go on get out of here
   get into the army
   sew yourself onto the colonel's shirt
   or the captain's fly   jackass
   don't you have any sense
   don't you read the papers
   why are you leaving now?

That kid walked out of here like he was the cat's pyjamas
   what are you wearing p j's for   you damn fool?
   why are you crying   you couldn't
   get another job anywhere anyways
   go march to the army's drummer
   be a man like all your dead uncles
   then think of something else to do

Lost him, sorry about that the president said
   he was a good boy
   never see one like him again
   Why don't you repeat that your honor
   why don't you sizzle up the meaning
   of that sentence for your breakfast
   why don't you stick him in a prayer
and count to ten before my wife gets you.

That boy is a puddle in Beirut the paper says
   scraped up for singing in church
   too bad   too bad is a terrible tune
   It's no song at all   how come you sing it?

I gave away that kidlike he was an old button
   Here old button get off ame
   I don't need you anymore
   go on get out of here
   get into the army
   sew yourself onto the colonel's shirt
   or the captain's fly   jackass
   don't you have any sense
   don't you read the papers
   why are you leaving now?

Grace Paley (b.1922)

BERNARD FARRELL   325

Dear Ewan, Áine and Christopher,

Thank you so much for your letter inviting me to be part of Lifelines. *May this edition prove to be as successful as its predecessors.*

The poem I have chosen is 'The Cottage Hospital' by John Betjeman.

I could stick a pin into The Contents of any John Betjeman collection and chances are that I'd like (and probably love) the selection. 'The Cottage Hospital' wasn't always a favourite but now, with time passing, I find that it has become more relevant and, perhaps, more frightening.

Apart from its theme and expression, I greatly admire its structure. The third stanza may initially seem remote and unconnected, but when the work is taken as a unit and the seeds so cleverly sown bear fruit, then everything falls perfectly into place. The poem, I think, holds the same attraction for me as the flame does for the moth. It is more than slightly dangerous.

With every good wish,
Bernard Farrell

The Cottage Hospital

At the end of a long-walled garden
    in a red provincial town,
A brick path led to a mulberry—
    scanty grass at its feet.
I lay under blackening branches
    where the mulberry leaves hung down
Sheltering ruby fruit globes
    from a Sunday-tea-time heat.
Apple and plum espaliers
    basked upon bricks of brown;
The air was swimming with insects,
    and children played in the street.

Out of this bright intentness
    into the mulberry shade
Musca domestica (housefly)
    swung from the August light
Slap into slithery rigging
    by the waiting spider made
Which spun the lithe elastic
    till the fly was shrouded tight.
Down came the hairy talons
    and horrible poison blade

And none of the garden noticed
    that fizzing, hopeless fight.

Say in what Cottage Hospital
    whose pale green walls resound
With the tap upon polished parquet
    of inflexible nurses' feet
Shall I myself be lying
    when they range the screens around?
And say shall I groan in dying,
    as I twist the sweaty sheet?
Or gasp for breath uncrying,
    as I feel my senses drown'd
While the air is swimming with insects
    and children play in the street?

John Betjeman (1906–1984)

CAROL ANN DUFFY   326

Dear All,

*'The Song of Wandering Aengus' by W B Yeats is my favourite poem.
I first read it when I was 15 or so and I still, thankfully, find it as
beautiful now as I did then. It was almost instantly memorable and the
last two lines, on that first reading, were like a small punch in the
stomach. I've recently taken great pleasure from a recording of the poem,
with music, by Christy Moore.*

Best wishes,
Carol Ann Duffy

['The Song of Wandering Aengus' was also chosen by Charles Haughey,
Seamus Brennan and Fiona Shaw in *Lifelines*.]

The Song of Wandering Aengus

I went out to the hazel wood,
Because a fire was in my head,
And cut and peeled a hazel wand,
And hooked a berry to a thread;
And when white moths were on the wing,
And moth-like stars were flickering out,
I dropped the berry in a stream
And caught a little silver trout.

When I had laid it on the floor
I went to blow the fire aflame,
But something rustled on the floor,
And some one called me by my name:

It had become a glimmering girl
With apple blossom in her hair
Who called me by my name and ran
And faded through the brightening air.

Though I am old with wandering
Through hollow lands and hilly lands,
I will find out where she has gone,
And kiss her lips and take her hands;
And walk among long dappled grass,
And pluck till time and times are done
The silver apples of the moon,
The golden apples of the sun.

W B Yeats (1865–1939)

JEAN KENNEDY SMITH   327

Embassy of the United States of America
Dublin
18 January 1994

Dear Students,

Thank you for inviting me to suggest a poem for inclusion in your 1994 Lifelines *anthology. I am pleased to be a part of such a worthwhile project that will benefit disadvantaged people in developing countries.*

Among my favorite poems is this one by Emily Dickinson (1830–1886):

We never know how high we are
Till we are asked to rise
And then if we are true to plan
Our statures touch the skies—

The Heroism we recite
Would be a normal thing
Did not ourselves the Cubits warp
For fear to be a King—

These lines, which emphasize our amazing capabilities and the indomitable nature of the human spirit, have always been inspirational for me. They are printed in the front of my book, Chronicles of Courage, *a collection of stories about people with disabilities and the importance of the arts in their lives.*

My very best wishes to you and the other students at Wesley College for success with this Lifelines *anthology. You are to be congratulated for this interesting endeavor.*

Sincerely,
Jean Kennedy Smith
Ambassador

DAVID MARCUS 328

6 January 1994

Dear Áine, Ewan and Christopher,

*(Although an ardent feminist, I still believe in putting ladies first!) —
I am delighted to be associated with your noble venture and thank you
for inviting me.*

*I enclose my choice, a poem by the American poet, E E Cummings. It
has no title — Cummings never gave his poems titles — and it is
absolutely vital that it be printed exactly as enclosed with the poet's
typographical oddities.*

Good luck to you all.

Yours,
David Marcus

mr youse needn't be so spry
concernin questions arty

each has his tastes but as for i
i likes a certain party

gimme the he-man's solid bliss
for youse ideas i'll match youse

a pretty girl who naked is
is worth a million statues

E E Cummings (1894–1962)

*The typograhpical experiments cultivated by the American poet, E E
Cummings, served to alienate many readers and critics. The loss was,
and still is, theirs. One of the most accomplished craftsmen of his age
and a lyric poet who had few superiors, he was a master of every mode.
The poem of his I have chosen would, in our silly politically correct times,
probably be reviled as male sexist. Male? But naturally; that's what he
was. Sexist? But that's to ignore his use of the sexual dichotomy to
express his view that life was more important than art. Ms youse needn't
be so spry.*

David Marcus

JOHN CAREY 329

Merton College
Oxford

Dear Committee,

Thank you for your letter.

I suppose my 'favourite' poem — that is, the one I happen to be thinking about most, varies from time to time. But the poem I say over to myself most often, I think, is Keats's 'To Autumn'. I love it because of its calming rhythms, and because, though it is about dying, it is not sad, but rich and comforting.

With best wishes,

Yours sincerely,
John Carey

['To Autumn' was also chosen by Neil Rudenstine in *Lifelines* and by Seán Lysaght in this volume. The poem appears in full on page 125.]

JOHN ARDEN 330

24 January 1994

Dear Ewan Gibson, Áine Jackson and Christopher Pillow,

Thank you for inviting me to choose a poem for Lifelines *— I enclose a combination of extracts from a poem and some interpolated explanation/ comment, which I hope is the sort of thing you want. All best wishes for the success of the project.*

Yours sincerely,
John Arden

'Speak Parrot', *written in 1521 by an English clergyman, John Skelton (?1460–1529). A poem of political defiance, an attack upon the power and corruption of the great minister, Cardinal Wolsey. Skelton was living in the Sanctuary of Westminster Abbey, London, where his friend the abbot promised to protect him against the Cardinal's vengeance; but even so he had to disguise his poem; his readers as well as himself needed protection; the true meaning would only have been clear to people of considerable learning; to anyone else (a police-informant, for example) it would seem to be nothing more dangerous than amusing nonsense-verse. The sort of writing later to be known (in the Soviet Union) as samizdat, a secret weapon against a tyrannical regime. Skelton puts his horror of Wolsey into the mouth of a parrot, a harmless creature who only repeats what he hears and cannot be held responsible for it. Our world is as corrupt as Skelton's, and writers who choose to say so can in many cases face as much peril as he did; he was an old man in 1521, and very brave. It is a long poem; I give only a few bits of it, in modernised English. The parrot begins by describing himself —*

With my beak bent, and my little wanton eye,
My feathers fresh as is the emerald green,
About my neck a circulet like the rich ruby,
My little legs, my feet both neat and clean.
I am a minion to wait upon a queen;
'My proper Parrot, my little pretty fool.'
With ladies I learn and go with them to school . . .

'Parrot, Parrot, Parrot, pretty popinjay!'
With my beak I can pick my little pretty toe;
My delight is solace, pleasure, disport and play;
Like a wanton, when I will, I reel to and fro.
Parrot can say, '*Caesar, ave,*' also;
But Parrot hath no favour to Esebon;
Above all other birds, set Parrot alone.

'Caesar, ave,' means 'Hail Caesar' — ie: Parrot is attacking the king's government, not the gullible young king. Esebon is a biblical name, Heshbon, a heathen city — ie: Wolsey's administration. Then Parrot becomes very obscure, surrealist, wild, for those who do not have the key —

O Esebon, Esebon, to thee is come again
Sihon, the regent *Amorreorum,*
And Og, that fat hog of Bashan, doth retain
The crafty *coistronus Cananeorum* . . .
Esebon, Marylebone, Whetstone-next-Barnet;
A trim-tram for an horse-mill it were a nice thing,
Dainties for damsels, chaffer far-fat.
Bo-ho doth bark well. Hough-ho he ruleth the ring;
From Scarpary to Tartary renown therein doth spring,
With 'He said,' and 'We said,' I wot now what I wot,
Quod magnus est dominus Judas Iscariot . . .

— and so on, for another 387 lines. I won't try to explain all the hidden meanings; but Og that fat hog is the notoriously corpulent Wolsey. The coistronus Cananeorum *(ie: the Canaanites' kitchen-boy) must be one of his officials. The last line translates as 'for Judas Iscariot is a great lord' — ie: the nation is ruled by treacherous villains, which was true then, and is true today of more countries than England. But only the pert little parrot dared say so.*

John Arden

COLM O'GAORA   331

25 February 1994

Dear Ewan, Áine, and Christopher,

Many thanks for inviting me to nominate my favourite poem for inclusion in the next edition of Lifelines *— I am flattered to be considered 'well-known'. I apologise for responding so late.*

My favourite poem is 'this is a rubbish of human rind' *by the American poet E E Cummings.*

I like and admire this poem because it is both bitter and beautiful, damning and redemptive, and has a powerfully elegiac edge to it, particularly in the two closing lines. In the space of four short stanzas it conjures images that echo long after the page has been turned.

With best wishes for the continued success of Lifelines.

Colm O'Gaora

from *Xaipe (1950)*

this is a rubbish of human rind
with a photograph
clutched in the half
of a hand and the word
love underlined

this is a girl who died in her mind
with a warm thick scream
and a keen cold groan
while the gadgets purred
and the gangsters dined

this is a deaf dumb church and blind
with an if in its soul
and a hole in its life
where the young bell tolled
and the old vine twined

this is a dog of no known kind
with one white eye
and one black eye
and the eyes of his eyes
are as lost as you'll find

E E Cummings (1894–1962)

ANNE MADDEN LE BROCQUY   332

*After marvelling at a very young Chinese calligrapher when I was ten
years old, my mother gave me* 170 Chinese Poems, *translated by
Arthur Waley. I read and reread of the sorrows, separations, exiles and
imprisonments expressed in these poems and came to love them and to
know many by heart. Here is one which did not sadden me.*

Plucking the Rushes
(A boy and a girl are sent to gather rushes for thatching)

Green rushes with red shoots,
Long leaves bending to the wind —
You and I in the same boat
Plucking rushes at the Five Lakes.
We started at dawn from the orchid-island;
We rested under the elms till noon.
You and I plucking rushes
Had not plucked a handful when night came!

Anonymous (fourth century)

Translated by Arthur Waley (1889–1966)

All best wishes to Lifelines *for a great success,*
Anne

CHARLES CAUSLEY   333

30 January 1994

Dear Ewan Gibson,

*I don't know whether the poem I choose might or might not be suitable
for the anthology — include it or don't include it, just as you wish. But
I think it would be* 'La Casada Infiel', *probably the best-known poem
by the Spanish poet and playwright Federico García Lorca.*

*The translation I prefer over all others is by Stephen Spender and J I
Gili. You'll probably know that Lorca was murdered at the age of 38 by
Falangists in Granada in 1936 towards the end of the Spanish civil war.
His body was never found.*

*It's not the function, I think, of any work of art to reveal all its secrets
at once. A poem isn't a piece of machinery. If we take it to pieces and
put it together again it may still give no reason why it works — nor is
it obliged to. It must always retain some of its secrets so that it may
continue to give out what Lorca himself called* sonidos negros, *black
sounds. However often we return to a work of art by a master we should*

still be able to make fresh discoveries. The poem should have, so to speak, the magical quality of self-renewal.

Lorca's lyrical narrative, now blowing cool, now blowing hot, has this quality. I first heard it read in Gibraltar over 50 years ago. However many times I've returned to it, it has never failed me.

Good wishes to you and your fellow-editors for your work, and all you do.

Yours sincerely,
Charles Causley

La Casada Infiel

Y que yo me la llevé al río
creyendo que era mozuela,
pero tenía marido.

Fué la noche de Santiago
y casi por compromiso.
Se apagaron los faroles
y se encendieron los grillos.
En las últimas esquinas
toqué sus pechos dormidos,
y se me abrieron de pronto
como ramos de jacintos.
El almidón de su enagua
me sonaba en el oído
como una pieza de seda
rasgada por diez cuchillos.
Sin luz de plata en sus copas
los árboles han crecido
y un horizonte de perros
ladra muy lejos del río.

Pasadas las zarzamoras,
los juncos y los espinos,
bajo su mata de pelo
hice un hoyo sobre el limo.
Yo me quité la corbata.
Ella se quitó el vestido.
Yo el cinturón con revólver.
Ella sus cuatro corpiños.
Ni nardos ni caracolas
tienen el cutis tan fino,
ni los cristales con luna
relumbran con ese brillo.
Sus muslos se me escapaban
como peces sorprendidos,
la mitad llenos de lumbre,
la mitad llenos de frío.

Aquella noche corrí
el mejor de los caminos,
montado en potra de nácar
sin bridas y sin estribos.
No quiero decir, por hombre,
las cosas que ella me dijo.
La luz del entendimiento
me hace ser muy comedido.
Sucia de besos y arena
yo me la llevé del río.
Con el aire se batían
las espadas de los lirios.

Me porté como quien soy.
Como un gitano legítimo.
La regalé un costurero
grande, de raso pajizo,
y no quise enamorarme
porque teniendo marido
me dijo que era mozuela
cuando la llevaba al río.

Federico García Lorca (1898–1936)

The Faithless Wife

And I took her to the river
thinking she was a maiden,
but she had a husband.

It was on Saint James's night
and almost as if prearranged.
The lanterns went out
and the crickets lighted up.
In the farthest corners
I touched her sleeping breasts,
and they opened to me suddenly
like spikes of hyacinth.
The starch of her petticoat
sounded in my ears
like a piece of silk
torn by ten knives.
Without silver light on their foliage
the trees had grown larger
and a horizon of dogs
barks very far from the river.

Past the blackberries,
the reeds and the hawthorn,
underneath her cluster of hair
I made a hollow in the earth.

I took off my tie.
She took off her dress.
I my belt with the revolver.
She her four bodices.
Nor nard nor conch
have skin so fine,
nor did crystals lit by moon
shine with this brilliance.
Her thighs escaped me
like startled fish,
half full of fire,
have full of cold.
That night I ran
on the best of the roads
mounted on a mare of nacre
without bridle or stirrups.
As a man, I won't repeat
the things she said to me.
The light of understanding
has made me most discreet.
Smeared with sand and kisses
I took her from the river.
With the air battled
the swords of the lilies.

I behaved as the person I am.
Like a proper gipsy.
I gave her a sewing basket, large,
of straw-coloured satin,
and I did not want to fall in love
because having a husband
she told me she was a maiden,
when I took her to the river.

Translated by Stephen Spender and J I Gili

SAM McAUGHTRY   334

*When I was a young man, if I thought very highly of a girl, I used to
pretend to her that I was the author of this. It is a measure of the purity
of the verse that the ladies all believed it to be from the Northern
Protestant Economy of Words School. Mind you, I took care not to claim
authorship of the verse to literary students! But, in all my reading, I
have never seen better use made of a quarter of a page. In fact, because
it was as beautiful as she, I gave it to my eventual true love, telling her
the rightful author's name.*

Sam McAughtry

from *Last Verses*

These verses weare made by Michaell Drayton Esquier Poett Lawreatt the night before hee dyed.

. . . Look, as your looking-glass by chance may fall,
Divide, and break in many pieces small
And yet shows forth the self-same face in all,

Proportions, features, graces, just the same,
And in the smallest piece as well the name
Of fairest one deserves as in the richest frame;

So all my thoughts are pieces but of you,
Which put together make a glass so true
As I therein no other's face but yours can view.

Michael Drayton (1563–1631)

JIM MAYS   335

Department of English
University College Dublin

12 April 1994

Dear Lifelines,

I have been working in Ireland again for only nine days. I brought one book, supposing the others would follow with the furniture. It is From this Condensery: The Complete Writing of Lorine Niedecker. *My enthusiasms come and go but Niedecker has been a fixture for a very long time.*

She lived most of her life (1903–70) at Blackhawk Island, near Fort Atkinson, Wisconsin. She wrote from the position of being a woman in that place, in relative isolation and obscurity, maintaining literary contacts largely through correspondence. Her early poems are like riddles, her later ones are longer and have a different music. The one I have chosen is short but has a version of the later sound, adding up here to an effect of cross-grained sweetness.

The poem is more than a statement about a feminized, American Narcissus. Half the meaning lies in the skill which contrived it, half in the recognition that such skill can be literally absorbing. If your readers like the poem as much as I do, they might also look out for Billy Mills and Catherine Walsh. They are the only Irish writers I know who begin where Niedecker leaves off.

Yours sincerely,
J C C Mays

My life is hung up
in the flood
   a wave-blurred
      portrait

Don't fall in love
with this face —
   it no longer exists
      in water
         we cannot fish

Lorine Niedecker (1903–1970)

JOSEPH BRODSKY   336

New York

11 April 1993

Dear Mr Gibson, Ms Jackson and Mr Pillow,

I would say that my favorite poem is 'Desert Places,' by Robert Frost. As for the reasons for my choice, my feelings about this poem are not reducible to a few lines. The poem is a few lines itself: you're better off reading them than anything I would have to say about them.

Yours sincerely,
Joseph Brodsky

Desert Places

Snow falling and night falling fast, oh, fast
In a field I looked into going past,
And the ground almost covered smooth in snow,
But a few weeds and stubble showing last.

The woods around it have it — it is theirs.
All animals are smothered in their lairs.
I am too absent-spirited to count;
The loneliness includes me unawares.

And lonely as it is, that loneliness
Will be more lonely ere it will be less —
A blanker whiteness of benighted snow
With no expression, nothing to express.

They cannot scare me with their empty spaces
Between stars — on stars where no human race is.
I have it in me so much nearer home
To scare myself with my own desert places.

Robert Frost (1874–1963)

SEOIRSE BODLEY   337

16 January 1994

'Canal Bank Walk' (Patrick Kavanagh)

Patrick Kavanagh's poem flows as effortlessly as the 'green waters of the canal'. Reading it I have the feeling that the technique of which he is so clearly the master is almost an irrelevance to him. What matters is the sense of the quotidian seen from a perspective so special as to transform the commonplace into an ecstatic vision of an other world always present here and now. Heaven and the world do not merely meet: they are one and the same. Yet for all its rhapsodic features and the risk of an abandonment that could easily have caused him to lose touch with the demands of shape and sense he completes the poem with a daring yet nonchalant command. But to comment on the poem at all is in a way to contradict his final two lines. His concern is ultimately with 'arguments that cannot be proven'. Seldom has the desire for that which cannot be expressed by logic been so logically and artistically expressed.

Thank you for asking me. Good luck with your fine project.

Yours sincerely,
Seoirse Bodley

['Canal Bank Walk' was also chosen by Bertie Ahern. The poem in full can be found on page 11.]

EMMA DONOGHUE   338

Dear Ewan, Áine, and Christopher,

I've heard of these excellent books before; best of luck with this year's. It's not often that poems get to fill hungry mouths.

My favourite poem is one of Emily Dickinson's that begins 'Wild Nights — Wild Nights!'

I've loved Dickinson's startling poems ever since my mother recited them to me when I was small. As a 14-year-old lesbian I happened to read somewhere that Emily Dickinson had been in love with her sister-in-law; this confirmed my hunch that writers didn't have to be 'normal', didn't have to obey any rules but their own hearts. 'Wild Nights' conjures up the mixture of danger and safety found in the best kind of love.

Good luck again, and thanks for asking me.

Emma Donoghue

Wild Nights — Wild Nights!
Were I with thee
Wild Nights should be
Our luxury!

Futile — the Winds —
To a Heart in port —
Done with the Compass —
Done with the Chart!

Rowing in Eden —
Ah, the Sea!
Might I but moor — Tonight —
In Thee!

Emily Dickinson (1830–1886)

DESMOND EGAN   339

13 January 1994

Dear Ewan, Áine and Christopher,

My favourite poets have not changed much: Machado, Hopkins, Herbert, Keats, Verlaine, Catullus, Kavanagh, Rilke, Tsvetayeva and Co. . . but my favourite poem constantly does, as a song does. So at the moment I think I would go for Gerard Manley Hopkins's 'As Kingfishers Catch Fire'. More and more I value insight in any work of art — what does talent matter, really? the world is full of it and it makes little enough difference — and this poem astonishes me. It also brims with feeling and of course the technique is still far ahead of most modern poetry (with or without inverted commas).

Looking back over your letter, I begin to wonder if you had intended me to choose a favourite poem out of my own; if this be the case, I think I might choose 'Peace'. Right now I would.

Congratulations on your enterprise and on your interest in helping poor children.

Kind regards.

Yours sincerely,
Desmond Egan

As Kingfishers Catch Fire, Dragonflies Dráw Fláme

As kingfishers catch fire, dragonflies dráw fláme;
As tumbled over rim in roundy wells
Stones ring; like each tucked string tells, each hung bell's
Bow swung finds tongue to fling out broad its name;
Each mortal thing does one thing and the same:

Deals out that being indoors each one dwells;
Selves — goes itself; *myself* it speaks and spells,
Crying *Whát I dó is me: for that I came.*

Í say móre: the just man justices;
Kéeps gráce: thát keeps all his goings graces;
Acts in God's eye what in God's eye he is —
Chríst — for Christ plays in ten thousand places,
Lovely in limbs, and lovely in eyes not his
To the Father through the features of men's faces.

Gerard Manley Hopkins (1844–1889)

Peace
For Seán MacBride

    just to go for a walk out the road
    just that
    under the deep trees
    which whisper of peace

    to break the bread of words
    with someone passing
    just that
    four of us round a pram
    and baby fingers asleep

    just to join the harmony
    the fields the blue everyday hills
    the puddles of daylight and

    you might hear a pheasant
    echo through the woods
    or plover may waver by
    as the evening poises with a blackbird
    on its table of hedge
    just that
    and here and there a gate
    a bungalow's bright window
    the smell of woodsmoke of lives

    just that!

    but Sweet Christ that
    is more than most of mankind can afford
    with the globe still plaited in its own
    crown of thorns

    too many starving eyes
    too many ancient children
    squatting among flies
    too many stockpiles of fear

too many dog jails too many generals
too many under torture by the impotent
screaming into the air we breathe

too many dreams stuck in money jams
too many mountains of butter selfishness
too many poor drowning in the streets
too many shantytowns on the outskirts of life

too many of us not sure what we want
so that we try to feed a habit for everything
until the ego puppets the militaries
mirror our own warring face

too little peace

Desmond Egan (b.1936)

EDWARD WALSH   340

University of Limerick
Ollscoil Luimnigh

14 January 1994

Dear Ewan, Áine and Christopher

Many thanks for your letter. My favourite poem is 'The Song of Wandering Aengus' *by William Butler Yeats (1865–1939).*

When legislation establishing the University of Limerick was enacted, preparations were being made to mark the event by the unveiling of a Foundation Stone, with the University of Limerick inscribed on one side and a few lines of poetry on the other. One Sunday I took a book of poetry out sailing with me on Lough Derg, and, anchored in the sunshine, went about the task of identifying some suitable lines. Finally I narrowed the choice to the lines by Yeats, now inscribed on the stone:

    'And pluck till time and times are done
    The silver apples of the moon
    The golden apples of the sun'

Wishing you every success with your project.

Yours sincerely,
Edward M Walsh
President

['The Song of Wandering Aengus' was also chosen by Fiona Shaw, Charles Haughey and Seamus Brennan in *Lifelines* and by Carol Ann Duffy in this volume. The poem appears in full on page 176.]

CONOR O'CALLAGHAN   341

18 January 1994

Dear Ewan, Áine and Christopher,

I'm not sure how I fit under the sub-title 'Letters from famous people'. But thank you for getting in touch, and I am pleased to be asked.

I've resisted the obvious temptation to be wilfully obscure, and have chosen a sonnet by Geoffrey Hill, from his great sequence 'Funeral Music'. I admire it because it is cold and hard. The closing images are breathtaking. The soul longs for a pure state beyond the complexities of human emotion, and the poet imagines a perfection he knows is impossible.

Geoffrey Hill's work is difficult, intimidating and deeply unfashionable. The man himself seems alarmingly reactionary: like Eliot, 'a classicist, a royalist, and an Anglo-Catholic'. The collected edition of his poems is the only book I ever stole, when I was 16. It has had a special place on my shelves ever since. When the poetry of others has been eroded by time, his will still be bright and undiminished, like quartz.

Thanks again, and the best of luck.

Conor O'Callaghan

from *Funeral Music*

IV
Let mind be more precious than soul; it will not
Endure. Soul grasps its price, begs its own peace,
Settles with tears and sweat, is possibly
Indestructible. That I can believe.
Though I would scorn the mere instinct of faith,
Expediency of assent, if I dared,
What I dare not is a waste history
Or void rule. Averroes, old heathen,
If only you had been right, if Intellect
Itself were absolute law, sufficient grace,
Our lives could be a myth of captivity
Which we might enter: an unpeopled region
Of ever new-fallen snow, a palace blazing
With perpetual silence as with torches.

Geoffrey Hill (b.1932)

GLORIA NAYLOR   342

Brooklyn
New York

26 June 1993

Dear Ewan Gibson,

*Thank you for your letter. I'm sending comments on Langston Hughes's
'A Dream Deferred' for the next collection. I wish you much success
with this collection as well.*

Sincerely,
Gloria Naylor

Harlem

What happens to a dream deferred?

> Does it dry up
> like a raisin in the sun?
> Or fester like a sore —
> And then run?
> Does it stink like rotten meat?
> Or crust and sugar over —
> like a syrupy sweet?

> Maybe it just sags
> like a heavy load.

> *Or does it explode?*

Langston Hughes (1902–1967)

*This is one of my favorite poems and I liked it so much that I used it as
an epigraph for my first novel,* The Women Of Brewster Place. *Part
of the 'humanness' of being human is our ability to dream. There may
be greater dreams for some, humbler dreams for others but, regardless
of the degradation in any given circumstance, hope is innate within the
human heart. So our ability to dream cannot be destroyed, even if it is
reduced to only planning for the next meal — or a desire to be left totally
alone. But here Langston Hughes talks about the dangers to the human
spirit when dreams are thwarted. The language appears simple at first,
but carefully examining each of the repercussions for a deferred dream,
we can chart the behavior for individuals, societies, or entire nations
that have despaired and given up.*

Gloria Naylor

CONOR BRADY   343

The Irish Times
11-15 D'Olier Street
Dublin 2

18 January 1994

Dear Ewan, Áine and Christopher,

Thank you for inviting me to contribute to your book. I am sure it will be a great success.

Yours sincerely,
Conor Brady
Editor

Winter Magic

A crumb of bread,
For such expenditure I've been repaid
With three clear silvery notes,
Three lingering notes,
Trilled from the little throat
Of one small bird,
And all the frost-bound earth
At once burst forth
In flowers of Spring,
And bridal dresses robed the trees
Tissued with sprays of blush-white blossom,
And the air was heavy
With the fresh earth's smell
And drowsy with the hum of honey bees —
Such magic lies in three clear rippling notes
Trilled by a little bird
In thanksgiving
For one small crumb of bread.

Anonymous

This little poem is part of an anthology compiled over many years by my father who died when I was a young boy. I do not know the author; perhaps he wrote it himself. It is dated 1939.

It is a reminder always for me of his gentle nature. And it evokes memories of winter mornings in childhood when he and I would spread crumbs on the window-sills for the robins.

Conor Brady

RÓISÍN CONROY   344

Attic Press
4 Upper Mount Street
Dublin 2

17 February 1994

Dear Ewan,

Thank you for your letter of invitation in connection with your collection of Lifelines.

I would like to submit, for your consideration, the enclosed poem by Mary Dorcey.

I am not sure what kind of detail you require. As you can see it is very personal and nearly speaks for itself. However it meant a great deal to me at a time of betrayal which I found absolutely shattering.

With best wishes and luck with your project.

Yours sincerely,
Róisín Conroy
Publisher

If Only She Had Told You Beforehand

It's not the thing itself
that stinks —
you said,
just that she did it
without any warning.

If she had told you
beforehand
(if the right ever knows
what the left is planning?)
it would have been
different . . .

if she had trusted —
confided . . .
(if she had known enough to tell
would she have felt enough to do it?)
even hinted . . .

if she had taken
the time —
sat you down and
explained the whole story

it would have been easy —
well prepared . . .
you might even
have laughed . . .

kissed their cheeks —
waved them off
as they climbed
the stairs
to your bed . . .

well
maybe not quite . . .
flowers
in their hair . . .

but it would have been
different —

if only
she had told you
beforehand.

Mary Dorcey (b.1950)

PAUL MULDOON   345

Princeton University
Princeton
New Jersey

3 February 1994

Dear Ewan Gibson,

*One of my favourite poems is 'The Taxis' by Louis MacNeice. I love its
negotiation of the thin line between nursery-rhyme and nightmare,
between humour and horror, between delight and dread, that's quite
unlike anything I know.*

With best wishes for your wonderful project.

Yours sincerely,
Paul Muldoon

The Taxis

In the first taxi he was alone tra-la,
No extras on the clock. He tipped ninepence
But the cabby, while he thanked him, looked askance
As though to suggest someone had bummed a ride.

In the second taxi he was alone tra-la
But the clock showed sixpence extra; he tipped according
And the cabby from out his muffler said: 'Make sure
You have left nothing behind tra-la between you'.

In the third taxi he was alone tra-la
But the tip-up seats were down and there was an extra
Charge of one-and-sixpence and an odd
Scent that reminded him of a trip to Cannes.

As for the fourth taxi, he was alone
Tra-la when he hailed it but the cabby looked
Through him and said: 'I can't tra-la well take
So many people, not to speak of the dog'.

Louis MacNeice (1907–1963)

TERENCE BROWN   346

School of English
Trinity College
Dublin 2

5 March 1994

Dear Ewan, Áine and Christopher,

Sorry I haven't replied before now. I've been away. A favourite poem is poem IV of T S Eliot's 'The Waste Land'. It is a piece of verbal music which wonderfully evokes the tidal movements of the sea and shows how language can create a compelling mood in a few brief lines when skilfully deployed.

Hope this is not too late.

Terence Brown

[The publishers were unable to obtain permission to print 'The Waste Land'.]

RICHARD GORMAN   347

Milano, Italia
26 January 1994

Hello — here's a small poem I like:

Poem

As the cat
climbed over
the top of

the jamcloset
first the right
forefoot

carefully
then the hind
stepped down

into the pit of
the empty
flowerpot

William Carlos Williams (1883–1963)

*I like the paced real-time quality in a small incident finely observed with
its references to halting music and Japanese Haiku.*

MÍCHEÁL Ó SÚILLEABHÁIN   348

University of Limerick
Ollscoil Luimnigh

30 January 1994

Dear Ewan, Áine and Christopher,

*Forgive my delay in responding to your letter due to pressure of work.
You and your colleagues are to be complimented for undertaking such
an imaginative project. I wish you well with it.*

*At the moment, my favourite poem is one by Seamus Heaney the title
of which I have forgotten! And to make matters worse I cannot lay my
hands on the book! But it is the first poem in either* The Haw Lantern
or Seeing Things. *In it Heaney tells of how his mother 'taught me to
hit/taught me to loosen/taught me between the hammer and the block to
face the music . . .' The poem is all about getting things 'angled right'
so that everything will come out OK. I love the poem because it is about
precise timing — something near to a musician's heart. I love especially*

the invocation — 'Teach me now to listen . . .' It reminds me that life could be like a good piece of music if only we were in touch more often with our own life-force, just as a musician can spin into an interactive circle of simultaneous playing and listening, becoming the sound itself.

Sonas oraibh,
Mícheál Ó Súilleabháin

from *Clearances*
in memoriam M.K.H., 1911–1984

She taught me what her uncle once taught her:
How easily the biggest coal block split
If you got the grain and hammer angled right.

The sound of that relaxed alluring blow,
Its co-opted and obliterated echo,
Taught me to hit, taught me to loosen,

Taught me between the hammer and the block
To face the music. Teach me now to listen,
To strike it rich behind the linear black.

Seamus Heaney (b.1939)

RORY BRENNAN   349

17 January 1994

My favourite poem keeps changing. The Muse may be notoriously fickle but the privilege of disloyalty can also extend to her admirers. Sometimes it's a poem by Auden, then one by MacNeice or again one by a lesser-known writer such as John Heath-Stubbs or Elizabeth Jennings.

The poem I have chosen is the one I like best, perhaps not quite the same thing. I first read it in a barber's shop in Terenure in Dublin, thirty-two years ago, so it is forever associated with the sound of clippers and passing traffic. I had just left school. Its relaxed quatrains seemed to express a sane reconciliation to the inevitable mixture of grief and joy that I knew would lie ahead.

The poem's second stanza refers to the First World War, in which Blunden was a junior officer. The third is perhaps out of favour with today's regime of 'political correctness'. Nonetheless I still admire the resilient fatalism of the poem and continue to read through the anthology I first found it in, The Penguin Book of English Verse. *The selfsame copy, not too bad for all the wear, is on my desk as I write.*

With best wishes,
Rory Brennan

Report on Experience

I have been young, and now am not too old;
And I have seen the righteous forsaken,
His health, his honour and his quality taken.
    This is not what we were formerly told.

I have seen a green country, useful to the race,
Knocked silly with guns and mines, its villages vanished,
Even the last rat and last kestrel banished —
    God bless us all, this was peculiar grace.

I knew Seraphina; Nature gave her hue,
Glance, sympathy, note, like one from Eden.
I saw her smile warp, heard her lyric deaden;
    She turned to harlotry; — this I took to be new.

Say what you will, our God sees how they run.
These disillusions are His curious proving
That He loves humanity and will go on loving;
    Over them are faith, life, virtue in the sun.

Edmund Blunden (1896–1974)

MICHAEL D HIGGINS   350

Oifig an Aire Ealaíon, Cultúir agus
Gaeltachta
(Office of the Minister for Arts
Culture and the Gaeltacht)

21 January 1994

Dear Ewan, Áine and Christopher,

Thank you very much for your letter inviting me to nominate a poem for the follow-up to Lifelines. *While it is difficult to nominate any one poem which I would regard as my favourite, I have given the matter some thought and I would like to nominate James Joyce's much neglected poem 'Puer' written on the occasion of the birth of his son and in my opinion more moving than Yeats's 'A Prayer for my Daughter'.*

I hope that the new publication is as interesting and as successful as the last edition of Lifelines *and I wish all of you involved in the project my sincere best wishes for its success and I commend most heartily all those involved in it.*

Yours sincerely,
Michael D

Michael D Higgins TD
Minister for Arts, Culture
and the Gaeltacht

Ecce Puer

Of the dark past
A child is born;
With joy and grief
My heart is torn.

Calm in his cradle
The living lies.
May love and mercy
Unclose his eyes!

Young life is breathed
On the glass;
The world that was not
Comes to pass.

A child is sleeping:
An old man gone.
O, father forsaken,
Forgive your son!

James Joyce (1882–1941)

FIONN O'LEARY   351

Radio 1
RTE
Dublin 4

18 January 1994

Dear Ewan, Áine and Christopher,

I didn't open your letter, with its kind invitation to contribute to Lifelines, *until last weekend, as I am trying to catch up with a backlog of correspondence to* Sounds Classical. *Apologies, then, for the delay.*

'To my unknown friend' *(translated by David McDuff) was written in the Small Zone, a special unit for women prisoners of conscience in Barashevo labour camp, after Irina Ratushinskaya had been sentenced in March 1983 to seven years' hard labour plus five years' internal exile. Her crime was 'anti-Soviet agitation and propaganda': otherwise, writing poetry.*

In this poem I hear the voice of the indomitable human spirit giving me courage. Despite the rigours of the labour camp, the lies of the system, separation from her husband, Irina transcends her own plight to forge solidarity with the oppressed everywhere, so 'don't be afraid . . .'

With best wishes,
Fionn O'Leary

To My Unknown Friend

Above my half of the world
The comets spread their tails.
In my half of the century
Half the world looks me in the eye.
In my hemisphere the wind's blowing,
There are feasts of plague without end.
But a searchlight shines in our faces,
And effaces the touch of death.
And our madness retreats from us,
And our sadness passes through us,
And we stand in the midst of our fates,
Setting our shoulders against the plague.
We shall hold it back with our selves,
We shall stride through the nightmare.
It will not get further than us — don't be afraid
On the other side of the globe!

Small Zone, 26 February 1984

Irina Ratushinskaya
Translated by David McDuff

JAY PARINI   352

*I first thought of the idea of becoming a poet myself when, at the age of
fifteen, I was handed a copy of 'Mowing' by an English teacher of mine
in Scranton, Pennsylvania. The lines sang in my head for days, and I
was thoroughly amazed. How was it possible, I thought, for a poem to
catch a mood so completely, and for the sound of the poem itself to mimic
its subject so perfectly? Those first two lines continue to astonish me:
'There was never a sound beside the wood but one, | And that was my
long scythe whispering to the ground.' I think of it often as I sit in my
study in Vermont, my pencil in hand, the only sound being the slight
scratch of lead on paper.*

*Frost understood the sacredness of work, and that 'The fact is the
sweetest dream that labor knows.' Whatever work we do, it must be
based in the actuality of experience, in the sensory world of sight, sound,
taste, smell, touch: the grittiness of things in their literal being. This is
'the sweetest dream' because it must be imagined, and the work of
imagining reality is 'the earnest love that laid the swale in rows.' We
work to shape reality, to make it new, and when the work is done, we set
it aside — or leave the hay 'to make' as Frost says in that remarkable
last line. One cuts the hay, then lets it to dry or 'make' in the sun.*

*Frost is a poet who could respond directly, without pretension, to his
immediate experience. He was a working farmer, and he cut a lot of hay
with a scythe. More than most poets he understood the nature of work,*

and how work done lovingly, for its own sake or the sake of others, is its own reward. 'What was it it whispered?' Frost wonders. He is not sure himself while he is doing the scything. The meaning of the act may follow, and it may not 'make' in the sun; meanwhile, 'Anything more than the truth would have seemed too weak' beside this labor which is, of course, a labor of love.

Jay Parini

Mowing

There was never a sound beside the wood but one,
And that was my long scythe whispering to the ground.
What was it it whispered? I knew not well myself;
Perhaps it was something about the heat of the sun,
Something, perhaps, about the lack of sound —
And that was why it whispered and did not speak.
It was no dream of the gift of idle hours,
Or easy gold at the hand of fay or elf:
Anything more than the truth would have seemed too weak
To the earnest love that laid the swale in rows,
Not without feeble-pointed spikes of flowers
(Pale orchises), and scared a bright green snake.
The fact is the sweetest dream that labor knows.
My long scythe whispered and left the hay to make.

Robert Frost (1874–1963)

KATHRYN HOLMQUIST   353

18 January 1994

Dear Ewan, Áine and Christopher,

My 'favourite' poem changes with nearly every book of poetry I read. Recently I came across some work by the Czech poet Miroslav Holub, who turned 70 last year. Holub has been a 'career poet' for 40 years while at the same time working as an immunologist and he has the gift of mingling artistic insight and scientific knowledge without being esoteric, something which we badly need at the cusp of the 21st century as discoveries in genetics transform our view of our own humanity. I particularly like 'Haemophilia/Los Angeles' because it captures the spiritual unease many of us feel around the sense that our 'fate' lies in our genes. The poem makes me a little homesick as it captures the buzzing feeling of a great American city, then transforms this into an image of the claustrophobia of the soul trapped in the frail, human body to create a compelling mood of sickness and exile.

Kathryn Holmquist

Haemophilia/Los Angeles

And so it circulates
from the San Bernardino Freeway
to the Santa Monica Freeway and
down to the San Diego Freeway and
up to the Golden State Freeway,

and so it circulates
in the vessels of the marine creature,
transparent creature,
unbelievable creature in the light
of the southern moon
like the footprint
of the last foot in the world,

and so it circulates
as if there were no other music
except Perpetual Motion,
as if there were no conductor
directing an orchestra of black angels
without a full score:

out of the grand piano floats
a pink C-sharp in the upper octave,
out of the violin
blood may trickle at any time,
and in the joints of the trombone
there swells a fear of the tiniest staccato,

as if there were no Dante
in a wheelchair,
holding a ball of cotton to his mouth,
afraid to speak a line
lest he perforate the meaning,

as if there were no genes
except the gene for defects
and emergency telephone calls,

and so it circulates
with the full, velvet hum of the disease,
circulates all hours of the day,
circulates all hours of the night
to the praise of non-clotting,

each blood cell carrying
four molecules of hope
that it might all be something
totally different
from what it is.

Miroslav Holub (b.1923)
Translated by Dana Hábová and David Young

ANNE DUNLOP   354

January 1994

Dear Ewan, Áine and Christopher,

My favourite poem is without doubt 'The Owl and the Pussycat' (went to sea in a beautiful pea green boat . . .).

Why? Because it was the first poem I ever learnt and I use it to this day as my party piece! Incidentally it's the only poem I can ever remember without getting the lines jumbled up.

I think you are doing a wonderful job producing Lifelines — *keep up the good work!*

Yours sincerely,
Anne Dunlop

The Owl and The Pussy Cat

The Owl and the Pussy-cat went to sea
    In a beautiful pea-green boat,
They took some honey, and plenty of money,
    Wrapped up in a five-pound note.
The Owl looked up to the stars above,
    And sang to a small guitar,
'O lovely Pussy! O Pussy, my love,
    What a beautiful Pussy you are,
        You are
        You are!
    What a beautiful Pussy you are!'

Pussy said to the Owl, 'You elegant fowl!
    How charmingly sweet you sing!
O let us be married! too long we have tarried:
    But what shall we do for a ring?'
They sailed away, for a year and a day,
    To the land where the Bong-tree grows
And there in a wood a Piggy-wig stood
    With a ring at the end of his nose,
        His nose,
        His nose,
    With a ring at the end of his nose.

'Dear Pig, are you willing to sell for one shilling
    Your ring?' Said the Piggy, 'I will.'
So they took it away, and were married next day
    By the Turkey who lives on the hill.
They dined on mince, and slices of quince,

Which they ate with a runcible spoon;
And hand in hand, on the edge of the sand,
They danced by the light of the moon,
The moon,
The moon,
They danced by the light of the moon.

Edward Lear (1812–1888)

JANE O'MALLEY   355

17 January 1994

Dear Ewan, Áine and Christopher,

Thank you for your invitation to contribute to Lifelines.

I have chosen 'At the Barbara Hepworth Carving Studio' *by Patrick O'Brien from his collected poems,* A Book of Genesis.

I have chosen this poem because it reflects my own experience of my many visits to the garden and studio.

I wish you well in your charitable work.

Sincerely,
Jane O'Malley

At the Barbara Hepworth Carving Studio, St Ives, Cornwall

I the sculptor, am the landscape.
            Barbara Hepworth.

We look through glass
from the memorial garden.
It is as death left it,
exhibiting the everyday chaos
from which she made edens
of stone and metal. Bereft, it

seems to wait some postponed
hour when the door will open
and she will take from the wall
a coat cauled in afterbirth of stone
and with sharp blows quicken
the cry of life, cut the umbilical

cord that binds her to unfinished
tasks. On the table are chisels
and hammers, in neat repose.
Over all, the air of a diminished

civilisation whose artifacts puzzle
the first explorers. A chosen

stone bulges in its pregnant
pause, and on the floor a red basin
has long given up the ghost of water.
Angles divide the gaunt
February sunlight which a machine
polishes to marmoreal spears.

There would be no surprise
were she to return, having found
in the protective curves of need,
or in beseeching trees, in the mysteries
of Cornish moor, the form this stone had bound
to itself, awaiting her loving deed.

Patrick O'Brien

MARY KENNEDY   356

Newsroom
RTE

12 January 1994

Dear Ewan, Áine and Chris,

Having read and enjoyed the collected edition of Lifelines, *I was delighted to receive your letter and would love to be included in the next edition. I, like so many others, would find it very hard to pick one poem as my favourite, but there's a little poem in Irish that I hold very dear, for its simplicity and the notion of childhood that it celebrates. It's always floating around in my head as a reminder, perhaps, of the importance of enjoying those 'sticky' days when children are small and innocent, unaware of the niceties of domestic life and unquestioning in their love. It's a pity really that they grow up so very quickly.*

Subh Milis

Bhí subh milis
Ar baschrann an dorais,
Ach mhúch me an corraí
Ionam a d'éirigh,
Mar smaoinigh me ar an lá,
A bheas an baschrann glan,
Agus an lámh bheag
Ar iarraidh.

Sweet Jam

There was sticky sweet jam
On the door handle,
But I suppressed
The anger that rose inside me,
Because I thought of the day,
When the handle would be clean,
And the tiny hand
Gone.

Seamus O'Neill

Best of luck with your project.

Sincerely,
Mary Kennedy

NIGEL HAWTHORNE   357

27 January 1994

Dear Ewan, Áine and Christopher,

I have chosen William Wordsworth's 'Composed Upon Westminster Bridge' *for your anthology.*

The view from the bridge is still majestic. It is still very exciting to see the lie of the river, and the strangely glamorous array of modern, classical and ecclesiastical buildings stretching round the bend of this great river — at night in particular.

The calm, on the other hand, has long since gone, and the mighty heart no longer lies still, but is awake for a good deal of the night. The poem symbolises how gradually we are despoiling the beauty of our cities and the beauty of our countryside by what we call progress.

My very good wishes for the success of the book.

Yours sincerely,
Nigel Hawthorne

Composed Upon Westminster Bridge
3 September 1802

Earth has not anything to show more fair:
Dull would he be of soul who could pass by
A sight so touching in its majesty:
This City now doth, like a garment, wear

The beauty of the morning; silent, bare,
Ships, towers, domes, theatres, and temples lie
Open unto the fields and to the sky,
All bright and glittering in the smokeless air.
Never did sun more beautifully steep
In his first splendour, valley, rock, or hill;
Ne'er saw I, never felt, a calm so deep!
The river glideth at his own sweet will:
Dear God! the very houses seem asleep;
And all that mighty heart is lying still!

William Wordsworth (1770–1850)

CATHAL Ó SEARCAIGH   358

Tír Chonaill

1 Márta 1994

My dear Ewan, Áine, Christopher,

*Maith domh an mhoill. Istigh tá an dán atá roghnaithe agam . . .
'Afterlives' le Derek Mahon. Tá obair ar dóigh á dhéanaimh agaibh
agus mólaim go hard na spéire sin. Tá súil agam go mbeidh an rath agus
an ráchaint cheanna ar an eagrán reatha de* Lifelines *agus a bhí ar na
cinn eile. Is léir go ndeachaigh ann smaoineadh agus an saothair i
bhfeidhm ar an phobal. Ádh mór oraibh triúr.*

Le dea ghuí.
Cathal Ó Searcaigh

*Some people invoke spirits. They are called spiritualists. Some people
invoke themselves. They are called poets. I belong to the second calling.
In recent times, though, I'm becoming more mediumistic. I'm letting
ancestral voices speak through me. This implies, for me anyway, a
longing for origins . . . a yearning for home, an attachment to place and
an awareness of its past. Home is the gaelic-speaking community of
Gleann An Átha, situated in the shadow of Mt Errigal, between Dún
Lúiche and Gort 'a Choirce in North West Donegal. This is the territory
of my people, the terrain of my imagination, my soulscape. Home! I
became acutely aware of that word thanks to Derek Mahon's poem. This
is how it happened. In the mid-seventies I was 'on the stray' in London,
drifting aimlessly, taking a walk on the wild side of life and of love. It
was the first time I looked down into that terrible dark pool — the
dubhlinn of the self. At times like that you realise that you're an abyss.
Within there's a deep unfathomable darkness. You get dizzy looking
down into yourself — into that Chasm of Silence. A poem becomes a
shout of defiance yelled in the face of that Silence. I found out that it was
much more rewarding to write bad poems than to read really great poems
. . . until somebody gave me a copy of Derek Mahon's collection* The

Snow Party. 'Afterlives', *the first poem in that collection, was a revelation, particularly the second part of it. The first time I read the word 'home' there in the last line, I got what I can only describe as a 'shock of recognition'. It was an awakening for me, an awakening from the anonymity of the city. I felt the word as a fierce longing to be reunited with something which I felt to be cut off from. Suddenly I felt deprived and dispossessed in the faceless society of the streets and I craved for a new sense of communion with my own hill-farming community. The word was a discovery for me but what is discovery only what we remove the cover from. It has always been there . . . only concealed. That poem sent me home to my own land and my own language. It was the beginning of my homecoming. For Mahon it's a poem about coming back to a turbulent and troubled city. On the rough seas of sectarian strife, poetry becomes, for some, the buoy of the Spirit.*

Gúrú maith agaibh:
*   le gean,*
till the desert sands freeze and the camels come
*   skating home.*

Cathal Ó Searcaigh

Afterlives
for James Simmons

I
I wake in a dark flat
To the soft roar of the world.
Pigeons neck on the white
Roofs as I draw the curtains
And look out over London
Rain-fresh in the morning light.

This is our element, the bright
Reason on which we rely
For the long term solutions.
The orators yap, and guns
Go off in a back street;
But the faith does not die

That in our time these things
Will amaze the literate children
In their non-sectarian schools
And the dark places be
Ablaze with love and poetry
When the power of good prevails.

What middle-class cunts we are
To imagine for one second
That our privileged ideals

Are divine wisdom, and the dim
Forms that kneel at noon
In the city not ourselves.

II
I am going home by sea
For the first time in years.
Somebody thumbs a guitar
On the dark deck, while a gull
Dreams at the masthead,
The moon-splashed waves exult.

At dawn the ship trembles, turns
In a wide arc to back
Shuddering up the grey lough
Past lightship and buoy,
Slipway and dry dock
Where a naked bulb burns;

And I step ashore in a fine rain
To a city so changed
By five years of war
I scarcely recognise
The places I grew up in,
The faces that try to explain.

But the hills are still the same
Grey-blue above Belfast.
Perhaps if I'd stayed behind
And lived it bomb by bomb
I might have grown up at last
And learnt what is meant by home.

Derek Mahon (b.1941)

GERALD DAWE   359

27 January 1994

*My choice of Dylan Thomas is for nostalgic reasons. He was one of the
very first poets I read when I was about thirteen. My grandmother,
whom we lived with, taught elocution on Wednesdays and Saturdays
so I heard a lot of poetry when I was very young. It was a real shock to
be on my own and read poetry for myself some time later. I filled up
science school-notebooks with poems by Yeats, Robert Lowell, D H
Lawrence and Dylan Thomas alongside desperate things of my own. The
poems of Dylan Thomas which I remember writing out include 'Light
Break Where No Sun Shines'. He is a marvellous poet and his spell
has not broken for me — not in a million years.*

Gerald Dawe

Light Breaks Where No Sun Shines

Light breaks where no sun shines;
Where no sea runs, the waters of the heart
Push in their tides;
And, broken ghosts with glow-worms in their heads,
The things of light
File through the flesh where no flesh decks the bones.

A candle in the thighs
Warms youth and seed and burns the seeds of age;
Where no seed stirs,
The fruit of man unwrinkles in the stars,
Bright as a fig;
Where no wax is, the candle shows its hairs.

Dawn breaks behind the eyes;
From poles of skull and toe the windy blood
Slides like a sea;
Nor fenced, nor staked, the gushers of the sky
Spout to the rod
Divining in a smile the oil of tears.

Night in the sockets rounds,
Like some pitch moon, the limit of the globes;
Day lights the bone;
Where no cold is, the skinning gales unpin
The winter's robes;
The film of spring is hanging from the lids.

Light breaks on secret lots,
On tips of thought where thoughts smell in the rain;
When logics die,
The secret of the soil grows through the eye,
And blood jumps in the sun;
Above the waste allotments the dawn halts.

Dylan Thomas (1914–1953)

CHRISTOPHER NOLAN   360

21 January 1994

Dear Ewan, Áine and Christopher,

Well done you three and I will of course join in in your grand venture.

My favourite poem is Gerard Manley Hopkins's lovely sonnet 'Pied Beauty'. My introduction to this poet's work came away back in 1978 when a fan in London sent me his own well-thumbed copy of Hopkins's poetry. He suggested that I read 'The Caged Skylark' and I did enjoying the comparison between the bird in the cage with my boy-poet's predicament as I sat confined within my frame. But as I sat there thinking my glance fell on the opposite page and I began to read 'Pied Beauty'. Remember now that I was just thirteen at the time and had never heard of Hopkins but as I gazed through this poem's kaleidoscope I was captivated, I had never ever experienced such musical language or such magical images.

Christy Nolan

P.S. Great good luck with your Lifelines!

Pied Beauty

Glory be to God for dappled things —
    For skies of couple-colour as a brinded cow;
        For rose-moles all in stipple upon trout that swim;
Fresh-firecoal chestnut-falls; finches' wings;
    Landscape plotted and pieced — fold, fallow, and
        plough;
    And áll trádes, their gear and tackle and trim.

All things counter, original, spare, strange;
    Whatever is fickle, freckled (who knows how?)
        With swift, slow; sweet, sour; adazzle, dim;
He fathers-forth whose beauty is past change:
        Praise him.

Gerard Manley Hopkins (1844–1889)

MARY O'MALLEY 361

22 January 1994

Dear Ewan, Áine and Christopher,

Lifelines *is the best anthology I've ever read by a mile and I'm delighted to contribute. So many poems clamour for attention — Eavan Boland's 'War Horse', Pablo Neruda's 'Barcarole', Shakespeare's sonnets, but I will name one poem which is vital to me now for its rhythm, its riskiness, the quality of its light. It became for me an incantation at a time of darkness and pain, when its images burned before me with a transforming power. That poem is Derek Walcott's 'Oceano Nox' and he invests it with a rare and distant tenderness. It is a meditation on darkness and it lifts with pure radiance. I also love it because it is beautiful to say.*

I think ye are wonderful to be making this act of faith and I hope ye make a fortune.

With every best wish,
Mary O'Malley

Oceano Nox
For Robert Lee

What sort of moon will float up through the almonds
like a bobbing marker in the surf of trees?
A quarter-moon, like an Iranian dagger?
A capitol with wide spheres of influence?
One with a birthmark like Gorbachev's head?
A local moon, full of its own importance,
a watchman's flashlight with fresh batteries,
startling the trickle from a kitchen drain,
pinning a crab to the hotel's wire fence,
changing its mind like a cat burglar,
probing locked harbours, rattling the foam's chain.

Calm as a kitchen clock without the hands
high on a cupboard shelf of this beach house,
the moon stares on a plastic tablecloth,
where she reprints the shadow of a mouse
bent like a friar nibbling his rosary's
berries with fingers quicker than his mouth;
then islands were the gems of an Infanta,
and tiny armoured ants, in Indian file,
hoisted their banners, singing 'Sancta, Sancta
Regina,' then scattered in armadas
to the cracked wedding cake of her fixed smile.

Her forehead bound as tightly as a nun's
or a black laundress who has pinned the sails,
forgotten, on a clothesline, she was once
the Virgin Queen whose radiance drew the snails
of her horned galleons with their silvery slime,
pale slugs in sand. Insomniac remorse.
Beyond all that now, and way past her prime
her mind is wandering in another tense;
she hears the cannon's surf, the palm frond's gales,
and sees, through the erasures of her face,
those wrecks she christened: *Invincible, Revenge.*

Oceano Nox. Night whispers to the Ocean.
A watchman in a constable's cloak patrols
the hotel's wire boundary. I answer his good night.
His flashlight swivels through a spume of salt,
it passes over the old hill of skulls
made by husked coconut shells, the original fault
unsettled by the shallows' dark commotion;
he sings a reggae in a moon so bright
you can read palms by it. A steel band rolls
glissandos of surf round the hotel pool's
gazebo, doubling the moon's arc light.

A wave of sound, an echo overhead
(not shaking the moon's oval in the pool),

that pulses in the memory, when, from school
to college, I cherished the theatre
of high Marlovian clouds, my heritage
of that great globe herself, and what I read
sank in like surf reopening the wet
pores of sand, and swirls in the cave's head,
till on this beach-house wall, centuries later,
I mutter the sea's lines, and they recede
to the emerald and ruby of a fading jet:

'Black is the beauty of the brightest day,'
black the circumference around her rings
that radiate from black invisibly,
black is the music which her round mouth sings,
black is the backcloth on which diadems shine,
black, night's perfection, which conceals its flaws
except the crack of the horizon's line;
now all is changing but my focus was
once on the full moon, not what surrounds the moon,
upon a watchman's flashlight not the watchman,
the mesmerizing wake of History.

I have rehearsed their beauty all this week,
and her white disk moves like a camera's lens
along the ebony of a high-boned cheek,
I mean Anne Daniels's, Lauretta Etienne's,
their bow-carved mouths, their half-globed eyes serene,
surfaces so polished that their skin would squeak
if you pushed your forefinger up the bone,
their laughter white as breakers in their grin,
too modest to be actresses, each one
wrapped in sea cotton, intact from Benin.

Oceano Nox. The clocks resume their motion,
a laser from the lighthouse skims a wave;
a different age is whispering to the ocean,
the fronds will take the old moon by the hand
and lead her gently into a cloud's grave;
I cross the darkened grass back to the house;
then all her radiance comes back again,
making the frogs sundials on the lawn;
there is a ring around her, meaning rain,
and meaning nothing more, in that blank face,
than History's innocence or its remorse.

So let her light dissolve into the sable
and velvet memory of a collared cloud,
dimming the square tiles on a kitchen table,
dulling the cheers of an applauding crowd
of breakers flinging whitecaps into space
when you close in the door and ram the latch, as
you think of women with their necks as supple

as bowing palms, and watch the mouse scuttle
back to its hole. A palm's nib scratches
the roof's parchment. At a brass lamp's base,
new rainflies, and the masts of wooden matches.

A scribbling plague of rainflies. Go to bed.
After the morning rain, the shuddering almond
will shake the sweat of nightmare from its bent head.
The surf will smooth the sand's page and even
the cumuli change their idea of heaven
as the sun wipes the nib of a palm frond,
and from the wet hills, parishes of birds
test a new tongue, because these are their shores,
while the old moon gapes at a loss for words
like any ghost at cockcrow, as a force
threshes the palms, lifting their hearts and yours.

Derek Walcott (b.1930)

BRIAN BOURKE   362

3 February 1994

Dear Everyone,

*Find enclosed poem and comment. I hope I am not too late for inclusion.
I was away I'm afraid.*

Yours sincerely,
Brian Bourke

from *The Passionate Pilgrimage*

Sonnet II

Scarce had the Sun dried up the dewy morn,
And scarce the herd gone to the hedge for shade,
When Cytherea, all in love forlorn,
A longing tarriance for Adonis made
Under an osier growing by a brook,
A brook where Adon used to cool his spleen:
Hot was the day: she hotter that did look
For his approach, that often there had been.
Anon he comes, and throws his mantle by,
And stood stark naked on the brook's green brim:
The Sun look'd on the world with glorious eye,
Yet not so wistly as this queen on him.
    He, spying her, bounced in, whereas he stood:
    'O Jove,' quoth she, 'why was not I a flood!'

William Shakespeare (1564–1616)

This sonnet is one of a few poems that keeps recurring in my memory complete and almost correct without becoming a satire or a nonsense. It is funny and bawdy, which leaves nothing for me to do, except remember it.

Brian Bourke

OLIVIA O'LEARY   363

'Prime Time'
Radio Telefís Éireann
Dublin 4

Dear Ewan, Áine, and Chris,

Thanks for your letter. My favourite poem is Louis MacNeice's 'Entirely'. Why?

We spend so much of life looking for the formula which makes sense of it all, thinking every so often we've found the secret. We never will, and if we did, life would become so predictable that we'd die of boredom. This poem says it all. It should probably be read with a Northern accent.

Sincerely,
Olivia O'Leary

Entirely

If we could get the hang of it entirely
    It would take too long;
All we know is the splash of words in passing
    And falling twigs of song,
And when we try to eavesdrop on the great
    Presences it is rarely
That by a stroke of luck we can appropriate
    Even a phrase entirely.

If we could find our happiness entirely
    In somebody else's arms
We should not fear the spears of the spring nor the city's
    Yammering fire alarms
But, as it is, the spears each year go through
    Our flesh and almost hourly
Bell or siren banishes the blue
    Eyes of Love entirely.

And if the world were black or white entirely
    And all the charts were plain
Instead of a mad weir of tigerish waters,
    A prism of delight and pain,

We might be surer where we wished to go
   Or again we might be merely
Bored but in brute reality there is no
   Road that is right entirely.

Louis MacNeice (1907–1963)

['Entirely' was also Hilary Orpen's choice in *Lifelines*.]

BERNADETTE GREEVY   364

27 January 1994

Dear Áine, Ewan and Christopher,

A very great poem containing within it lines redolent of my professional life-style has to be my choice. I refer to the epic poem 'Ulysses' by Alfred Lord Tennyson, two sections of which contain particular sentiments that are deeply moving and significant to me.

Congratulations on your inspired idea and on the wonderful results you have already achieved in helping those in desperate need throughout the Third World.

Yours sincerely,
Bernadette Greevy

from *Ulysses*

I cannot rest from travel: I will drink
Life to the lees: all times I have enjoy'd
Greatly, have suffer'd greatly, both with those
That loved me, and alone; on shore and when
Thro' scudding drifts the rainy Hyades
Vext the dim sea: I am become a name;
For always roaming with a hungry heart
Much have I seen and known; cities of men
And manners, climates, councils, governments,
Myself not least, but honour'd of them all . . .

Tho' much is taken, much abides; and tho'
We are not now that strength which in old days
Moved earth and heaven; that which we are, we are;
One equal temper of heroic hearts,
Made weak by time and fate, but strong in will
To strive, to seek, to find, and not to yield.

Alfred Lord Tennyson (1809-1892)

STEVE MacDONOGH   365

'Young Poets' *by Nicanor Parra*

I have so many favourite poems, and most of them are very long, but I can think of none that comes to my mind quite as often as this eight-line poem by the Chilean poet, Nicanor Parra. Despite its brevity it succeeds in holding a number of different, even contradictory elements in balance; in this it attains a truth that is like a helping hand on the tiller. Almost all the poems that mean a lot to me include some kind of reference to the focal events and processes of our unhappy century, the first World War and the Holocaust, and 'Young Poets' succeeds in offering positive direction from under the shadow of disaster, while also provoking a chuckle at the end.

Steve MacDonogh

Young Poets

Write as you will
In whatever style you like
Too much blood has run under the bridge
To go on believing
That only one road is right.

In poetry everything is permitted.

With only this condition, of course:
You have to improve on the blank page.

Nicanor Parra (b.1914)
Translated by Miller Williams

EAMON GRENNAN   366

Vassar College
Poughkeepsie
New York

3 February 1994

Dear Ewan, Áine and Chris,

This astounding sonnet is high on the list of my favorite poems because of the way it manages to treat its subject — the death of one of Hopkins's parishioners — in a manner both tender and rugged. I also love it because of the vivid, economic, and apt portrait it gives of the blacksmith himself, 'Big-boned and hardy-handsome,' and because of the dexterity and speed with which it moves from objective description to direct, intimate address — from 'Sickness broke him,' to 'Child, Felix, poor

Felix Randal.' There's such great swift sureness of speech in it, too, which you can hear in the athletic balance it can hold between formal restraints and emotional outburst. What also leaves me mesmerised with admiration is the way Hopkins manages to mix — in an utterly unsentimental way — religious consolation and real human pain: they can temper but never, for him, cancel one another. And that great last line strikes home with the effect of a series of sharp, decisive, final hammer-blows — violent and musical — leaving us with that 'bright and battering sandal' which could be forged for Pegasus himself. The fact of so many things (emotional, spiritual, intellectual, technical) all working so well together, in a poem that is itself partly a celebration of work, never ceases to be a wonder and a satisfaction to me.

Many thanks for asking me to participate in this good work of yours. Blessings on it.

Eamon Grennan

Felix Randal

Felix Randal the farrier, O he is dead then? my duty all ended,
Who have watched his mould of man, big-boned and hardy–
    handsome
Pining, pining, till time when reason rambled in it and some
Fatal four disorders, fleshed there, all contended?

Sickness broke him. Impatient he cursed at first, but mended
Being anointed and all; though a heavenlier heart began some
Months earlier, since I had our sweet reprieve and ransom
Tendered to him. Ah well, God rest him all road ever he
    offended!

This seeing the sick endears them to us, us too it endears.
My tongue had taught thee comfort, touch had quenched thy
    tears,
Thy tears that touched my heart, child, Felix, poor Felix Randal;

How far from then forethought of, all thy more boisterous
    years,
When thou at the random grim forge, powerful amidst peers,
Didst fettle for the great grey drayhorse his bright and
    battering sandal!

Gerard Manley Hopkins (1844–1889)

['Felix Randal' was also chosen by Cyril Cusack in *Lifelines*.]

DONALD HALL   367

8 March 1993

Dear Gibson/Jackson/Pillow,

A good idea. My favorite poem (as of today) is Marvell's 'Horatian Ode'. (I am aware that it makes uncomfortable reference to Irish history!)

Reasons? Poetry exists to say the unsayable, to compound the uncompoundable, to embody the simultaneous presence of opposed feelings and ideas that logic cannot acknowledge as simultaneous. In Marvell's poem, the opposite intensities — say, in awkward summary, love for victim and awe for murderer — incorporate themselves at extremes.

Yours truly,
Donald Hall

An Horation Ode upon Cromwell's Return from Ireland

The forward youth that would appear
Must now forsake his muses dear,
    Nor in the shadows sing
    His numbers languishing.
'Tis time to leave the books in dust,
And oil the unusèd armour's rust:
    Removing from the wall
    The corslet of the hall.
So restless Cromwell could not cease
In the inglorious arts of peace,
    But through adventurous war
    Urgèd his active star.
And, like the three-forked lightning, first
Breaking the clouds where it was nursed,
    Did thorough his own side
    His fiery way divide.
(For 'tis all one to courage high
The emulous or enemy:
    And with such to inclose
    Is more than to oppose.)
Then burning through the air he went,
And palaces and temples rent:
    And Caesar's head at last
    Did through his laurels blast.
'Tis madness to resist or blame
The force of angry heaven's flame:

And, if we would speak true,
Much to the man is due,
Who, from his private gardens, where
He lived reservèd and austere,
As if his highest plot
To plant the bergamot,
Could by industrious valour climb
To ruin the great work of time,
And cast the kingdoms old
Into another mould.
Though justice against fate complain,
And plead the ancient rights in vain:
But those do hold or break
As men are strong or weak.
Nature, that hateth emptiness,
Allows of penetration less:
And therefore must make room
Where greater spirits come.
What field of all the Civil Wars,
Where his were not the deepest scars?
And Hampton shows what part
He had of wiser art,
Where, twining subtle fears with hope,
He wove a net of such a scope,
That Charles himself might chase
To Carisbrooke's narrow case:
That thence the royal actor born
The tragic scaffold might adorn:
While round the armèd bands
Did clap their bloody hands.
He nothing common did or mean
Upon that memorable scene:
But with his keener eye
The axe's edge did try:
Nor called the gods with vulgar spite
To vindicate his helpless right,
But bowed his comely head,
Down, as upon a bed.
This was that memorable hour
Which first assured the forcèd power.
So when they did design
The Capitol's first line,
A bleeding head where they begun,
Did fright the architects to run;
And yet in that the State
Foresaw its happy fate.
And now the Irish are ashamed
To see themselves in one year tamed:
So much one man can do,

That does both act and know.
They can affirm his praises best,
And have, though overcome, confessed
    How good he is, how just,
    And fit for highest trust:
Nor yet grown stiffer with command,
But still in the Republic's hand:
    How fit he is to sway
    That can so well obey.
He to the Commons' feet presents
A kingdom, for his first year's rents:
    And, what he may, forbears
    His fame, to make it theirs:
And has his sword and spoils ungirt,
To lay them at the public's skirt.
    So when the falcon high
    Falls heavy from the sky,
She, having killed, no more does search
But on the next green bough to perch,
    Where, when he first does lure,
    The falc'ner has her sure.
What may not then our isle presume
While Victory his crest does plume?
    What may not others fear
    If thus he crowns each year?
A Caesar, he, ere long to Gaul,
To Italy an Hannibal,
    And to all states not free
    Shall climactéric be.
The Pict no shelter now shall find
Within his parti-coloured mind,
    But from this valour sad
    Shrink underneath the plaid:
Happy, if in the tufted brake
The English hunter him mistake,
    Nor lay his hounds in near
    The Caledonian deer.
But thou, the Wars' and Fortune's son,
March indefatigably on,
    And for the last effect
    Still keep thy sword erect:
Besides the force it has to fright
The spirits of the shady night,
    The same arts that did gain
    A power, must it maintain.

Andrew Marvell (1621–1678)

VONA GROARKE   368

Newman House
18 January 1994

Dear Ewan, Áine and Christopher,

I have chosen the poem 'Manners' by Elizabeth Bishop, which I love for its obvious simplicity. It records an age and a state of mind entirely without cynicism: a secure, small world in which no-one can lose his way. The child-like speaking voice is brilliantly achieved with rudimentary, sing-song rhymes which accommodate the jolly generosity and good faith of the child and her grandfather.

I also like it for its not-so-obvious complexities. Hovering at the edge of its simplicity is something much darker, suggested by the obscured faces of the passengers in the cars: a future in which the values of the child and her grandfather will be as outmoded as their wagon seat; an impersonal, technological world which will have no place for the gentle intimacy of manners. The poem marks the belated transition from the nineteenth to the twentieth centuries, and from innocence to painful experience. Its success lies, I think, in doing so without the slightest trace of either rhetoric or sentiment.

I wish you success with your new Lifelines, *and congratulations on your work so far.*

Best wishes,
Vona Groarke
Curator

Manners
For a Child of 1918

My grandfather said to me
as we sat on the wagon seat,
'Be sure to remember to always
speak to everyone you meet.'

We met a stranger on foot.
My grandfather's whip tapped his hat.
'Good day, sir. Good day. A fine day.'
And I said it and bowed where I sat.

Then we overtook a boy we knew
with his big pet crow on his shoulder.
'Always offer everyone a ride;
don't forget that when you get older,'

my grandfather said. So Willy
climbed up with us, but the crow

gave a 'Caw!' and flew off. I was worried.
How would he know where to go?

But he flew a little way at a time
from fence post to fence post, ahead;
and when Willy whistled he answered.
'A fine bird,' my grandfather said,

'and he's well brought up. See, he answers
nicely when he's spoken to.
Man or beast, that's good manners.
Be sure that you both always do.'

When automobiles went by,
the dust hid the people's faces,
but we shouted 'Good day! Good day!
Fine day!' at the top of our voices.

When we came to Hustler Hill,
he said that the mare was tired,
so we all got down and walked,
as our good manners required.

Elizabeth Bishop (1911–1979)

SEÁN Ó TUAMA   369

Roinn Na Nua-Ghaeilge
(Department of Modern Irish)
Coláiste na hOllscoile Corcaigh
(University College Cork)

14 Féabhra 1994

Dear Ewan, Áine and Christopher,

Sorry for the delay in answering your letter. 'Caoineadh Airt Uí
Laoghaire' / 'The Lament for Art O'Leary' *is my favourite poem, and
Eibhlín Dhubh Ní Chonaill's only known composition.*

*It is much too long for you to print; so I picked out a few excerpts and
the translation by Eilís Dillon.*

*I like this poem above all others for its devastatingly intimate revelation
of a heart breaking. It passes through a whole range of emotions — from
bitterness to grief — with a startling intensity.* 'Caoineadh Airt Uí
Laoghaire' *is not only a cry against death, but it is the greatest
affirmation known to me of a woman's love for a man.*

Beir beannacht,
Seán Ó Tuama

as *Caoineadh Airt Uí Laoghaire*

I
Mo ghrá go daingean tu!
Lá dá bhfaca thu
ag ceann tí an mhargaidh,
thug mo shúil aire dhuit,
thug mo chroí taitneamh duit,
d'éalaíos óm charaid leat
i bhfad ó bhaile leat.

Is domhsa nárbh aithreach:
Chuiris parlús á ghealadh dhom,
rúmanna á mbreacadh dhom,
bácús á dheargadh dhom,
brící á gceapadh dhom,
rósta ar bhearaibh dom,
mairt á leagadh dhom;
codladh i gclúmh lachan dom
go dtíodh an t-eadartha
nó thairis dá dtaitneadh liom.

Mo chara go daingean tu!
is cuimhin lem aigne
an lá breá earraigh úd,
gur bhreá thíodh hata dhuit
faoi bhanda óir tarraingthe;
claíomh cinn airgid,
lámh dheas chalma,
rompsáil bhagarthach —
fir-chritheagla
ar námhaid chealgach —
tú i gcóir chun falaracht
is each caol ceannann fút.
D'umhlaídís Sasanaigh
síos go talamh duit,
is ní ar mhaithe leat
ach le haon-chorp eagla,
cé gur leo a cailleadh tu,
a mhuirnín mh'anama . . .

Mo chara thu go daingean!
is nuair thiocfaidh chūgham abhaile
Conchúr beag an cheana
is Fear Ó Laoghaire, an leanbh,
fiafróid díom go tapaidh
cár fhágas féin a n-athair.
'Neosad dóibh faoi mhairg
gur fhágas i gCill na Martar.

Glaofaid siad ar a n-athair,
is ní bheidh sé acu le freagairt . . .

Mo chara thu go daingean!
is níor chreideas riamh dod mharbh
gur tháinig chūgham do chapall
is a srianta léi go talamh,
is fuil do chroí ar a leacain
siar go t'iallait ghreanta
mar a mbítheá id shuí 's id sheasamh.
Thugas léim go tairsigh,
an dara léim go geata,
an tríú léim ar do chapall.

Do bhuaileas go luath mo bhasa
is do bhaineas as na reathaibh
chomh maith is bhí sé agam,
go bhfuaras romham tu marbh
cois toirín ísil aitinn,
gan Pápa gan easpag,
gan cléireach gan sagart
do léifeadh ort an tsailm,
ach seanbhean chríonna chaite
do leath ort binn dá fallaing —
do chuid fola leat 'na sraithibh;
is níor fhanas le hí ghlanadh
ach í ól suas lem basaibh.

Mo ghrá thu go daingean!
is éirigh suas id sheasamh
is tar liom féin abhaile,
go gcuirfeam mairt á leagadh,
go nglaofam ar chóisir fhairsing,
go mbeidh againn ceol á spreagadh,
go gcóireod duitse leaba
faoi bhairlíní geala,
faoi chuilteanna breátha breaca,
a bhainfidh asat allas
in ionad an fhuachta a ghlacais.

Eibhlín Dhubh Ní Chonaill (mid to late eighteenth century)

from *The Lament for Art O'Leary*

I
My love forever!
The day I first saw you
At the end of the market-house,
My eye observed you,
My heart approved you,
I fled from my father with you,
Far from my home with you.

II
I never repented it:
You whitened a parlour for me,
Painted rooms for me,
Reddened ovens for me,
Baked fine bread for me,
Basted meat for me,
Slaughtered beasts for me;
I slept in ducks' feathers
Till midday milking-time,
Or more if it pleased me.

III
My friend forever!
My mind remembers
That fine spring day
How well your hat suited you,
Bright gold banded,
Sword silver-hilted —
Right hand steady —
Threatening aspect —
Trembling terror
On treacherous enemy —
You poised for a canter
On your slender bay horse.
The Saxons bowed to you,
Down to the ground to you,
Not for love of you
But for deadly fear of you,
Though you lost your life to them,
Oh my soul's darling . . .

V
My friend you were forever!
When they will come home to me,
Gentle little Conor
And Farr O'Leary, the baby,
They will question me so quickly,
Where did I leave their father.
I'll answer in my anguish
That I left him in Killnamartyr.
They will call out to their father;
And he won't be there to answer . . .

VII

My friend you were forever!
I knew nothing of your murder
Till your horse came to the stable
With the reins beneath her trailing,
And your heart's blood on her shoulders
Staining the tooled saddle
Where you used to sit and stand.
My first leap reached the threshold,
My second reached the gateway,
My third leap reached the saddle.

VIII

I struck my hands together
And I made the bay horse gallop
As fast as I was able,
Till I found you dead before me
Beside a little furze-bush.
Without Pope or bishop,
Without priest or cleric
To read the death-psalms for you,
But a spent old woman only
Who spread her cloak to shroud you —
Your heart's blood was still flowing;
I did not stay to wipe it
But filled my hands and drank it.

IX

My love you'll be forever!
Rise up from where you're lying
And we'll be going homewards.
We'll have a bullock slaughtered,
We'll call our friends together,
We'll get the music going.
I'll make a fine bed ready
With sheets of snow-white linen,
And fine embroidered covers
That will bring the sweat out through you
Instead of the cold that's on you!

Translated by Eilís Dillon

NICK HORNBY   370

3 February 1994

Dear Ewan Gibson, Áine Jackson and Chris Pillow,

My favourite poem is 'Gravy', by Raymond Carver, from the book A New Path to the Waterfall. *Carver was dying of cancer when he wrote the poem, but I love its absolute determination to celebrate: he had nearly died of alcoholism ten years before, but gave up drinking, met the woman with whom he spent the last, very happy, decade of his life, and produced several volumes of wonderful short stories and poems. So 'Gravy' is about being given a second chance, and appreciating that chance for what it was. I find it very moving and very humbling, because I know that this was written by someone who was a better human being than more or less all of us.*

I hope this is OK, and let me know if I can be of any further help (I'd like to buy one, for example).

Best wishes and good luck,

Nick Hornby

Gravy

No other word will do. For that's what it was. Gravy.
Gravy, these past ten years.
Alive, sober, working, loving and
being loved by a good woman. Eleven years
ago he was told he had six months to live
at the rate he was going. And he was going
nowhere but down. So he changed his ways
somehow. He quit drinking! And the rest?
After that it was *all* gravy, every minute
of it, up to and including when he was told about,
well, some things that were breaking down and
building up inside his head. 'Don't weep for me,'
he said to his friends. 'I'm a lucky man.
I've had ten years longer than I or anyone
expected. Pure gravy. And don't forget it.'

Raymond Carver (1939–1988)

EILÍS NÍ DHUIBHNE 371

25 January 1994

Dear Ewan, Áine and Christopher,

Thank you very much for your letter, asking me to send you the name of my favourite poem for Lifelines. *Of course I am very happy to do this, and appreciate very much being asked.*

Like most people, probably, I have a number of favourite poems, including poems that I loved when I first read them and which made an impact on me at the time, and poems, sometimes the same, that go through my head very often. If I were picking one from the first group, it would be 'When you are old and grey and full of sleep', *the poem by Yeats based on a sonnet by Ronsard, which my husband quoted to me when he proposed. It is the ideal poem for this situation. Who could resist* 'But I have loved the pilgrim soul in you...'? *In fact, I think love poems are the most primary and natural kinds of poem. Those and nature poems. The one I will finally select as my favourite is one in which love and nature are combined:* 'Leaba Shíoda', *by Nuala Ní Dhomhnaill. I like that because it is an honest, unabashedly romantic and passionate poem of a woman's love for a man, the kind of poem you sometimes get as a traditional song but seldom as a literary poem by an Irishwoman. The bit I like best is the 'skin — like milk being poured from jugs at dinnertime'. I think that, and many of the other images, are lovely.*

Good luck with the project.

Eilís Ní Dhuibhne

When You are Old

When you are old and grey and full of sleep,
And nodding by the fire, take down this book,
And slowly read, and dream of the soft look
Your eyes had once, and of their shadows deep;

How many loved your moments of glad grace,
And loved your beauty with love false or true,
But one man loved the pilgrim soul in you,
And loved the sorrows of your changing face;

And bending down beside the glowing bars,
Murmur, a little sadly, how Love fled
And paced upon the mountains overhead
And hid his face amid a crowd of stars.

W B Yeats (1865–1939)

['When You Are Old' was also chosen by Anthony Clare in *Lifelines*.]

Leaba Shíoda

Do chóireoinn leaba duit
i Leaba Shíoda
sa bhféar ard
faoi iomrascáil na gcrann
is bheadh do chraiceann ann
mar shíoda ar shíoda
sa doircheacht
am lonnaithe na leamhan.

Craiceann a shníonn
go gléineach thar do ghéaga
mar bhainne á dháil as crúiscíní
am lóin
is tréad gabhar ag gabháil thar chnocáin
do chuid gruaige
cnocáin ar a bhfuil faillte arda
is dhá ghleann atá domhain.

Is bheadh do bheola taise
ar mhilseacht shiúcra
tráthnóna is sinn ag spaisteoireacht
cois abhann
is na gaotha meala
ag séideadh thar an Sionna
is na fiúisí ag beannú duit
ceann ar cheann.

Na fiúisí ag ísliú
a gceann maorga
ag umhlú síos don áilleacht
os a gcomhair
is do phriocfainn péire acu
mar shiogairlíní
is do mhaiseoinn do chluasa
mar bhrídeog.

Ó, chóireoinn leaba duit
i Leaba Shíoda
le hamhascarnach an lae
i ndeireadh thall
is ba mhór an pléisiúr dúinn
bheith géaga ar ghéaga
ag iomrascáil
am lonnaithe na leamhan.

Nuala Ní Dhomhnaill (b.1952)

Labasheedy (The Silken Bed)

I'd make a bed for you
in Labasheedy
in the tall grass
under the wrestling trees
where your skin
would be silk upon silk
in the darkness
when the moths are coming down.

Skin which glistens
shining over your limbs
like milk being poured
from jugs at dinnertime;
your hair is a herd of goats
moving over rolling hills,
hills that have high cliffs
and two ravines.

And your damp lips
would be as sweet as sugar
at evening and we walking
by the riverside
with honeyed breezes
blowing over the Shannon
and the fuchsias bowing down to you
one by one.

The fuchsias bending low
their solemn heads
in obeisance to the beauty
in front of them
I would pick a pair of flowers
as pendant earrings
to adorn you
like a bride in shining clothes.

O I'd make a bed for you
in Labasheedy,
in the twilight hour
with evening falling slow
and what a pleasure it would be
to have our limbs entwine
wrestling
while the moths are coming down.

Translated by the author

BRIAN LEYDEN · 372

Ewan Gibson, Áine Jackson, Christopher Pillow,

*What to choose? There is Patrick Kavanagh's master-work, 'The Great
Hunger'. A poem I love, though big and awkward like the man himself.
And I treat it as a poem to read not recite. No. It will have to be W B
Yeats. The young and the living poets object. But if I give in to those
clamouring voices this letter will never be written. 'He Wishes for the
Cloths of Heaven' is easily remembered, heartfelt and utterly
Romantic. Not exactly a party piece, but I have found it useful when
cornered by in-laws and relations who tell me being a writer is fine, but
would I not like a proper job?*

Yours sincerely,
Brian Leyden

MICHAEL MORTELL · 373

7 March 1994

Dear Ewan, Áine and Christopher,

*Thank you for your letter. I deem it a great compliment to be included
in your anthology.*

*'He Wishes for the Cloths of Heaven' by W B Yeats has been a poem
close to my heart since I first read it about fifteen years ago.*

*In this short poem Yeats captures for me the two great abiding elements
of love — its magic and its frailty.*

Wishing you every success with your venture.

Michael Mortell

JUDITH WOODWORTH · 374

April 1994

Dear Ewan, Áine and Christopher,

*I was really delighted to receive your letter requesting me to contribute
to your new edition of 'Lifelines'. To be honest, I am not a great reader
of poetry books. However, I was given two copies of 'Lifelines' last year;
one by Wesley College when I had the great pleasure of presenting prizes
at Prize Day. These two copies are placed strategically around the house
and I have now discovered the joy of reading poems at odd quiet moments
of the day, whilst also enjoying the comments accompanying them.*

Poetry has always been significant to me in the context of its setting to music. Of all the many songs I am familiar with, either from performing them myself or listening to others performing them, one particular song and poem continues to haunt me. W B Yeats's 'He Wishes for the Cloths of Heaven' is set to music by the English composer Thomas Frederick Dunhill. In this simple and evocative setting the composer I feel has enhanced Yeats's poem, so that the poignancy of the words linger on in the memory.

Wishing you continued success with this wonderful project.

Yours sincerely,
Judith Woodworth

He Wishes for the Cloths of Heaven

Had I the heavens' embroidered cloths,
Enwrought with golden and silver light,
The blue and the dim and the dark cloths
Of night and light and the half-light,
I would spread the cloths under your feet:
But I, being poor, have only my dreams;
I have spread my dreams under your feet;
Tread softly because you tread on my dreams.

W B Yeats (1865–1939)

CIARÁN Mac MATHÚNA   375

RTE

February 1994

'Solitude' by Robin Flower

Robin Flower was an Englishman with a deep love of Ireland and its Gaelic tradition. He was a distinguished scholar and worked for some years compiling The Catalogue of Irish Manuscripts *in the British Museum.*

But Robin Flower's interest in Gaelic Ireland was not confined to the dusty volumes in the Museum; for him the living speech of the Gaelic world was equally important. In this he found an oral literature which he saw as a rich part of an old European civilisation.

From 1910 onwards for about 20 years he spent long holidays in the Great Blasket, a Gaelic speaking island off the Kerry coast, three miles out on the Atlantic, 'the ultimate shore of the old world' as he described it himself.

The people of the Great Blasket made Flower one of themselves and from them he wrote down their folktales and folksongs and translated into English one of the great classic books on life on the Blaskets, written in Irish by his friend Tomás O'Crohan (An tOileánach, The Islandman), who lived there all his life.

But Robin Flower was a writer and a poet in his own right and his book The Western Island *or* The Great Blasket *is a delightful account in prose of his own experiences there and also includes some of his original poems.*

'Solitude' is one of these poems and evokes the loneliness and strange unearthly experience he felt on the Great Blasket when 'a mist came from the sea and took the world away.' But all is well as the sun breaks through and the mountain peaks of Slemish and Brandon appear again in their high glory and seem to be physical symbols of a timeless, mystical world.

Ciarán Mac Mathúna

Solitude

They could not stack the turf in that wet spring,
And the cold nights were icy in our bones,
And so we burned furze and the rusted bracken.
I climbed the hill alone
And by the old fort gathered in the sun
Red fern and crackling furze;
And, as I worked, a mist came from the sea
And took the world away,
And left me islanded in that high air,
Where the trenched doon broods silent on the hill.
I do not know what shapes were in the mist,
But solitude was made more solitary
By some re-risen memory of the earth
That gathered round my loneliness,
And threatened with the dead my living breath.
I could have cried aloud for my sharp fear,
But the mist thinned and withered, and the sun
At one swift stride came through.
They passed those shadowy threats,
And the great company of Ireland's hills,
Brandon and Slemish and the lesser brethren,
Stood up in the bright air,
And on the other side the sea,
The illimitable Atlantic, rolled and shone.

Robin Flower (1881–1946)

MARGRIT CRUICKSHANK   376

28 January 1994

Dear Ewan, Áine and Christopher,

Thank you for inviting me to contribute a favourite poem to the next Lifelines. *I would be delighted, both because the money you raise goes to help others and because the previous* Lifelines *were such fascinating anthologies, full of old favourites and, for me anyway, exciting new discoveries.*

Choosing one poem is almost impossible. But this one by the Czech writer Miroslav Holub seems very suitable for the times we live in.

Good luck,
Margrit Cruickshank

The Door

Go and open the door.
    Maybe outside there's
    a tree, or a wood,
    a garden,
    or a magic city.

Go and open the door.
    Maybe a dog's rummaging.
    Maybe you'll see a face,
or an eye,
or the picture
                of a picture.

Go and open the door.
    If there's a fog
    it will clear.

Go and open the door.
    Even if there's only
    the darkness ticking,
    even if there's only
    the hollow wind,
    even if
        nothing
                is there,
go and open the door.

At least
there'll be
a draught.

Miroslav Holub (b.1923)
Translated by Ian Milner

JOHN BRUTON   377

Dail Éireann
Baile Átha Cliath, 2
(Dublin 2)

28 February 1994

Dear Ewan,

Thank you for your letter and I apologise for the delay in replying.

*I am happy to enclose a poem which I enjoy by Micheal O'Siadhail. It is
'History' and my reason for this choice is that it is a good poem about
an important subject and Micheal is a personal friend of mine.*

Wishing you every success with your Project.

With kindest regards.

Yours sincerely,
John Bruton
Leader Fine Gael

from *The Chosen Garden*
IV Turns and Returns

History

And we keep beginning afresh
an endless history
as if this odyssey
had never happened before. Yes,

ours was a spoiled generation
secure, even tepid
somehow untested —
no plague or war, torture or starvation.

Look how some were keeping faith
in a gulag while we
fumbled out our destiny,
walking our easy under-urban path.

So it wasn't their route (wince
at the thought). Still,
freedom was a crucible,
blundering chalkless tour in labyrinths.

Maybe we grope the same journey
scooping the oracular
in scandals of the particular
light we throw on some greater story.

Why does the word keep taking flesh?
A nameless dream
wild stratagem
wanting to shape our venture. O Gilgamesh

forever traveller, your myth brooding
in us, we grapple
with redemption's fable.
O Scheherazade healing a cuckolded king.

Micheal O'Siadhail (b.1947)

FAY WELDON   378

20 January 1994

Dear Ewan Gibson,

How about Kipling's 'If'? An old fashioned poem, suggesting out of date self-control, and very stiff-upper-lipped, but nevertheless it had a profound influence.

With best wishes,
Fay Weldon

If—

If you can keep your head when all about you
    Are losing theirs and blaming it on you,
If you can trust yourself when all men doubt you,
    But make allowance for their doubting too;
If you can wait and not be tired by waiting,
    Or being lied about, don't deal in lies,
Or being hated, don't give way to hating,
    And yet don't look too good, nor talk too wise:

If you can dream — and not make dreams your master;
    If you can think — and not make thoughts your aim;
If you can meet with Triumph and Disaster
    And treat those two impostors just the same;
If you can bear to hear the truth you've spoken
    Twisted by knaves to make a trap for fools,
Or watch the things you gave your life to, broken,
    And stoop and build 'em up with worn-out tools:

If you can make one heap of all your winnings
    And risk it on one turn of pitch-and-toss,
And lose, and start again at your beginnings
    And never breathe a word about your loss;
If you can force your heart and nerve and sinew
    To serve your turn long after they are gone,
And so hold on when there is nothing in you
    Except the Will which says to them: 'Hold on!'

If you can talk with crowds and keep your virtue,
    Or walk with Kings — nor lose the common touch,
If neither foes nor loving friends can hurt you,
    If all men count with you, but none too much;
If you can fill the unforgiving minute
    With sixty seconds' worth of distance run,
Yours is the Earth and everything that's in it,
    And — which is more — you'll be a Man, my son!

Rudyard Kipling (1865–1936)

TOM PAULIN   379

28 January 1994

Dear Ewan, Áine and Christopher,

It's hard to say which poem out of the many I love is a favourite, but when I was a young student I read Yeats's 'The Cold Heaven' and something clicked. The recognition has lasted and deepened — the cold passion of Yeats's lyricism is entangled with historical experience as the ghost is sent out naked on the roads. Sent where? To hell or Connaught? Across the Irish Sea or the Atlantic? Does the spirit wander like mad Sweeney across Ulster? Does it gaze out on the snowy Himalayas like Kim and the lama in Kipling's great novel? No answer. The homeless suffering in Yeats's poem — Lear and the Fool on the heath — haunt me, even as I write this.

Good luck and every good wish,
Tom Paulin

The Cold Heaven

Suddenly I saw the cold and rook-delighting heaven
That seemed as though ice burned and was but the
        more ice,
And thereupon imagination and heart were driven
So wild that every casual thought of that and this
Vanished, and left but memories, that should be out
        of season
With the hot blood of youth, of love crossed long ago;
And I took all the blame out of all sense and reason,
Until I cried and trembled and rocked to and fro,
Riddled with light. Ah! when the ghost begins to
        quicken,
Confusion of the death-bed over, is it sent
Out naked on the roads, as the books say, and stricken
By the injustice of the skies for punishment?

W B Yeats (1865–1939)

TIM GOULDING   380

26 January 1994

Dear Ewan, Áine and Christopher

Congratulations on your worthy project. Thanks also for choosing my participation.

I have chosen 'Inversnaid' by Gerard Manley Hopkins. This poem straightaway lands me beside the river Dargle where I grew up. I passed one summer and autumn there, painting fifty pictures of its various aspects. It is a little more than a 'burn' but its 'rollrock highroad' rampages through the Dargle Glen before it spreads out more discreetly for its final effluence. Hopkins' poem captures the song of the river with its alternate rhythms. His musical verse is crammed with visual observation, befitting one whose first ambition was to be a painter. His cry for the preservation of wilderness is all the more poignant today. Above all, though, I'm inspired by his glimpse of the Divine in nature. These are hymns to the 'Elan Vital'.

Tim Goulding

Inversnaid

This darksome burn, horseback brown,
His rollrock highroad roaring down,
In coop and in comb the fleece of his foam
Flutes and low to the lake falls home.

A windpuff-bonnet of fáwn-fróth
Turns and twindles over the broth
Of a pool so pitchblack, féll-frówning,
It rounds and rounds Despair to drowning.

Degged with dew, dappled with dew
Are the groins of the braes that the brook treads through,
Wiry heathpacks, flitches of fern,
And the beadbonny ash that sits over the burn.

What would the world be, once bereft
Of wet and of wildness? Let them be left,
O let them be left, wildness and wet;
Long live the weeds and the wilderness yet.

Gerard Manley Hopkins (1844–1889)

PROINNSÍAS Ó DUINN   381

RTE Concert Orchestra
10 March 1994

Dear Students,

Many thanks for your letter.

As an orchestral conductor I deal indirectly on a regular basis with both poetry and prose. It is necessary for me in this capacity to be enthusiastic about the actual work in hand at any given time and to sell it as the most important work ever written! Because of this, it is difficult to settle on one particular poem as my favourite.

Several works spring to mind and I must confess the powerful poem of Cardinal Newman 'The Dream of Gerontius' would have to be high on the list. This poem is written from inside the mind of a dying man as he lies, dreaming of the journey his soul takes to the unseen world, and the manner in which it is received by the agents of the Almighty. The subject concerns us all and its riveting fascination is probably enhanced because nobody in the history of mankind can claim to actually know the answers or scenario. Newman cleverly communicates his own views and deep faith using the dream of a dying man as a vehicle.

For some time now I have been writing the music for a musical based on the life of the English lyricist, writer, and painter, Edward Lear. In each case the lyrics of the musical numbers are the actual writings of Lear. His most famous nonsense verse is, perhaps, 'The Owl and the Pussy-cat'. Here is another poet who wrote nonsense verses to amuse children and, indeed, succeeded admirably. I must confess to having tremendous regard for any writer, poet or composer who can make people smile.

However, if you have to study the life of a writer such as Lear, and dwell on the text for long periods as I have had to do in attempting to set his words to music, you frequently find that behind the obvious and immediate impact that brings a smile, there lies a deeper undercurrent. In this case, Lear talking about himself.

In the poem 'The Duck and the Kangaroo' we read the humorous and most unlikely conversation between the two. The intention is to make us smile and he succeeds. Lear never married and had very low self-esteem because of his appearance. He loved children and among the many he met and for whom he wrote was one named Gussie. He admitted that if circumstances were different — if he were better looking and more deserving, and if the age difference did not exist — he would have married Gussie. A situation somewhat like the Duck and the Kangaroo. In the musical this becomes a poignant duet because we see that Lear is speaking his thoughts and aspirations through the Duck and that the Kangaroo is Gussie who would rescue him from his lonely and sad life.

To set up this interpretation for the audience Anne Makower, who wrote the book, gave Lear the following line just as the music starts: '... Gussie, when you grow up, you must marry someone not like me at all, but someone like you and young like you and beautiful like you. Now promise me, Gussie, that you'll do that.'

The Duck and the Kangaroo

(Lear)   Said the Duck to the Kangaroo,
              'Good gracious! How you hop!
              Over the fields and water too,
              As if you never would stop!
              My life is a bore in this nasty pond,
              And I long to go out in the world beyond!
              I wish I could hop like you!'
              Said the Duck to the Kangaroo.

              'Please give me a ride on your back!'
              Said the Duck to the Kangaroo.
              'I would sit quite still and say nothing but 'Quack',
              The whole of the long day through!
              And we'd go to the Dee and the Jelly Bo Lee,
              Over the land and over the sea; —
              Please take me a ride! O do!'
              Said the Duck to the Kangaroo.

(Gussie)   Said the Kangaroo to the Duck,
              'This requires some little reflection;
              Perhaps on the whole it might bring me luck,
              And there seems but one objection,
              Which is, if you'll let me speak so bold,
              Your feet are unpleasantly wet and cold,
              And would probably give me the roo —
              Matiz!' said the Kangaroo.

(Lear)   (Said the Duck), 'As I sat on the rocks,
              (I have thought over that) —
              I have thought over that completely,
              And I bought four pairs of worsted socks
              Which fit my webbed feet neatly.
              And to keep out the cold I've bought a cloak,
              And every day a cigar I'll smoke,
              All to follow my own dear true
              Love of a Kangaroo!'

(Gussie)   (Said the Kangaroo), 'I'm ready!
              All in the moonlight pale;
              But to balance me well, dear Duck, sit steady!
              And quite at the end of my tail!'

(Both)   So away they went with a hop and a bound,
                (And they) hopped the whole world three times
                round;
                And who so happy, — O who,
                As the Duck and the Kangaroo?

(Gussie curls up against Lear and goes to sleep)

(Lear)   'My life is a bore in this nasty pond,
                And I long to go out in the world beyond.
                I wish I could hop like you!'

Many thanks and best wishes,
Proinnsías Ó Duinn

MARY MORRISSY   382

24 January 1994

Dear Ewan, Áine and Christopher,

Thank you for your letter inviting me to participate in the Lifelines *anthology. I hesitate before nominating my favourite poem, as I am constantly making new poetic discoveries, but* 'Reference Back' *by Philip Larkin was one of my first favourites. It captures for me both the awkward distance between people and the lucky coincidence of connection. I like too the delicate sense of anticipated loss the poem evokes, and its poignant air of lament. And, of course, those two great lines:–*

    'We are not suited to the long perspectives
    Open at each instant of our lives.'

How true!

With every good wish for your venture,
Mary Morrissy

Reference Back

That was a pretty one, I heard you call
From the unsatisfactory hall
To the unsatisfactory room where I
Played record after record, idly,
Wasting my time at home, that you
Looked so much forward to.

Oliver's *Riverside Blues,* it was. And now
I shall, I suppose, always remember how
The flock of notes those antique negroes blew
Out of Chicago air into
A huge remembering pre-electric horn

The year after I was born
Three decades later made this sudden bridge
From your unsatisfactory age
To my unsatisfactory prime.

Truly, though our element is time,
We are not suited to the long perspectives
Open at each instant of our lives.
They link us to our losses: worse,
They show us what we have as it once was,
Blindingly undiminished, just as though
By acting differently we could have kept it so.

Philip Larkin (1922–1985)

PAUL ANDREWS   383

28 February 1994

Dear Ewan, Áine, Christopher,

Your letter brought me joy, in several ways. Lifelines *has been my favourite anthology for the last two years. I am delighted to know you are carrying on the work, and through it saving the voiceless in the Third World. It made my day to be included in your list, which has become a Who's Who of poetry-readers. It is a rare gift to spread joy around. Keep it up!*

The choice is hard, but I'll opt for Louis MacNeice's 'Prayer before Birth', hoping it is unchosen by others, and that I will not find under my letter 'This was also Ian Paisley's choice; see page xxx'.

It is not merely that Louis was a fellow-Ulsterman, innured to a grey climate, but hungry for 'sky to sing to me, birds and a white light in the back of my mind to guide me'. More than that, he touches the fear, anger and yearning for life that drive us to prayer. In your collection it is a prayer for the millions of Third World children who need to be protected, provided, consoled, forgiven, heard, and given life. It must be spoken with passion.

Paul Andrews

['Prayer before Birth' was also Agnès Bernelle's choice. The poem in full can be found on page 155.]

JOHN CREEDON   384

RTE

12 January 1994

Greetings All!

Enclosed one of my favourite poems. I have many but this is the first I ever learned — taught to me in 2nd class North Mon., Cork, by a kind and gentle Christian Brother named Brother Gill — a Wexford man, I think. It's a very simple poem but valuable for young children because it shows that inside every oul' fella beats the heart of a boy! The poem is also 100% guaranteed Irish!

Hope this does the trick. Good luck with the project.

In haste,
John Creedon

Danny Murphy

He was as old as old can be,
His little eyes could scarcely see,
His mouth was sunken in between
His nose and chin, and he was lean
And twisted up and withered quite
So that he couldn't walk aright.

His pipe was always going out,
And then he'd have to search about
In all his pockets, and he'd mow
— O, deary me! and, musha now!
And then he'd light his pipe, and then
He'd let it go clean out again.

He couldn't dance or jump or run,
Or ever have a bit of fun
Like me and Susan, when we shout
And jump and throw ourselves about:
— But when he laughed, then you could see
He was as young as young could be!

James Stephens (1882–1950)

EITHNE FITZGERALD   385

Minister of State, Office of the Tánaiste
Government Buildings, Dublin 2

25 January 1994

Dear Lifelines,

Thank you for asking me to contribute to the next edition of Lifelines. *Well done on this innovative way to help the Third World.*

I have chosen the poem 'Generation' *by Maureen Gordon.*

Like Rumpole and his Wordsworth, I enjoyed the poems I studied in school for their rhythm and use of language, poems full of verve like 'Lepanto', and the romantic poetry of Shelley and Yeats. In recent years I have particularly liked to read women poets like Eavan Boland, dealing with women's experiences in a way which was completely absent from my school curriculum.

Maureen Gordon is a poet whose talent for writing was developed in the Writers' Group in DATE, the Dundrum Adult Education project. Maureen's poem 'Generation' *speaks of a universal theme for women, the passing of the childbearing years and finding new outlets for our creativity.*

May I wish you every success with the project.

Yours sincerely,
Eithne Fitzgerald
Minister of State

Generation

After the moon had claimed me for her daughter,
I gave up writing poetry.
Netted in her sling,
swung on her tides,
my body floated
through mindless seasons of fecundity.

Now it is jetsam,
beached,
spent seaweed drying in the Autumn sun,
unsought conceptions quicken in my mind,
burden and swell,
demand deliverance.

As the mind darkens
and oblivion looms,
already I can see

round the next bend
the spiral rising into the unknown,
the unimaginable.
In what future womb
will my freed spirit
be required to seed?

Maureen Gordon

TESS GALLAGHER   386

1 May 1993

Dear Ewan Gibson, et al,

Thank you for your letter.

*Your project seems quite a good one and I will enclose a copy of the poem
'What the Doctor Said,' by Raymond Carver, which is from his last
book entitled* A New Path to the Waterfall.

*Now as to why this is a favorite poem of mine: Raymond Carver was
able to write this poem in the aftermath of having received the dire news
that his lung cancer, which had progressed to the brain, had then spread
to the one remaining lung. What's amazing to me is that horror, humor
and mortality all coexist in this poem. The humanity of the speaker in
the poem is what astounds me every time I re-read the poem. I feel the
predicament of the doctor having to deliver such news and trying to
clock himself in the facticity of counting the tumors. I feel the razor sharp
irony of the speaker, how it coexists with his desperate need to cling to
hope, and then the amazing way in which the speaker grasps the hands
of the very one who has delivered the news of his death. It is as if he has
seen the highest choice and, in a way, vanquished death by thanking the
messenger who has by then begun to assume an almost ridiculous air.
It is the speaker whose stature is enlarged, even if it is 'habit' which
delivers him from that impossible, yet unavoidable news. Ray wrote the
poem and then fulfilled its news with his death barely two months later,
on 2 August 1988. Except for the Buddhist monks who used to write a
brief haiku, then put down their pens and die, I don't know any
contemporary example of a writer giving us such a poem under the
pressure of his own imminent death. I love its spiritual dimension which
is delivered so offhandedly that it takes hold of us the way sunlight takes
hold of roses and weeds alike.*

*I hope this is sufficient to explain my predilection for this poem by my
late husband.*

Sincere best wishes,
Tess Gallagher

What the Doctor Said

He said it doesn't look good
he said it looks bad in fact real bad
he said I counted thirty-two of them on one lung before
I quit counting them
I said I'm glad I wouldn't want to know
about any more being there than that
he said are you a religious man do you kneel down
in forest groves and let yourself ask for help
when you come to a waterfall
mist blowing against your face and arms
do you stop and ask for understanding at those moments
I said not yet but I intend to start today
he said I'm real sorry he said
I wish I had some other kind of news to give you
I said Amen and he said something else
I didn't catch and not knowing what else to do
and not wanting him to have to repeat it
and me to have to fully digest it
I just looked at him
for a minute and he looked back it was then
I jumped up and shook hands with this man who'd just given me
something no one else on earth had ever given me
I may even have thanked him habit being so strong

Raymond Carver (1939–1988)

R S THOMAS   387

Friends,

I choose a fragment by W B Yeats as expressing in one short verse homo sapiens's problem in the 20th century.

Cofion cynes
R S Thomas

from *Fragments*

I
Locke sank into a swoon;
The Garden died;
God took the spinning-jenny
Out of his side.

William Butler Yeats (1865–1939)

CHARLES TYRRELL   388

Dear Ewan, Áine and Christopher,

I hope I'm not too late with my response to your request. The poem I chose is Paul Durcan's 'The Mantelpiece' *from his last collection —* Give me Your Hand.

Best of luck with the project.

Yours sincerely,
Charles Tyrrell

The Mantelpiece
after Vuillard

Staring into the marble, I stray into it
Exploring its pores, its veins, its stains, its moles.
A block of marble on legs of marble.
Is it an altar?
Am I going to die?
Where is she? Will she ever come back?
Who is she? What is her name?
What kind of a woman
Would have an altar for a mantelpiece?
Would rescue a down-and-out at her gate
And put him to sleep in her own bed?

When she does come back in the late afternoon
She does not speak except to say
'It's May!'
She puts a glass vase of Queen Anne's lace
And daisies on the mantelpiece,
A single poppy, a bramble blossom,
Medicine bottles with labels
Prescribing for me when and how to take them.
She reiterates 'It's May!'
As if she herself is the May.
She hands me a book entitled 'Howard's End'.
How does she know that my name is Howard?
She puts out a clothes horse
Draping it with white cotton nighties.
I put out a finger with which to trace the marble
But trace her instead — trace her cheekbone.
Is your mantelpiece an altar?
She smiles: Are you my spring lamb?
I am.

That was five and a half years ago.
The world that is the case is everything and new.
O my drowned spring lamb!
O my wild, wild mantelpiece!

Paul Durcan (b.1944)

'The Mantelpiece'

This recent poem by Paul Durcan was written in response to a painting I've long admired by Edouard Vuillard called 'The Mantelpiece'. Vuillard and his contemporary and fellow Frenchman Pierre Bonnard were masters at painting the intimate, incidental domestic situation and transforming it into something a lot more profound. I fear that this painting of the mantelpiece will never be quite the same for me now that Paul Durcan has applied his whacky imagination to it. The last line takes the biscuit.

Charles Tyrrell

TERRY DOLAN   389

University College Dublin
Department of English
Old and Middle English

17 March 1994

Dear Ewan, Áine and Christopher,

Very sorry I have taken so long to send you this. I hope it is not too late — but here goes, anyway.

Very best wishes, many thanks, and good luck.

Yours sincerely,
Terry Dolan

When I studied English Literature as an undergraduate I never read even one line of American poetry or prose, much to my shame and regret. Years later a friend in Dublin introduced me to the writings of Jack Kerouac, Allen Ginsberg, Emily Dickinson, William Carlos Williams and, of course, Walt Whitman, among many others. I was thrilled with discovery after discovery. I even went to the City Lights Bookshop while on business in San Francisco and sat and read Ginsberg's Howl *in the midst of the browsers.*

More than any other poet, Walt Whitman's strength, honesty, compelling rhythm, disciplined pace, and perfect choice of words lead me to select a piece of his 'Song of Myself' *as my choice for inclusion*

*in your anthology. These lines tell me so much about the energy,
loneliness, self-reliance, and austerity of the sophisticated American
mind.*

Very best wishes,
Terry Dolan
Professor Terence Dolan

from *Song of Myself*

1

I celebrate myself, and sing myself,
And what I assume you shall assume,
For every atom belonging to me as good belongs to you.

I loafe and invite my soul,
I lean and loafe at my ease observing a spear of summer grass.
My tongue, every atom of my blood, form'd from this soil, this air,
Born here of parents born here from parents the same, and
      their parents the same,
I, now thirty-seven years old in perfect health begin,
Hoping to cease not till death.

Creeds and schools in abeyance,
Retiring back a while sufficed at what they are, but never
      forgotten,
I harbor for good or bad, I permit to speak at every hazard,
Nature without check with original energy.

2

Houses and rooms are full of perfumes, the shelves are
      crowded with perfumes,
I breathe the fragrance myself and know it and like it,
The distillation would intoxicate me also, but I shall not let it.

The atmosphere is not a perfume, it has no taste of the
      distillation, it is odorless,
It is for my mouth forever, I am in love with it,
I will go to the bank by the wood and become undisguised and
      naked,
I am mad for it to be in contact with me.

The smoke of my own breath,
Echoes, ripples, buzz'd whispers, love-root, silk-thread, crotch
      and vine,
My respiration and inspiration, the beating of my heart, the
      passing of blood and air through my lungs,
The sniff of green leaves and dry leaves, and of the shore and
      dark-color'd sea-rocks, and of hay in the barn,
The sound of the belch'd words of my voice loos'd to the
      eddies of the wind,

A few light kisses, a few embraces, a reaching around of arms,
The play of shine and shade on the trees as the supple boughs
    wag,
The delight alone or in the rush of the streets, or along the
    fields and hillsides,
The feeling of health, the full-noon trill, the song of me rising
    from bed and meeting the sun.

Have you reckon'd a thousand acres much? have you reckon'd
    the earth much?
Have you practis'd so long to learn to read?
Have you felt so proud to get at the meaning of poems?

Stop this day and night with me and you shall possess the
    origin of all poems,
You shall possess the good of the earth and sun, (there are
    millions of suns left,)
You shall no longer take things at second or third hand, nor
    look through the eyes of the dead, nor feed on the spectres
    in books,
You shall not look through my eyes either, nor take things
    from me,
You shall listen to all sides and filter them from your self.

3
I have heard what the talkers were talking, the talk of the
    beginning and the end,
But I do not talk of the beginning or the end.

There was never any more inception than there is now,
Nor any more youth or age than there is now,
And will never be any more perfection than there is now,
Nor any more heaven or hell than there is now.
Urge and urge and urge,
Always the procreant urge of the world.

Out of the dimness opposite equals advance, always substance
    and increase, always sex,
Always a knit of identity, always distinction, always a breed of
    life.

To elaborate is no avail, learn'd and unlearn'd feel that it is so.

Sure as the most certain sure, plumb in the uprights, well
    entretied, braced in the beams,
Stout as a horse, affectionate, haughty, electrical,
I and this mystery here we stand.

Clear and sweet is my soul, and clear and sweet is all that is
    not my soul.

Lack one lacks both, and the unseen is proved by the seen,
Till that becomes unseen and receives proof in its turn.

Showing the best and dividing it from the worst age vexes age,
Knowing the perfect fitness and equanimity of things, while
    they discuss I am silent, and go bathe and admire myself.

Welcome is every organ and attribute of me, and of any man
    hearty and clean,
Not an inch nor a particle of an inch is vile, and none shall be
    less familiar than the rest.

I am satisfied—I see, dance, laugh, sing;
As the hugging and loving bed-fellow sleeps at my side
    through the night, and withdraws at the peep of the day with
    stealthy tread,
Leaving me baskets cover'd with white towels swelling the
    house with their plenty,
Shall I postpone my acceptation and realization and scream at
    my eyes,
That they turn from gazing after and down the road,
And forthwith cipher and show me to a cent,
Exactly the value of one and exactly the value of two, and
    which is ahead?

4
Trippers and askers surround me,
People I meet, the effect upon me of my early life or the ward
    and city I live in, or the nation,
The latest dates, discoveries, inventions, societies, authors old
    and new,
My dinner, dress, associates, looks, compliments, dues,
The real or fancied indifference of some man or woman I love,
The sickness of one of my folks or of myself, or ill-doing or loss
    or lack of money, or depressions or exaltations,
Battles, the horrors of fratricidal war, the fever of doubtful
    news, the fitful events;
These come to me days and nights and go from me again,
But they are not the Me myself.

Apart from the pulling and hauling stands what I am,
Stands amused, complacent, compassionating, idle, unitary,
Looks down, is erect, or bends an arm on an impalpable
    certain rest,
Looking with side-curved head curious what will come next,
Both in and out of the game and watching and wondering at it.

Backward I see in my own days where I sweated through fog
    with linguists and contenders,
I have no mockings or arguments, I witness and wait.

5
I believe in you my soul, the other I am must not abase itself
    to you,
And you must not be abased to the other.

Loafe with me on the grass, loose the stop from your throat,
Not words, not music or rhyme I want, not custom or lecture,
    not even the best,
Only the lull I like, the hum of your valvèd voice.

I mind how once we lay such a transparent summer morning,
How you settled your head athwart my hips and gently turn'd
    over upon me,
And parted the shirt from my bosom-bone, and plunged your
    tongue to my bare-stript heart,
And reach'd till you felt my beard, and reach'd till you held
    my feet.

Swiftly arose and spread around me the peace and knowledge
    that pass all the argument of the earth,
And I know that the hand of God is the promise of my own,
And I know that the spirit of God is the brother of my own,
And that all the men ever born are also my brothers, and the
    women my sisters and lovers,
And that a kelson of the creation is love,
And limitless are leaves stiff or drooping in the fields,
And brown ants in the little wells beneath them,
And mossy scabs of the worm fence, heap'd stones, elder,
    mullein and pokeweed

6
A child said *What is the grass?* fetching it to me with full hands;
How could I answer the child? I do not know what it is any
    more than he.

I guess it must be the flag of my disposition, out of hopeful
    green stuff woven.

Or I guess it is the handkerchief of the Lord,
A scented gift and remembrancer designedly dropt,
Bearing the owner's name someway in the corners, that we
    may see and remark, and say *Whose?*

Or I guess the grass is itself a child, the produced babe of the
    vegetation.

Or I guess it is a uniform hieroglyphic,
And it means, Sprouting alike in broad zones and narrow
    zones,
Growing among black folks as among white,
Kanuck, Tuckahoe, Congressman, Cuff, I give them the same, I
    receive them the same.

And now it seems to me the beautiful uncut hair of graves.

Tenderly will I use you curling grass,
It may be you transpire from the breasts of young men,
It may be if I had known them I would have loved them,

It may be you are from old people, or from offspring taken
    soon out of their mothers' laps
And here you are the mothers' laps.

This grass is very dark to be from the white heads of old
    mothers,
Darker than the colorless beards of old men,
Dark to come from under the faint red roofs of mouths,

O I perceive after all so many uttering tongues,
And I perceive they do not come from the roofs of mouths for
    nothing.

I wish I could translate the hints about the dead young men
    and women,
And the hints about old men and mothers, and the offspring
    taken soon out of their laps.

What do you think has become of the young and old men?
And what do you think has become of the women and
    children?

They are alive and well somewhere,
The smallest sprout shows there is really no death,
And if ever there was it led forward life, and does not wait at
    the end to arrest it,
And ceas'd the moment life appear'd.

All goes onward and outward, nothing collapses,
And to die is different from what any one supposed, and
    luckier.

****

49
And as to you Death, and you bitter hug of mortality, it is idle
    to try to alarm me.

To his work without flinching the accoucheur comes,
I see the elder-hand pressing receiving supporting,
I recline by the sills of the exquisite flexible doors,
And mark the outlet, and mark the relief and escape.

And as to you Corpse I think you are good manure, but that
    does not offend me,
I smell the white roses sweet-scented and growing,
I reach to the leafy lips, I reach to the polish'd breasts of melons.

And as to you Life I reckon you are the leavings of many deaths,
(No doubt I have died myself ten thousand times before.)

I hear you whispering there O stars of heaven,
O suns—O grass of graves—O perpetual transfers and
    promotions,
If you do not say any thing how can I say any thing?

Of the turbid pool that lies in the autumn forest,
Of the moon that descends the steeps of the soughing twilight,
Toss, sparkles of day and dusk—toss on the black stems that
    decay in the muck,
Toss to the moaning gibberish of the dry limbs.

I ascend from the moon, I ascend from the night,
I perceive that the ghastly glimmer is noonday sunbeams
    reflected,
And debouch to the steady and central from the offspring
    great or small.

50
There is that in me—I do not know what it is—but I know
    it is in me.

Wrench'd and sweaty—calm and cool then my body becomes,
I sleep—I sleep long.

I do not know it—it is without name—it is a word unsaid,
It is not in any dictionary, utterance, symbol.

Something it swings on more than the earth I swing on,
To it the creation is the friend whose embracing awakes me.

Perhaps I might tell more. Outlines! I plead for my brothers
    and sisters.

Do you see O my brothers and sisters?
It is not chaos or death—it is form, union, plan—it is eternal
    life—it is Happiness.

51
The past and present wilt—I have fill'd them, emptied them,
And proceed to fill my next fold of the future.

Listener up there! what have you to confide to me?
Look in my face while I snuff the sidle of evening.
(Talk honestly, no one else hears you, and I stay only a minute
    longer.)

Do I contradict myself?
Very well then I contradict myself,
(I am large, I contain multitudes.)
I concentrate toward them that are nigh, I wait on the
    door-slab.

Who has done his day's work? who will soonest be through
    with his supper?
Who wishes to walk with me?

Will you speak before I am gone? will you prove already
    too late?

52

The spotted hawk swoops by and accuses me, he complains of
   my gab and my loitering.

I too am not a bit tamed, I too am untranslatable,
I sound my barbaric yawp over the roofs of the world.

The last scud of day holds back for me,
It flings my likeness after the rest and true as any on the
   shadow'd wilds,
It coaxes me to the vapor and the dusk.

I depart as air, I shake my white locks at the runaway sun,
I effuse my flesh in eddies, and drift it in lacy jags.

I bequeath myself to the dirt to grow from the grass I love,
If you want me again look for me under your boot-soles.

You will hardly know who I am or what I mean,
But I shall be good health to you nevertheless,
And filter and fibre your blood.

Failing to fetch me at first keep encouraged,
Missing me one place search another,
I stop somewhere waiting for you.

Walt Whitman (1819–1892)

ANNE LE MARQUAND HARTIGAN   390

21 March 1994

Dear Ewan Gibson, Áine Jackson, Christopher Pillow,

*I have found great difficulty in choosing a favourite poem, it is a bit like
being a child when we asked each other what was our favourite colour.
(I always said black as I felt it was left out.) Really, even then I didn't
like the idea of favourites. And, it is impossible with poetry.*

*Poems feed us in different ways, at different times. I can be bowled over
by a poem. They can hit me in the guts, have music that entrances and
enwraps me in its magic.*

*I so wanted to put in a poem by Emily Dickinson, or Robert Frost, or
William Blake, or Agnes Nemes Nagy, a poem by John B Keane, Emily
Brontë, and so many more. T S Eliot was very important to me in my
teens. Shakespeare, how can I do without him? Bawdy and raw Chaucer,
the poetry of the medieval mystery plays. The wonderful lyric poems of
Fleur Adcock, and her humour! The many women poets of now that need
to be heard.*

*I chose 'Limbo', by Seamus Heaney. When I first read it in the '70s it
shook and moved me. It is not a comfortable poem, it is bleak but*

*beautifully made as we expect always from Heaney. The terrible fact of
'Limbo' is still here with us, babies still die as it seems to their mothers
there is no loving place for their children or themselves. Until this ends
forever how are we a civilized or a Christian nation? Because two babies
were found dead in the last few months is the reason why I have chosen
'Limbo'. This fact and the poem are both terrible and real.*

*A true poet has many voices, singing of life and death, love and hate,
warmth, sensuousness, and the cruelty of this world. Seamus Heaney
has all these voices. In 'Limbo' he shows a beautiful and a chill power.*

*My thanks for inviting me to make a contribution to your book. I wish
you very well in such a warming venture, it is good to be part of it.*

Yours sincerely,
Anne Le Marquand Hartigan

Limbo

Fishermen at Ballyshannon
Netted an infant last night
Along with the salmon.
An illegitimate spawning,

A small one thrown back
To the waters. But I'm sure
As she stood in the shallows
Ducking him tenderly

Till the frozen knobs of her wrists
Were dead as the gravel,
He was a minnow with hooks
Tearing her open.

She waded in under
The sign of her cross.
He was hauled in with the fish.
Now limbo will be

A cold glitter of souls
Through some far briny zone.
Even Christ's palms, unhealed,
Smart and cannot fish there.

Seamus Heaney (b.1939)

TIM PIGOTT-SMITH   391

9 March 1994

Dear Ewan, Áine and Christopher,

I'm sorry to have been so slow replying to your letter, but I have been very busy.

I can't say that there is a favourite poem because there are many that I like but I adore William Shakespeare's Sonnet, which begins:

'When my love swears that she is made of truth'.

I like it because it is passionate and tender and funny.

All the best and hope the book sells well.

Yours sincerely,
Tim Pigott-Smith

CXXXVIII

When my love swears that she is made of truth,
I do believe her though I know she lies,
That she might think me some untutored youth,
Unlearnèd in the world's false subtleties.
Thus vainly thinking that she thinks me young,
Although she knows my days are past the best,
Simply I credit her false-speaking tongue;
On both sides thus is simple truth suppressed.
But wherefore says she not she is unjust?
And wherefore say not I that I am old?
O, love's best habit is in seeming trust,
And age in love loves not to have years told.
      Therefore I lie with her, and she with me,
      And in our faults by lies we flattered be.

William Shakespeare (1564–1616)

JULIE BURCHILL   392

My favourite modern poet is Carol Ann Duffy, whose latest book is Mean Time. *But my favourite poem of all time is* 'The Raven' *by Edgar Allan Poe. I first read it when I was twelve, at a time when I was convinced I didn't like poetry, and it was so much like the Vincent Price films I loved —* The Fall of the House of Usher, The Masque of the Red Death — *that I went for it immediately. Now I can see that it is as well as being gorgeously Gothic actually a very funny and sly poem about the human capacity for self-torment; once the narrator has cottoned on that all the raven can say is 'Nevermore', he starts tormenting himself by asking the bird if he will ever see his lost love, Lenore, again, and if he will ever by happy. But the only word the raven knows is 'Nevermore' and the narrator loses his rag.*

Julie Burchill

The Raven

Once upon a midnight dreary, while I pondered, weak and
    weary,
Over many a quaint and curious volume of forgotten lore—
While I nodded, nearly napping, suddenly there came a
    tapping,
As of some one gently rapping, rapping at my chamber door.
'Tis some visitor,' I muttered, 'tapping at my chamber door—
              Only this and nothing more.'

Ah, distinctly I remember it was in the bleak December,
And each separate dying ember wrought its ghost upon the
    floor.
Eagerly I wished the morrow; —vainly I had sought to borrow
From my books surcease of sorrow—sorrow for the lost Lenore—
For the rare and radiant maiden whom the angels name Lenore —
              Nameless here for evermore.

And the silken sad uncertain rustling of each purple curtain
Thrilled me—filled me with fantastic terrors never felt before;
So that now, to still the beating of my heart, I stood repeating:
'Tis some visitor entreating entrance at my chamber door—
Some late visitor entreating entrance at my chamber door;
              This it is and nothing more.'

Presently my soul grew stronger; hesitating then no longer,
'Sir,' said I, 'or Madam, truly your forgiveness I implore;
But the fact is I was napping, and so gently you came rapping,
And so faintly you came tapping, tapping at my chamber door,
That I scarce was sure I heard you' —here I opened wide the
    door;—
              Darkness there and nothing more.

Deep into that darkness peering, long I stood there wondering,
    fearing,
Doubting, dreaming dreams no mortals ever dared to dream
    before;
But the silence was unbroken, and the stillness gave no token,
And the only word there spoken was the whispered word,
    'Lenore!'
This I whispered, and an echo murmured back the word,
    'Lenore!'—
              Merely this and nothing more.

Back into the chamber turning, all my soul within me burning,
Soon again I heard a tapping something louder than before.
'Surely,' said I, 'surely that is something at my window lattice;
Let me see, then, what thereat is, and this mystery explore—
Let my heart be still a moment, and this mystery explore;—
          'Tis the wind and nothing more.'

Open here I flung the shutter, when, with many a flirt and
    flutter,
In there stepped a stately Raven of the saintly days of yore.
Not the least obeisance made he; not a minute stopped or
    stayed he,
But, with mien of lord or lady, perched above my chamber
    door—
Perched upon a bust of Pallas just above my chamber door—
          Perched, and sat, and nothing more.

Then this ebony bird beguiling my sad fancy into smiling,
By the grave and stern decorum of the countenance it wore,
'Though thy crest be shorn and shaven, thou,' I said, 'art sure
    no craven,
Ghastly grim and ancient Raven wandering from the Nightly
    shore—
Tell me what thy lordly name is on the Night's Plutonian
    shore!'
          Quoth the Raven, 'Nevermore.'

Much I marvelled this ungainly fowl to hear discourse so
    plainly,
Though its answer little meaning—little relevancy bore;
For we cannot help agreeing that no living human being
Ever yet was blessed with seeing bird above his chamber
    door—
Bird or beast upon the sculptured bust above his chamber door,
          With such name as 'Nevermore.'

But the Raven, sitting lonely on that placid bust, spoke only
That one word, as if his soul in that one word he did outpour.
Nothing farther then he uttered; not a feather then he
    fluttered—
Till I scarcely more than muttered: 'Other friends have flown
    before—
On the morrow *he* will leave me as my Hopes have flown
    before.'
          Then the bird said, 'Nevermore.'

Startled at the stillness broken by reply so aptly spoken,
'Doubtless,' said I, 'what it utters is its only stock and store,
Caught from some unhappy master whom unmerciful Disaster
Followed fast and followed faster till his songs one burden bore—
Till the dirges of his Hope that melancholy burden bore
          Of "Never—nevermore." '

But the Raven still beguiling all my sad soul into smiling,
Straight I wheeled a cushioned seat in front of bird and bust
    and door;
Then, upon the velvet sinking, I betook myself to linking
Fancy unto fancy, thinking what this ominous bird of yore—
What this grim, ungainly, ghastly, gaunt, and ominous bird
    of yore
                    Meant in croaking 'Nevermore.'

This I sat engaged in guessing, but no syllable expressing
To the fowl whose fiery eyes now burned into my bosom's
    core;
This and more I sat divining, with my head at ease reclining
On the cushion's velvet lining that the lamp-light gloated o'er,
But whose velvet violet lining with the lamp-light gloating o'er
                    She shall press, ah, nevermore!

Then, methought, the air grew denser, perfumed from an
    unseen censer
Swung by Seraphim whose foot-falls tinkled on the tufted floor.
'Wretch,' I cried, 'thy God hath lent thee—by these angels he
    hath sent thee
Respite—respite and nepenthe from thy memories of Lenore!
Quaff, oh quaff this kind nepenthe and forget this lost Lenore!'
                    Quoth the Raven, 'Nevermore.'

'Prophet!' said I, 'thing of evil!—prophet still, if bird or devil!—
Whether Tempter sent, or whethertempest tossed thee here
    ashore,
Desolate, yet all undaunted, on this desert land enchanted—
On this home by Horror haunted,—tell me truly, I implore—
Is there—*is* there balm in Gilead?—tell me—tell me, I implore!'
                    Quoth the Raven, 'Nevermore.'

'Prophet!' said I, 'thing of evil!—prophet still, if bird or devil!
By that heaven that bends above us—by that God we both
    adore—
Tell this soul with sorrow laden if, within the distant Aidenn,
It shall clasp a sainted maiden whom the angels name Lenore—
Clasp a rare and radiant maiden whom the angels name
    Lenore.'
                    Quoth the Raven, 'Nevermore.'

'Be that word our sign of parting, bird or fiend!' I shrieked,
    upstarting—
'Get thee back into the tempest and the Night's Plutonian
    shore!
Leave no black plume as a token of that lie thy soul hath
    spoken!
Leave my loneliness unbroken!—quit the bust above my door!
Take thy beak from out my heart, and take thy form from off
    my door!'
                    Quoth the Raven, 'Nevermore.'

And the Raven, never flitting, still is sitting, still is sitting
On the pallid bust of Pallas just above my chamber door;
And his eyes have all the seeming of a demon's that is
    dreaming,
And the lamp-light o'er him streaming throws his shadow
    on the floor;
And my soul from out that shadow that lies floating on the
    floor
                  Shall be lifted—nevermore!

Edgar Allan Poe (1809–1849)

VIKRAM SETH   393

Noida
India

19 February 1994

One *of my favourite poems is Henry King's 'Exequy' written on the
death of his young wife. Every time I read it — and I do not read it too
often — I find it intolerably moving. It is rhymed, it is reasoned, and
below its decorous language lie the depths of barely resigned despair.*

Vikram Seth

The Exequy. To his Matchlesse never to be forgotten Friend

Accept thou Shrine of my dead Saint,
Insteed of Dirges this complaint;
And for sweet flowres to crown thy hearse,
Receive a strew of weeping verse
From thy griev'd friend, whom thou might'st see
Quite melted into tears for thee.

    Dear loss ! since thy untimely fate
My task hath been to meditate
On thee, on thee: thou art the book,
The library whereon I look
Though almost blind. For thee (lov'd clay)
I languish out, not live the day,
Using no other exercise
But what I practise with mine eyes:
By which wet glasses I find out
How lazily time creeps about
To one that mourns: this, onely this
My exercise and bus'ness is:
So I compute the weary houres
With sighs dissolved into showres.

Nor wonder if my time go thus
Backward and most preposterous;
Thou hast benighted me, thy set
This Eve of blackness did beget,
Who was't my day, (though overcast
Before thou had'st thy Noon-tide past)
And I remember must in tears,
Thou scarce had'st seen so many years
As Day tells houres. By thy cleer Sun
My life and fortune first did run;
But thou wilt never more appear
Folded within my Hemisphear,
Since both thy light and motion
Like a fled Star is fall'n and gon,
And twixt me and my soules dear wish
The earth now interposed is,
Which such a strange eclipse doth make
As ne're was read in Almanake.

I could allow thee for a time
To darken me and my sad Clime,
Were it a month, a year, or ten,
I would thy exile live till then;
And all that space my mirth adjourn,
So thou wouldst promise to return;
And putting off thy ashy shrowd
At length disperse this sorrows cloud.

But woe is me ! the longest date
Too narrow is to calculate
These empty hopes: never shall I
Be so much blest as to descry
A glimpse of thee, till that day come
Which shall the earth to cinders doome,
And a fierce Feaver must calcine
The body of this world like thine,
(My little World!). That fit of fire
Once off, our bodies shall aspire
To our soules bliss: then we shall rise
And view of our selves with cleerer eyes
In that calm Region, where no night
Can hide us from each others sight.

Mean time, thou hast her, earth: much good
May my harm do thee. Since it stood
With Heavens will I might not call
Her longer mine, I give thee all
My short-liv'd right and interest
In her, whom living I lov'd best:
With a most free and bounteous grief,
I give thee what I could not keep.

Be kind to her, and prethee look
Thou write into thy Dooms-day book
Each parcell of this Rarity
Which in thy Casket shrin'd doth ly:
See that you make thy reck'ning streight,
And yield her back again by weight;
For thou must audit on thy trust
Each graine and atome of this dust,
As thou wilt answer *Him* that lent,
Not gave thee, my dear Monument.

So close the ground, and 'bout her shade
Black curtains draw, my *Bride* is laid.

Sleep on my *Love* in thy cold bed
Never to be disquieted!
My last good night! Thou wilt not wake
Till I thy fate shall overtake:
Till age, or grief, or sickness must
Marry my body to that dust
It so much loves; and fill the room
My heart keeps empty in thy Tomb.
Stay for me there; I will not faile
To meet thee in that hollow Vale.
And think not much of my delay;
I am already on the way,
And follow thee with all the speed
Desire can make, or sorrows breed.
Each minute is a short degree,
And ev'ry houre a step towards thee.
At night when I betake to rest,
Next morn I rise neerer my West
Of life, almost by eight houres saile,
Than when sleep breath'd his drowsie gale.

Thus from the Sun my Bottom stears,
And my dayes Compass downward bears:
Nor labour I to stemme the tide
Through which to *Thee* I swiftly glide.

Tis true, with shame and grief I yield,
Thou like the *Vann* first took'st the field,
And gotten hast the victory
In thus adventuring to dy
Before me, whose more years might crave
A just precedence in the grave.
But heark! My pulse like a soft Drum
Beats my approach, tells *Thee* I come;
And slow howere my marches be,
I shall at last sit down by *Thee*.

    The thought of this bids me go on,
And wait my dissolution
With hope and comfort. *Dear* (forgive
The crime) I am content to live
Divided, with but half a heart,
Till we shall meet and never part.

Henry King (1592–1669)

SHARON O'BRIEN   394

28 March 1994

Dear Ewan, Áine and Christopher,

You wanted an early reply to your kind letter requesting that I tell you of my favorite poem, and I apologize for not having responded sooner. My energy ebbs and flows — perhaps more in midlife? — and sometimes I find myself just fulfilling my daily tasks and putting off adventures, like writing to you, that would be nourishing for me.

The poem I'm choosing, George Herbert's 'The Flower,' is about this kind of ebb and flow, which is why I like it. I wrote my undergraduate thesis on Herbert — something my friends, who were dealing with D H Lawrence and Virginia Woolf, found hard to understand. But something in me has always responded to his poetry. The conventional view, I think, is that 'The Flower' is about the soul's experience of the absence and presence of God, a cycle of deprivation and renewal that Herbert likens to the cycle of the seasons. But I read the poem as about depression and creativity. The state of numbness and absence Herbert describes is like depression, an emotional and psychological state in which the will is dead, the imagination frozen. And when depression lifts, and the world returns to us, we feel transformed, and it is hard to remember the selves we were before ('Grief melts away/Like snow in May/As if there were no such cold thing.') Similarly, when we are depressed, we cannot imagine leaving this underworld for the surface where life goes on ('Who would have thought my shriveld heart/Could have recovered greenness? It was gone/Quite underground.')

But what I love about 'The Flower,' and what I like to imagine when I enter into states of depression, is that life is going on under the surface. As Herbert says, the flowers have gone to see their 'mother-root,' and he imagines root and potential flower, throughout the winter of depression, in a cozy underworld unknown to the conscious self, engaging in a sort of psychic housekeeping. ('Where they together/All the hard weather, keep house unknown.')

So, although I do not read this poem from a Christian perspective, I find its rhythm of death and rebirth a hopeful story for me, and for all of us, during periods of hard weather: deep in the unconscious, perhaps, there

*is some housekeeping going on that will lead us, some day, to once more
'smell the dew and rain/And relish versing.'*

*I wish you luck with your venture, and look forward to seeing your new
edition of* Lifelines. *Thank you for having included me.*

Sincerely,
Sharon O'Brien

The Flower

How fresh, O Lord, how sweet and clean
Are thy returns! ev'n as the flowers in spring;
    To which, besides their own demean,
The late-past frosts tributes of pleasure bring.
                    Grief melts away
                    Like snow in May,
As if there were no such cold thing.

Who would have thought my shrivel'd heart
Could have recover'd greennesse? It was gone
    Quite under ground; as flowers depart
To see their mother-root, when they have blown;
                    Where they together
                    All the hard weather,
Dead to the world, keep house unknown.

These are thy wonders, Lord of power,
Killing and quickning, bring down to hell
    And up to heaven in an houre;
Making a chiming of a passing-bell.
                    We say amisse,
                    This or that is:
Thy word is all, if we could spell.

O that I once past changing were,
Fast in thy Paradise, where no flower can wither!
    Many a spring I shoot up fair,
Offring at heav'n, growing and groning thither:
                    Nor doth my flower
                    Want a spring-showre,
My sinnes and I joining together.

But while I grow in a straight line,
Still upwards bent, as if heav'n were mine own,
    Thy anger comes, and I decline:
What frost to that? what pole is not the zone,
                    Where all things burn,
                    When thou dost turn,
And the least frown of thine is shown?

And now in age I bud again,
After so many deaths I live and write;
    I once more smell the dew and rain,
And relish versing: O my onely light,
                It cannot be
                That I am he
On whom thy tempests fell all night.

These are thy wonders, Lord of love,
To make us see we are but flowers that glide:
    Which when we once can finde and prove,
Thou hast a garden for us, where to bide.
                Who would be more,
                Swelling through store,
    Forfeit their Paradise by their pride.

George Herbert (1593–1633)

CHARLES WRIGHT   395

Department of English
University of Virginia
Charlottesville
Virginia 22903

11 May 1993

Dear Gibson, Jackson and Pillow,

Thank you for your invitation to send a favorite poem for inclusion in Lifelines. *It is, of course, very difficult to decide on one's absolutely favorite poem, as none of them are ever what they set out to be, or were conceived as, or haven't been forever disabled somehow or somewhat by the author's own hand. Still, one is grateful for minor successes. Most of my own 'favorites' are too long for anthologies, i.e. 43 pages in one case, 8 in another and 3 to 4 in several others. The one I do include — a relatively early one (around 1976, I should imagine) — has the great advantage of brevity (it is one 'piece' of a 46 piece, book length poem called* China Trace*), it is part of something larger than itself, but still of itself. It began with a misreading of a sentence in Gerard Manley Hopkins's diaries — he said, 'I want to be busied with God,' which I read as 'I want to be bruised with God' — a poet I much admire, it says just about all I have to say on the subject under examination (there may be a God, but it's not personal) and, last but surely not least, I still have some affection for it after all these years. I hope you will be able to use it in your anthology. Thank you for writing.*

Sincerely,
Charles Wright

Clear Night

Clear night, thumb-top of a moon, a back-lit sky.
Moon-fingers lay down their same routine
On the side deck and the threshold, the white keys and the
    black keys.
Bird hush and bird song. A cassia flower falls.

I want to be bruised by God.
I want to be strung up in a strong light and singled out.
I want to be stretched, like music wrung from a dropped seed.
I want to be entered and picked clean.

And the wind says 'What?' to me.
And the castor beans, with their little earrings of death, say
    'What?' to me.
And the stars start out on their cold slide through the dark.
And the gears notch and the engines wheel.

Charles Wright (b.1935)

GABRIEL FITZMAURICE   396

24 January 1994

Dear Ewan, Áine and Christopher,

Many thanks for your invitation to submit a favourite poem for your consideration. I am honoured.

I have so very many favourite poems, and a number of favourite poets, that to choose one above another is a bit like choosing between my children! So, apart from saying that almost everything by Emily Dickinson, and a lot of Seán Ó Ríordáin immediately spring to mind, I'll go for something else.

I believe in poetry, in its power to influence and enlighten people, in its power to make us examine our lives. One such piece has always moved me. It's from Chapter 6 of Saint Matthew's Gospel, from The Sermon on the Mount. *(In fact, Brenda and I chose it as the Gospel reading for our wedding.) It is a hymn to living in the present. It is a calling to the good: if we are right with ourselves, we will be right with the world. There's a good God in Whose love we live. I've puzzled and pondered over this text for years trying to square it with the troubles of this world, and can only conclude that, ultimately, they are of our own making. If we are our brothers' keepers, we should look after each other. Anyway, here is the text. It's from the King James Version of 1611.*

I wish you all the best with the new Lifelines. *You are doing the world of good — not only for the Developing World, but also for the developing world of poetry! God bless the work!*

Gabriel Fitzmaurice

from *The Gospel according to St Matthew*

Translated out of the original tongues and with the former translations
diligently compared and revised. By His Majesty's Special command.
Authorised King James Version.

Therefore I say unto you, Take no thought for your life,
what ye shall eat, or what ye shall drink; nor yet for your
body, what ye shall put on. Is not the life more than meat,
and the body than raiment?

Behold the fowls of the air: for they sow not, neither do
they reap, nor gather into barns; yet your heavenly Father
feedeth them. Are ye not much better than they?

Which of you by taking thought can add one cubit unto his
stature?

And why take ye thought for raiment? Consider the lilies of
the field, how they grow; they toil not, neither do they spin.

And yet I say unto you, That even Solomon in all his glory
was not arrayed like one of these.

Wherefore, if God so clothe the grass of the field, which
today is, and tomorrow is cast into the oven, *shall he* not
much more *clothe* you, O ye of little faith?

Therefore take no thought, saying, What shall we eat? or, What
shall we drink? or, Wherewithal shall we be clothed?

(For after all these things do the Gentiles seek:) for your
heavenly Father knoweth that ye have need of all these things.

But seek ye first the kingdom of God, and his righteousness;
and all these things shall be added unto you.

Take therefore no thought for the morrow: for the morrow
shall take thought for the things of itself. Sufficient unto the
day *is* the evil thereof.

Matthew 6: 25-34

MARK JOYCE   397

14 January 1994

Dear Áine, Ewan and Chris,

*I've chosen one of Wallace Stevens' last poems 'Not Ideas about the
Thing but the Thing Itself', it still makes me dizzy when I read it.*

*Thanks for the invite to contribute. It's a wonderful project, good luck
with it.*

Yours
Mark Joyce

Not Ideas about the Thing but the Thing Itself

At the earliest ending of winter,
In March, a scrawny cry from outside
Seemed like a sound in his mind.

He knew that he heard it,
A bird's cry, at daylight or before,
In the early March wind.

The sun was rising at six,
No longer a battered panache above snow. . .
It would have been outside.

It was not from the vast ventriloquism
Of sleep's faded papier-mâché . . .
The sun was coming from outside.

That scrawny cry—it was
A chorister whose c preceded the choir.
It was part of the colossal sun,

Surrounded by its choral rings,
Still far away. It was like
A new knowledge of reality.

Wallace Stevens (1879–1955)

KATIE DONOVAN   398

'Gan do Chuid Éadaigh' / 'Nude' by Nuala Ní Dhomhnaill is one of
my favourite poems. I like the poet's subversion of the perspective of the
traditional love poem, wherein a male poet gives an admiring description
of his beloved's physical charms. Instead we have a female poet casting
a loving and appreciative eye on her man's nakedness. She takes on the
authoritative role of observer, which is so often presumed to be a male
preserve. I like her frank expression of fierce and exultant possessiveness
towards her lover's body. Her tongue-in-cheek-tone takes pleasure in
flouting the convention that only men should admit to these feelings.

I enjoy the fact that her male translator, Paul Muldoon, enters the
fun-loving spirit of the poem (I am assuming that the 'la-di-da' is his
inspired addition). No doubt reassuring for many men, this poem shows
that so-called cave man appeal can't hold a candle to silky snow-white
skin with its own distinctive scent.

Ní Dhomhnaill writes openly about the body in a way that Irish women
poets have not done before, perhaps because, like Virginia Woolf, they
encountered a block in their imaginations when it came to writing about
a subject which was considered taboo: unclean, improper. Mary
O'Malley, Mary O'Donnell and Maighread Medbh are other Irish poets
who are following in her footsteps.

Our cultural heritage includes legendary women of earth goddess proportions such as the lusty warrior, Queen Medbh, and Cuchulainn's wife, 'great-bladdered Emer'. These women were not shy about the physical side of their lives. Perhaps the wheel is turning full circle, and we are shrugging off a relatively recent, imported strain of prudery. The great number of Irish women poets writing today, and the wide scope of their subject matter, augurs well for the future.

Katie Donovan

Gan do Chuid Éadaigh

Is fearr liom tú
gan do chuid éadaigh ort,
do léine shíoda
is do charabhat,
do scáth fearthainne faoi t'ascaill
is do chulaith
trí phíosa faiseanta
le barr feabhais táilliúrachta,

do bhróga ar a mbíonn
i gcónaí snas,
do lámhainní craiceann eilite
ar do bhois,
do hata *crombie*
feircthe ar fhaobhar na cluaise—
ní chuireann siad aon ruainne
le do thuairisc,

mar thíos fúthu
i ngan fhios don slua
tá corp gan mhaisle, mháchail
nó míbhua
lúfaireacht ainmhí allta,
cat mór a bhíonn amuigh
san oíche
is a fhágann sceimhle ina mharbhshruth.

Do ghuailne leathan fairsing
is do thaobh
chomh slim le sneachta séidte
ar an sliabh;
do dhrom, do bhásta singil
is i do ghabhal
an rúta
go bhfuil barr pléisiúrtha ann.

Do chraiceann atá chomh dorcha
is slim

le síoda go mbeadh tiús veilbhite
ina shníomh
is é ar chumhracht airgid luachra
nó meadhg na habhann
go ndeirtear faoi
go bhfuil suathadh fear is ban ann.

Mar sin is dá bhrí sin
is tú ag rince liom anocht
cé go mb'fhearr liom tú
gan do chuid éadaigh ort,
b'fhéidir nárbh aon díobháil duit
gléasadh anois ar an dtoirt
in ionad leath ban Éireann
a mhilleadh is a lot.

Nuala Ní Dhomhnaill (b.1952)

Nude

The long and short
of it is I'd far rather see you nude—
your silk shirt
and natty

tie, the brolly under your oxter
in case of a rainy day,
the three-piece seersucker
suit that's so incredibly trendy,

your snazzy loafers
and, la-di-da,
a pair of gloves
made from the skin of a doe,

then, to top it all, a crombie hat
set at a rak-
ish angle — none of these add
up to more than the icing on the cake.

For, unbeknownst to the rest
of the world, behind the outward
show lies a body unsurpassed
for beauty, without so much as a wart

or blemish, but the brill-
iant slink of a wild animal, a dream-
cat, say, on the prowl,
leaving murder and mayhem

in its wake. Your broad, sinewy
shoulders and your flank
smooth as the snow
on a snow-bank.

Your back, your slender waist,
and, of course,
the root that is the very seat
of pleasure, the pleasure-source.

Your skin so dark, my beloved,
and soft
as silk with a hint of velvet
in its weft,

smelling as it does of meadowsweet
or 'watermead'
that has the power, or so it's said,
to drive men and women mad.

For that reason alone, if for no other,
when you come with me to the dance tonight
(though, as you know, I'd much prefer
to see you nude)

it would probably be best
for you to pull on your pants and vest
rather than send
half the women of Ireland totally round the bend.

Translated by Paul Muldoon

ART COSGROVE   399

University College Dublin

31 January 1994

Dear Ewan, Áine and Christopher,

Thank you for your invitation to me to contribute to Lifelines.

My suggestion is: 'The Song of the Strange Ascetic' — a light-hearted but provocative piece by G K Chesterton.

With best wishes for the success of your enterprise.

Yours sincerely,
Art Cosgrove
President

The Song of the Strange Ascetic

If I had been a Heathen,
    I'd have praised the purple vine,
My slaves should dig the vineyards,
    And I would drink the wine.
But Higgins is a Heathen,
    And his slaves grow lean and grey,
That he may drink some tepid milk
    Exactly twice a day.

If I had been a Heathen,
    I'd have crowned Neœra's curls,
And filled my life with love affairs,
    My house with dancing girls;
But Higgins is a Heathen,
    And to lecture rooms is forced,
Where his aunts, who are not married,
    Demand to be divorced.

If I had been a Heathen,
    I'd have sent my armies forth,
And dragged behind my chariots
    The Chieftains of the North.
But Higgins is a Heathen,
    And he drives the dreary quill,
To lend the poor that funny cash
    That makes them poorer still.

If I had been a Heathen,
    I'd have piled my pyre on high,
And in a great red whirlwind
    Gone roaring to the sky;
But Higgins is a Heathen,
    And a richer man than I:
And they put him in an oven,
    Just as if he were a pie.

Now who that runs can read it,
    The riddle that I write,
Of why this poor old sinner,
    Should sin without delight—?
But I, I cannot read it
    (Although I run and run),
Of them that do not have the faith,
    And will not have the fun.

G K Chesterton (1874–1936)

ALISON DYE

400

18 April 1994

Dear Ewan, Áine and Chris,

Thank you very much for your letter asking for a favourite poem.

I was surprised to discover that my first reaction to your request was to travel in my mind not to poetry I read in the present day, but to a poem I first knew and loved almost thirty years ago in college, a poem that took hold of me and apparently never let go, called up now by your letter.

The poem is 'Kubla Khan' by Samuel Taylor Coleridge (1772–1843).

Its first lines, indelibly imprinted on my unconscious, are:

In Xanadu did Kubla Khan
A stately pleasure dome decree:
Where Alph, the sacred river, ran
Through caverns measureless to man
    Down to a sunless sea.

I am not a poet, and certainly not a critic of poetry, so my reasons for responding so deeply to 'Kubla Khan' are not in any way academic. I remain enthralled with its stunning, shining, dream-like images of peace and light — but also gripped by its ominous, foreboding sense of dread which makes one worry indeed for the beauty and romance ('. . . All should cry, Beware! Beware! . . . And close your eyes with holy dread . . .'). The 'miracle of rare device, A sunny pleasure-dome with caves of ice' also contains the foreshadowing, to my eyes and ears, of much darker prospects: the ocean into which the sacred river runs is 'lifeless' and 'sunless', and as it reaches this sea from the caverns measureless to man, 'Kubla heard from far/Ancestral voices prophesying war!'

I find the language of the poem absolutely riveting. One is caught off balance by the subtle, seductive way in which it brings alive, and together, the opposing forces of death and life, peace and war, light and dark. One cannot be complacent in the stately pleasure dome, although the poem tempts one to float along: darkness is nibbling at the pleasing surface. Things are not as they seem.

For me, the juxtaposition of the two possibilities creates a complex, provocative, and irreconcilable tension — perhaps this is why I have never forgotten the poem.

I am also struck as I write this that 'Kubla Khan' may be quite appropriate to the interest of Lifelines: our relative plenty is in stark contrast to the suffering your anthology seeks to help relieve. Both exist, and one is very difficult indeed to reconcile with the other. Again, a relatively rosy state of being is at odds with realities elsewhere that cannot be denied.

I am afraid I have written far more than the few lines you asked for. My apologies.

I am also enclosing a copy of my first novel, which I would like to donate to the school, in the hopes of encouraging new young writers.

Best wishes with your project, and I am certainly grateful that you thought to include me.

Yours sincerely,
Alison Dye

Kubla Khan

In Xanadu did Kubla Khan
A stately pleasure-dome decree:
Where Alph, the sacred river, ran
Through caverns measureless to man
    Down to a sunless sea.
So twice five miles of fertile ground
With walls and towers were girdled round:
And there were gardens bright with sinuous rills,
Where blossomed many an incense-bearing tree;
And here were forests ancient as the hills,
Enfolding sunny spots of greenery.

But oh! that deep romantic chasm which slanted
Down the green hill athwart a cedarn cover!
A savage place! as holy and enchanted
As e'er beneath a waning moon was haunted
By woman wailing for her demon-lover!
And from this chasm, with ceaseless turmoil seething,
As if this earth in fast thick pants were breathing,
A mighty fountain momently was forced:
Amid whose swift half-intermitted burst
Huge fragments vaulted like rebounding hail,
Or chaffy grain beneath the thresher's flail:
And 'mid these dancing rocks at once and ever
It flung up momently the sacred river.
Five miles meandering with a mazy motion
Through wood and dale the sacred river ran,
Then reached the caverns measureless to man,
And sank in tumult to a lifeless ocean:
And 'mid this tumult Kubla heard from far
Ancestral voices prophesying war!
    The shadow of the dome of pleasure
    Floated midway on the waves;
    Where was heard the mingled measure
    From the fountain and the caves.
It was a miracle of rare device,
A sunny pleasure-dome with caves of ice!

      A damsel with a dulcimer
      In a vision once I saw:
      It was an Abyssinian maid,
      And on her dulcimer she played,
      Singing of Mount Abora.
      Could I revive within me
      Her symphony and song,
      To such a deep delight 'twould win me,
That with music loud and long,
I would build that dome in air,
That sunny dome! those caves of ice!
And all who heard should see them there,
And all should cry, Beware! Beware!
His flashing eyes, his floating hair!
Weave a circle round him thrice,
And close your eyes with holy dread,
For he on honey-dew hath fed,
And drunk the milk of Paradise.

Samuel Taylor Coleridge (1772–1843)

NIALL STOKES   401

When I was growing up, we were always taught that our physical and our spiritual yearnings were completely separate. And not just separate but irreconcilable. Our spiritual or religious impulses, we were informed again and again in different ways were essentially good. They were to be nurtured, developed and expressed, at every opportunity. The biggest problem which we were likely to encounter in this great and worthy enterprise would in fact be presented by our physical, sensual desires. These were to be discouraged, repressed and ultimately routed. They were the enemy of spirituality. They were essentially bad.

In this dualistic view of the world, sex was the root possibly not of all but certainly of most evil. I could never accept this. Some resilient instinct burned strongly enough to reject the weight of the fearsome indoctrination we were subjected to. Desire, sensuality, sexual expression — these to me felt intrinsically like good things. Why should they be branded otherwise?

Confirmation of these feelings was hard to come by in art and literature. In a world of dogmatism and blunt commandments, we learned about the sins of the flesh and most of the poetry and novels we were fed reinforced the message. Ultimately this would be one of the great attractions for me of rock 'n' roll — a milieu where the concept of sin was turned inside out and the pleasures of the flesh were celebrated. But to those who were uncomfortable with the received dualism, to encounter a poet like John Donne was a startling, life-affirming revelation . . .

Here was a man who began writing in the 16th Century who spoke in a wonderfully contemporary voice. It seemed to me, in my teens, as I began to grapple with aesthetic questions, that one of the great challenges facing artists in the 20th Century was to achieve the reconciliation of body and soul, of the sensual and the cerebral, the erotic and the spiritual — and yet when I read 'The Sunne Rising' and 'To His Mistris Going to Bed' I realised that John Donne had achieved precisely this balance all of 400 years ago.

'To His Mistris Going to Bed' is cinematic in its power. It draws you in to a moment of shared intimacy without ever becoming cloying. The tone is humorous at times but never raffish. Desire is celebrated audaciously and yet with great dignity. And there is, finally, a mystical quality about the poem's evocation of the universe of pleasure which unfolds through the wonderful uninhibited meeting of man and woman as equals in the act of sexual passion and love.

Dualism be damned! This *is where it's at.*

Niall Stokes
Editor, Hot Press

To His Mistris Going to Bed

Come, Madam, come, all rest my powers defy,
Until I labour, I in labour lie.
The foe oft-times having the foe in sight,
Is tired with standing though they never fight.
Off with that girdle, like heaven's zone glistering,
But a far fairer world encompassing.
Unpin that spangled breastplate which you wear,
That th' eyes of busy fools may be stopped there.
Unlace yourself, for that harmonious chime
Tells me from you, that now 'tis your bed time.
Off with that happy busk, which I envy,
That still can be, and still can stand so nigh.
Your gown going off, such beauteous state reveals,
As when from flowery meads th' hill's shadow steals.
Off with that wiry coronet and show
The hairy diadem which on you doth grow;
Now off with those shoes, and then safely tread
In this love's hallowed temple, this soft bed.
In such white robes heaven's angels used to be
Received by men; thou angel bring'st with thee
A heaven like Mahomet's paradise; and though
Ill spirits walk in white, we easily know
By this these angels from an evil sprite,
Those set our hairs, but these our flesh upright.
    Licence my roving hands, and let them go
Before, behind, between, above, below.

O my America, my new found land,
My kingdom, safeliest when with one man manned,
My mine of precious stones, my empery,
How blessed am I in this discovering thee!
To enter in these bonds, is to be free;
Then where my hand is set, my seal shall be.
    Full nakedness, all joys are due to thee.
As souls unbodied, bodies unclothed must be,
To taste whole joys. Gems which you women use
Are like Atlanta's balls, cast in men's views,
That when a fool's eye lighteth on a gem,
His earthly soul may covet theirs, not them.
Like pictures, or like books' gay coverings made
For laymen, are all women thus arrayed;
Themselves are mystic books, which only we
Whom their imputed grace will dignify
Must see revealed. Then since I may know,
As liberally, as to a midwife, show
Thyself: cast all, yea, this white linen hence,
Here is no penance, much less innocence.
    To teach thee, I am naked first, why then
What needst thou have more covering than a man.

John Donne (1572–1631)

ÁINE MILLER   402

Dear Ewan, Áine and Chris,

Thank you for asking me to contribute to Lifelines *and congratulations on such a worthwhile venture. I'm delighted to be a part of it.*

I knew at once from whose poetry I should make my choice. But which poem? A glance out the window at a spring tide of daisies and dandelion decided me. I have chosen 'An Easter Garland' *by Carol Rumens.*

I love this poem for the strong, but beautifully controlled, emotional connections it makes. Even transfigured by tears, nature is crude in its suddenness, brash in its ability to burst in on the grieving. Offended by it, and defined, we withdraw to an upper room of private memory. Into this time of silence and waiting comes another shock, this time a resurrection, and we cope by clothing it in the homely garb of metaphor.

I return to this poem again and again and always with that little sigh of acquiescence which marks my response to good poetry.

Thank you again for the opportunity to pay tribute to a fine poet and indulge myself at the same time. Please let me know when you publish and give me the chance to purchase copies.

Yours sincerely,
Áine Miller

An Easter Garland

1
The flowers did not seem to unfurl from slow bulbs.
They were suddenly there,
shivering swimmers on the edge of a gala
— nude whites and yellows shocking the raw air.
They'd switched themselves on like streetlamps
waking at dawn, feeling wrong,
to blaze nervously all day at the chalky sky.
Are they masks, the frills on bruised babies?
I can't believe in them,
as I can't believe in the spruces and lawns and bricks
they publicise, the misted light of front lounges
twinned all the way down the road,
twinned like their occupants, little weather-house people
who hide inside and do now show their tears
— the moisture that drives one sadly to a doorway.

2
My father explained the workings of the weather-house
as if he seriously loved such things,
told me why Grandpa kept a blackening tress
of seaweed in the hall.
He was an expert on atmosphere,
having known a weight of dampness
— the fog in a sick brother's lungs
where he lost his childhood; later, the soft squalls
of marriage and the wordier silences.

In the atmosphere of the fire
that took him back to bone
and beyond bone, he smiled.
The cellophaned flowers outside
went a slower way, their sweat
dappling the linings of their glassy hoods.

3
My orphaned grass
is standing on tip-toe to look for you.
Your last gift to a work-shy daughter
was to play-out and regather
the slow thread of your breath
behind the rattling blades,
crossing always to darker green,
till the lawn was a well-washed quilt
drying, the palest on the line,
and you rested over the handlebars
like a schoolboy, freewheeling
through your decades of green-scented, blue,
suburban English twilights.

4
In the lonely garden of the page
something has happened to your silence.
The stone cloud has rolled off.
You make yourself known
as innocently abrupt
as the flared wings of the almond,
cherry, magnolia;
and I, though stupid with regret,
would not be far wrong
if I took you for the gardener.

Carol Rumens (b.1944)

MARY DORCEY   403

26 April 1994

Dear Áine, Ewan and Christopher,

Thank you for asking me to select a poem for your book and for waiting so patiently for my response.

Like many other contributors I found it impossible to choose one favourite poem. So, lest I delay for another day, I have decided to surrender the struggle — I include two poems I love and appeal to your wisdom to carry out the onerous task of choice.

The first is by the Russian poet Marina Tsvetayeva — whose work I discovered during my last year at school published in the Penguin Modern European Poets series. I was mitching from exams one day, reading poetry in a Grafton Street bookshop when I came across this poem. I loved her from that moment on — her passion, her vision, her marvellous language.

She was born in Moscow in 1892. Opposed the revolution and was exiled. Spent many years in Prague and Paris. When she returned to Russia in 1939 following her husband Efron (who was shot soon afterwards) she found herself without friends and work. At the outbreak of war with Germany she was evacuated to Yelabuga and there in 1941 she hanged herself.

She said of writing: I don't love life as such; for me it begins to signify, that is to acquire weight and meaning only when it is transformed, that is — in art. If I were to be beyond the ocean, into Paradise, and forbidden to write, I would refuse the ocean and Paradise.

The second is by the contemporary American poet Irena Klepfisz. I like it for its special, maybe Jewish blend of worldly wisdom; toughness and compassion. Being Jewish, feminist and lesbian she knows something about the graft and joy of surviving!

With all good wishes and thanks for last year's wonderful collection.

Mary Dorcey

'Not That Passion Is Deceitful Or Imaginary!'

5

Not that passion is deceitful or imaginary!
It doesn't lie. Simply, it doesn't last!
If only we could come into this world as though
we were common people in love

be sensible, see things as they are: this
is just a hill, just a bump in the ground.
(And yet they say it is by the pull of
abysses, that you measure height.)

In the heaps of gorse, coloured dim
among islands of tortured pines...
(In delirium/above the level of
life)
      — Take me then. I'm yours.

Instead only the gentle mercies of
domesticity — chicks twittering —
because we came down into this world who
once lived at the height of heaven: in love.

Marina Tsvetayeva (1892–1941)

Dedication from *Bashert*
[ba-shert (Yiddish); inevitable, (pre) destined]

These words are dedicated to those who died
These words are dedicated to those who died
because they had no love and felt alone in the world
because they were afraid to be alone and tried to stick it out
because they could not ask
because they were shunned
because they were sick and their bodies could not resist the
      disease
because they played it safe
because they had no connections
because they had no faith
because they felt they did not belong and wanted to die

These words are dedicated to those who died
because they were loners and liked it
because they acquired friends and drew others to them
because they took risks
because they were stubborn and refused to give up
because they asked for too much

These words are dedicated to those who died
because a card was lost and a number was skipped
because a bed was denied
because a place was filled and no other place was left

These words are dedicated to those who died
because someone did not follow through

because someone was overworked and forgot
because someone left everything to God
because someone was late
because someone did not arrive at all
because someone told them to wait and they just couldn't any
    longer
These words are dedicated to those who died
because death is a punishment
because death is a reward
because death is the final rest
because death is eternal rage
These words are dedicated to those who died

Bashert

These words are dedicated to those who survived
These words are dedicated to those who survived
because their second grade teacher gave them books
because they did not draw attention to themselves and got lost
    in the shuffle
because they knew someone who knew someone else who
    could help them and bumped into them on a corner on a
    Thursday afternoon
because they played it safe
because they were lucky

These words are dedicated to those who survived
because they knew how to cut corners
because they drew attention to themselves and always got
    picked
because they took risks
because they had no principles and were hard

These words are dedicated to those who survived
because they refused to give up and defied statistics
because they had faith and trusted in God
because they expected the worst and were always prepared
because they were angry
because they could ask
because they mooched off others and saved their strength
because they endured humiliation
because they turned the other cheek
because they looked the other way

These words are dedicated to those who survived
because life is a wilderness and they were savage
because life is an awakening and they were alert
because life is a flowering and they blossomed
because life is a struggle and they struggled
because life is a gift and they were free to accept it

These words are dedicated to those who survived

Bashert

Irena Klepfisz

BARRY McGOVERN   404

2 May 1994

Dear Ewan, Áine and Christopher,

I find it impossible to say that this poem or that is my favourite. I love poetry and have many favourites. It often depends upon the mood I'm in. And as my friends will tell you I am a man of many moods.

Here is a poem I enjoy. It's by the poet Patrick MacDonogh who died some years ago.

Keep up the good work,

Yours,
Barry McGovern

No Mean City

Though naughty flesh will multiply
Our chief delight is in division;
Whatever of Divinity
We all are Doctors of Derision.
Content to risk a far salvation
For the quick coinage of a laugh
We cut, to make wit's reputation,
Our total of two friends by half.

Patrick MacDonogh (1902–1961)

EITHNE CARR   405

14 May 1994

Dear Ewan, Áine and Chris,

Thank you so much for your letter. Congratulations to you all for continuing the good work of Lifelines.

My choice of poem for you is Patrick Kavanagh's 'Advent'. Last Christmas copies of this were given out at Barna Church in Galway, and since then I have had my copy pinned up over my kitchen table. Each time I read it, and I often do, some different image stands out for me. The poem renews my hope and belief in the beauty of the everyday.

With all good wishes,
Eithne Carr

Advent

We have tested and tasted too much, lover—
Through a chink too wide there comes in no wonder.
But here in the Advent-darkened room
Where the dry black bread and the sugarless tea
Of penance will charm back the luxury
Of a child's soul, we'll return to Doom
The knowledge we stole but could not use.

And the newness that was in every stale thing
When we looked at it as children: the spirit-shocking
Wonder in a black slanting Ulster hill
Or the prophetic astonishment in the tedious talking
Of an old fool will awake for us and bring
You and me to the yard gate to watch the whins
And the bog-holes, cart-tracks, old stables where Time begins.

O after Christmas we'll have no need to go searching
For the difference that sets an old phrase burning—
We'll hear it in the whispered argument of a churning
Or in the streets where the village boys are lurching.
And we'll hear it among decent men too
Who barrow dung in gardens under trees,
Wherever life pours ordinary plenty.
Won't we be rich, my love and I, and please
God we shall not ask for reason's payment,
The why of heart-breaking strangeness in dreeping hedges
Nor analyse God's breath in common statement.
We have thrown into the dust-bin the clay-minted wages
Of pleasure, knowledge and the conscious hour—
And Christ comes with a January flower.

Patrick Kavanagh (1904–1967)

DANIEL HALPERN   406

The Ecco Press, Antaeus
Hopewell, New Jersey

11 May 1994

Dear Mr Gibson,

*In response to your letter. Rather than commenting on a single poem —
although for the purposes of your project I will select Yeats's 'A Prayer
for My Daughter' — I wish to comment very briefly about 'favorite
poems'.*

*There are many poems that have deep personal meaning for me, that are
capable of revealing material not part of the ordinary, not part of
discursive, practical thinking, the necessary (and calming) dailiness of*

moving from one place to another in order to complete the good day.
These poems are resource and reward — respite from the commonplace
but not antithetical to it. They are compositions that allow our language
to speak as it might in heaven, if heaven exists — a heavenly dialogue.
Alternately, the language of these poems has been worked in such a
fashion as to raise what may indeed originate in the commonplace into
something sacred and transfigured. These are poems I return to as one
more religious might return on the sabbath to the chosen place of worship
— to be via incense and liturgy in the presence of a higher authority.

Sincerely,
Daniel Halpern

A Prayer for my Daugher

Once more the storm is howling, and half hid
Under this cradle-hood and coverlid
My child sleeps on. There is no obstacle
But Gregory's wood and one bare hill
Whereby the haystack- and roof-levelling wind,
Bred on the Atlantic, can be stayed;
And for an hour I have walked and prayed
Because of the great gloom that is in my mind.

I have walked and prayed for this young child an hour
And heard the sea-wind scream upon the tower,
And under the arches of the bridge, and scream
In the elms above the flooded stream;
Imagining in excited reverie
That the future years had come,
Dancing to a frenzied drum,
Out of the murderous innocence of the sea.

May she be granted beauty and yet not
Beauty to make a stranger's eye distraught,
Or hers before a looking-glass, for such,
Being made beautiful overmuch,
Consider beauty a sufficient end,
Lose natural kindness and maybe
The heart-revealing intimacy
That chooses right, and never find a friend.

Helen being chosen found life flat and dull
And later had much trouble from a fool,
While that great Queen, that rose out of the spray,
Being fatherless could have her way
Yet chose a bandy-leggèd smith for man.
It's certain that fine women eat
A crazy salad with their meat
Whereby the Horn of Plenty is undone.

In courtesy I'd have her chiefly learned;
Hearts are not had as a gift but hearts are earned
By those that are not entirely beautiful;
Yet many, that have played the fool
For beauty's very self, has charm made wise,
And many a poor man that has roved,
Loved and thought himself beloved,
From a glad kindness cannot take his eyes.

May she become a flourishing hidden tree
That all her thoughts may like the linnet be,
And have no business but dispensing round
Their magnanimities of sound,
Nor but in merriment begin a chase,
Nor but in merriment a quarrel.
O may she live like some green laurel
Rooted in one dear perpetual place.

My mind, because the minds that I have loved,
The sort of beauty that I have approved,
Prosper but little, has dried up of late,
Yet knows that to be choked with hate
May well be of all evil chances chief.
If there's no hatred in a mind
Assault and battery of the wind
Can never tear the linnet from the leaf.

An intellectual hatred is the worst,
So let her think opinions are accursed.
Have I not seen the loveliest woman born
Out of the mouth of Plenty's horn,
Because of her opinionated mind
Barter that horn and every good
By quiet natures understood
For an old bellows full of angry wind?

Considering that, all hatred driven hence,
The soul recovers radical innocence
And learns at last that it is self-delighting,
Self-appeasing, self-affrighting,
And that its own sweet will is Heaven's will;
She can, though every face should scowl
And every windy quarter howl
Or every bellows burst, be happy still.

And may her bridegroom bring her to a house
Where all's accustomed, ceremonious;
For arrogance and hatred are the wares
Peddled in the thoroughfares.
How but in custom and in ceremony
Are innocence and beauty born?
Ceremony's a name for the rich horn,
And custom for the spreading laurel tree.

William Butler Yeats (1865–1939)

PHILIP KING 407

'I am Stretched on Your Grave' *was translated from the Irish by Frank O'Connor in a book of translations called,* The Little Monasteries. *I got a copy of* The Little Monasteries *in 1976 and was immediately struck by Frank O'Connor's translation of 'Tá mé sínte ar do thuama'. The poem stuck in my memory and I began tossing the words at concerts with Scullion, of whom I was a member at the time. I later became aware of the Irish sean-nós song which I heard sung by the late Diarmuid Ó Suilleabháin, a great singer from Cúil Aodha. It is a love song without parallel. It captures that terrible sense of loss when a loved one dies.*

Best regards,
Philip King

I am Stretched on Your Grave

I am stretched on your grave
And would lie there forever
If your hands were in mine
I'd be sure we'd not sever.
My appletree, my brightness
'Tis time we were together
For I smell of the earth
And am worn by the weather.

When my family thinks
That I'm safe in my bed
From night until morning
I am stretched at your head.
Calling out into the air with
Tears hot and wild
My grief for the girl that
I loved as a child.

Do you remember the
Night we were lost
In the shade of the blackthorn
And the chill of the frost.
Thanks be to Jesus we
Did what was right
And your maidenhead still
Is a pillar of light.

The priests and the friars
Approach me in dread
Because I still love you
My love, and you're dead.

I still will be your shelter
Through rain and through storm
But with you in your cold grave
I cannot sleep warm.

I am stretched on your grave
And would lie there forever
If your hands were in mine
I'd be sure we'd not sever.
My appletree, my brightness
'Tis time we were together
For I smell of the earth
And am worn by the weather.

Anonymous (eighteenth century)
Translated from the Irish by Frank O'Connor (1903–1966)

VERONICA BOLAY   408

8 May 1994

Dear Ewan Gibson, Áine Jackson and Christopher Pillow,

Thank you very much for this invitation! As a child I imagined about a chance like this only now I say this is impossible. I have many favourite poems. I am a reader (addict) of poems, anyway I decided for this one:

'Rain — Birdoswald' by Frances Horovitz (1938–1985)

I love in this poem the balance and the vibrations between human being, animals and nature. It is something I try to approach in my life and in my work.

Horovitz' mind and her finely honed language take me, her reader, by the hand, not going on an 'ego-trip' but to meet the 'I' and the 'You'. While death watches our lives. And our lives sense death.

The line 'We sense each other's quiet' is a marvel — in a world where 'flaunting it all' stays priority. Also this rain-trance I have experienced very often living amidst the 40 green shades.

Congratulations to **Lifelines,** *my admiration to the ones involved and good luck to your individual lives!*

Kind regards,
Veronica (Bolay)

Of course I'm looking forward . . . !

Rain — Birdoswald

I stand under a leafless tree
more still, in this mouse-pattering
    thrum of rain,
than cattle shifting in the field.
    It is more dark than light.
A Chinese painter's brush of deepening grey
    moves in a subtle tide.

The beasts are darker islands now.
Wet-stained and silvered by the rain
    they suffer night,
marooned as still as stone or tree.
    We sense each other's quiet.

Almost, death could come
inevitable, unstrange
    as is this dusk and rain,
and I should be no more
    myself, than raindrops
glimmering in last light
    on black ash buds

or night beasts in a winter field.

Frances Horovitz (1938–1985)

IMOGEN STUART   409

8 May 1994

Dear Ewan, Áine and Christopher,

My friend Maria Simonds-Gooding who was a contributor to one of your last Lifelines *showed me last night the 1992 edition which I think is splendid. I wish you an equally great success on the coming* Lifelines.

Reasons for my choice of poetry: During the war when I was a child still, we were little distracted by material goods, outings and parties. It was a time where one rather preserved what one had than seek new horizons.

During those difficult years my father read to me and my sister many poems. It is from these years that I still enjoy poetry: I love Monk Gibbon's poem 'From Disciple to Master' for its great simplicity and for the choice of words with its beautiful imagery.

My good wishes,

Yours sincerely,
Imogen Stuart

From Disciple to Master

My life is like a dream:
I do not know
How it began, nor yet
How it will go

Out of the night a bird
Has quickly flown
Across the lighted room
And now is gone.

Into the dark again
From whence it came
So the old druids said,
And I, the same.

But we are not content,
I, like them too,
Questioning all I meet,
Seek something new.

Saying to each who comes,
'So much is clear,
But if you know of more,
I wait to hear.

'The dark, the lighted room,
The bird which flies
Are not enough for man
Who one day dies.

'Are not enough for man
That bird which came
Out of the dark, and must
Return again.

'If you know more besides,
Tell what you know,
O wise and travelled souls,
Before I go.'

Monk Gibbon (1896–1987)

JOHN SHINNORS   410

Dear Ewan Gibson,

Thank you for your letter. The poem is the Yeats piece — 'The Stolen Child'.

My response to it is like that of viewing a beautifully executed work of art but whose subject matter is disturbing and despairing.

*The poem has never given me any pleasure but its eerie and unsettling
content always leave me with an unparalleled, morbid curiosity about
escape.*

Yours sincerely,
John Shinnors

The Stolen Child

Where dips the rocky highland
Of Sleuth Wood in the lake,
There lies a leafy island
Where flapping herons wake
The drowsy water-rats;
There we've hid our faery vats,
Full of berries
And of reddest stolen cherries.
Come away, O human child!
To the waters and the wild
With a faery, hand in hand,
For the world's more full of weeping than you can
        understand.

Where the wave of moonlight glosses
The dim grey sands with light,
Far off by furthest Rosses
We foot it all the night,
Weaving olden dances,
Mingling hands and mingling glances
Till the moon has taken flight;
To and fro we leap
And chase the frothy bubbles,
While the world is full of troubles
And is anxious in its sleep.
Come away, O human child!
To the waters and the wild
With a faery, hand in hand,
For the world's more full of weeping than you can
        understand.

Where the wandering water gushes
From the hills above Glen-Car,
In pools among the rushes
That scarce could bathe a star,
We seek for slumbering trout
And whispering in their ears
Give them unquiet dreams;
Leaning softly out

From ferns that drop their tears
Over the young streams.
Come away, O human child!
To the waters and the wild
With a faery, hand in hand,
For the world's more full of weeping than you can
    understand.

Away with us he's going,
The solemn-eyed:
He'll hear no more the lowing
Of the calves on the warm hillside
Or the kettle on the hob
Sing peace into his breast,
Or see the brown mice bob,
Round and round the oatmeal-chest.
For he comes, the human child,
To the waters and the wild
With a faery, hand in hand,
From a world more full of weeping than he can
    understand.

William Butler Yeats (1865–1939)
['The Stolen Child' was also Gerrit van Gelderen's and Mary Mooney's choice
in *Lifelines*.]

JOHN BEHAN   411

8 May 1994

Dear Friends,

Thank you for your letter re Lifelines.

My favourite poem is 'Peace' by Patrick Kavanagh.

When I was very young I spent all my holidays on a farm in Co. Laois,
which was the home of my grandparents, my father, aunts and uncles.
Some of my earliest and best memories belong to that period of my life.
The poem 'Peace' reflects very accurately the ethos of that time;
everything was simple, the pace and way of life slow. There was a direct
contact with the earth and animals and the way of life, to my child's eye
was both monumental and eternal. The time was the nineteen forties,
when the poem was written. The poem reflects to me the time and place
as I felt it to be then, and having now reached my fifty-fifth year, the
final two lines have a more profound effect on me than ever.

I thoroughly support your efforts and enclose a cheque for £20.

Yours sincerely,
John Behan

Peace

And sometimes I am sorry when the grass
Is growing over the stones in quiet hollows
And the cocksfoot leans across the rutted cart-pass
That I am not the voice of country fellows
Who now are standing by some headland talking
Of turnips and potatoes or young corn
Or turf banks stripped for victory.
Here Peace is still hawking
His coloured combs and scarves and beads of horn.

Upon a headland by a whinny hedge
A hare sits looking down a leaf-lapped furrow
There's an old plough upside-down on a weedy ridge
And someone is shouldering home a saddle-harrow.
Out of that childhood country what fools climb
To fight with tyrants Love and Life and Time?

Patrick Kavanagh (1904–1967)

ELEANOR McEVOY   412

12 May 1994

Dear Ewan, Áine and Christopher,

*Many thanks for your letter, please forgive me for not writing sooner,
I've been away for some time and I'm only catching up now.*

*It's very difficult to pick one favourite poem, when I have so many
favourites! However, I have chosen a poem by Sir Thomas Wyatt which
I love.*

I greatly enjoyed reading the first Lifelines *compilation. It's a
wonderful project for a worthy cause. Best of luck with this one.*

Eleanor McEvoy

*The Lover's Lute cannot be blamed though
it sing of his Lady's Unkindness*

Blame not my lute for he must sound
Of this or that as liketh me;
For lack of wit the lute is bound
To give such tunes as pleaseth me.
Though my songs be somewhat strange
And speaks such words as touch thy change
    Blame not my lute.

My lute, alas, doth not offend
Though that perforce he must agree
To sound such tunes as I intend
To sing to them that heareth me.
Then though my songs be somewhat plain
And toucheth some that use to feign
    Blame not my lute.

My lute and strings may not deny
But as I strike they must obey,
Break not them then so wrongfully
But wreak thyself some wiser way.
And though the songs which I indite
Do quit thy change with rightful spite
    Blame not my lute.

Spite asketh spite and changing change
And falsed faith must needs be known.
The faults so great, the case so strange
Of right it must abroad be blown.
Then since that by thine own desert
My songs do tell how true thou art
    Blame not my lute.

Blame but thyself that hast misdone
And well deserved to have blame.
Change thou thy way, so evil begun
And then my lute shall sound that same,
But if till then my fingers play
By thy desert their wonted way
    Blame not my lute.

Farewell, unknown, for though thou break
My strings in spite with great disdain
Yet have I found out for thy sake
Strings for to string my lute again.
And if perchance this foolish rhyme
Do make thee blush at any time
    Blame not my lute.

Thomas Wyatt (1503–1542)

JENNY JOSEPH   413

Dear Ewan Gibson, Áine Jackson and Christopher Pillow,

I have just got back from two months in America to find your letter and I am so sorry that, through nobody's fault, you have not had a reply about your excellent project.

I would feel honoured to be able to contribute to your Lifelines *if it helps in any way. I particularly support projects to maintain clean water supplies to people.*

'The House was Quiet and the World was Calm' *by Wallace Stevens*

What causes us to like certain poems is often as little to do with reasons and literary judgement as other matters of taste. My reaction to words, on the page as well as spoken, is a physiological one no less than that to pictures and music. I react to what I call grammar, the ways of words, as I do to combinations of shapes and colours and food. In this poem I find the progress of the separate sentences somehow pleasing to my inner ear, as if a step is made, tested, and then another very carefully added. The grammatical structure itself exemplifies this quiet watchful concentration on getting at the meaning, as when you are watching animals feeding at dusk you have to be still enough and concentrated, for them to feel you are part of the night.

More clearly, I like this poem because I love summer nights when it is balmy enough to leave doors and windows open all night and not know it, no separation between inner and outer; and because it reminds me of the extreme yet somehow peaceful excitement of feeling what one is thinking, one's bloodstream involved with the presence of the writer of the book one has taken to an upper window to catch the last of the light on such a summer night.

The House was Quiet and the World was Calm

The house was quiet and the world was calm.
The reader became the book; and summer night

Was like the conscious being of the book.
The house was quiet and the world was calm.

The words were spoken as if there was no book,
Except that the reader leaned above the page,

Wanted to lean, wanted much most to be
The scholar to whom his book is true, to whom

The summer night is like a perfection of thought.
The house was quiet because it had to be.

The quiet was part of the meaning, part of the mind:
The access of perfection to the page.

And the world was calm. The truth in a calm world,
In which there is no other meaning, itself

Is calm, itself is summer and night, itself
Is the reader leaning late and reading there.

Wallace Stevens (1879–1955)

from *The Prelude* by William Wordsworth
Bk. X. Residence in France

To say what I like about Wordsworth's Prelude *would take as much space as one of the fourteen books of that great epic. It should be read through as a narrative, preferably in no shorter sections than a book at a time, at least the first couple of readings. The cumulative roll of Wordsworth's narrative line, his superb ear, his command of vocabulary of course give pleasure. I personally like* The Prelude *perhaps because it is a work I've read closely and often, at first in my teens; and I think my own thinking about human beings in society (i.e. my political development) developed through reading Wordsworth. I have picked out some lines from Book X but at least from the beginning of the book should be read to give the context. The lines exemplify Wordsworth's mastery at exact, moving psychological analysis and description of human thinking and feeling. I value Wordsworth for his honesty. With George Orwell, Samuel Johnson and Virginia Woolf, he is the most honest writer I know. In* The Prelude *he takes us through a political education. He sets down, not a particular dogma, but what it feels like to think and feel politically. Heart-rending sadness at the Revolution betrayed, at hope lost, the idealist disillusioned, the true patriot helpless — these are portrayed in these books of* The Prelude *as nowhere else I know in English literature except for George Orwell's* Homage to Catalonia *and the ending of William Morris's* A Dream of John Ball, *surely the saddest end to a book in English.*

from *The Prelude*
Book X. Residence in France [1850 version]

What, then, were my emotions, when in arms
Britain put forth her freeborn strength in league,
Oh, pity and shame! with those confederate Powers!
Not in my single self alone I found,
But in the minds of all ingenuous youth,
Change and subversion from that hour. No shock
Given to my moral nature had I known
Down to that very moment; neither lapse
Nor turn of sentiment that might be named
A revolution, save at this one time;
All else was progress on the self-same path
On which, with a diversity of pace,
I had been travelling: this a stride at once
Into another region. As a light
And pliant harebell, swinging in the breeze
On some grey rock — its birthplace — so had I
Wantoned, fast rooted on the ancient tower
Of my belovèd country, wishing not
A happier fortune than to wither there:
Now was I from that pleasant station torn

And tossed about in whirlwind. I rejoiced,
Yea, afterwards — truth most painful to record!—
Exulted, in the triumph of my soul,
When Englishmen by thousands were o'erthrown,
Left without glory on the field, or driven,
Brave hearts! to shameful flight. It was a grief, —
Grief call it not, 'twas anything but that, —
A conflict of sensations without name,
Of which *he* only, who may love the sight
Of a village steeple, as I do, can judge,
When, in the congregation bending all
To their great Father, prayers were offered up,
Or praises for our country's victories;
And, 'mid the simple worshippers, perchance
I only, like an uninvited guest
Whom no one owned, sate silent, shall I add,
Fed on the day of vengeance yet to come?

William Wordsworth (1770–1850)

*I'm sure the above is too long. I found it impossible to do 3 'sound bites'
per great work. I thought that as it's students doing it they could learn
something of the poems, not just my personal feelings.*

Yours sincerely,
Jenny Joseph

TREVOR GEOGHEGAN   414

16 May 1994

Dear Ewan, Áine and Christopher,

*Thank you for your letter. I am sorry for not replying sooner but I have
been away.*

*I would be delighted to take part in your project and I thank you for
including me.*

*The poems and poetry that I like are many, but a poet whom I find a
great affinity with is Brian Mooney. He lives and works on the Burren
in Co. Clare. It is a landscape that I am very fond of and in recent years
I have painted it a great deal.*

*Brian's poetry has also been influenced by the landscape and for that
reason I have chosen a poem called 'Divine Heraldry'.*

Very best wishes,
Trevor Geoghegan

Divine Heraldry

Orion is out, his court
A camelot of stars; clouds run
Like shadows among all inky night;
Carilloning. Old dromedaries,
My hillsides, the cattle move in
Caravan along, the verdant earth
Their song, grey and azure
The pavement
Of their paths incline towards
Morning, ascendant, the ebb and
The webbing,
Helio's mute stare. And the night
Sundering.

Brian Mooney

ANNE KENNEDY   415

Dear Ewan, Áine and Christopher,

Thank you for inviting me to participate in Lifelines.

I have chosen as my favourite poem, 'The River-Merchant's Wife: A Letter', written by the Chinese poet Li Po c. 750. This vivid poem about a young wife's longing for her absent husband has been translated many times into many languages, but this 'free' version by Ezra Pound is justly famous. It is a brilliant evocation of youthful longing. It was not until you asked me to choose a favourite poem, that I realised what an influence this one has been on my own writing.

The use of detail — the bamboo stilts, blue plums, the river of swirling eddies, the monkeys, moss, paired butterflies and narrows make this poem as alive in the 20th century as it was in the 8th.

The use of place names appeals to me, but most of all I love the poignant understatement of the teenage wife's longing for her absent husband.

The very best of luck with your project.

Warm wishes,
Anne Kennedy

The River-Merchant's Wife: A Letter

While my hair was still cut straight across my forehead
I played about the front gate, pulling flowers.
You came by on bamboo stilts, playing horse,
You walked about my seat, playing with blue plums.
And we went on living in the village of Chokan:
Two small people, without dislike or suspicion.

At fourteen I married My Lord you.
I never laughed, being bashful.
Lowering my head, I looked at the wall.
Called to, a thousand times, I never looked back.

At fifteen I stopped scowling,
I desired my dust to be mingled with yours
Forever and forever and forever.
Why should I climb the lookout?

At sixteen you departed.
You went into far Ku-to-yen by the river of swirling eddies,
And you have been gone five months.
The monkeys make sorrowful noise overhead.

You dragged your feet when you went out.
By the gate now, the moss is grown, the different mosses,
Too deep to clear them away!
The leaves fall early this autumn, in wind.
The paired butterflies are already yellow with August
Over the grass in the West garden;
They hurt me. I grow older.
If you are coming down through the narrows of the river Kiang,
Please let me know beforehand,
And I will come out to meet you
                As far as Cho-fu-Sa.

Li Po (701–762)
Translated from the Chinese by Ezra Pound (1885–1972)

MÁIRE GEOGHEGAN-QUINN   416

Offig an Aire Dlí agus Cirt
(Office of the Minister for Justice)
Baile Átha Cliath
(Dublin)

My favourite comes from the Greek poet, Cavafy. The first time I came across it — quoted in a novel — I was startled by how it summed up one aspect of political life: the need to have a hatred. Cavafy's study of a people who have lost their own sense of direction and of mission is subtle and detailed. It looks at their fascination with baubles and symbols of office, and at how they project this fascination onto the barbarians. And it looks at how, without real imperatives of their own, they not only relinquish power to a threatening stereotype, but they allow their own identity to be defined by the threat.

The anti-climax is infinitely sad.

I hope this collection of poetry is as successful as earlier editions.

Yours sincerely,
Máire Geoghegan-Quinn
Minister for Justice

Waiting for the Barbarians

What are we waiting for, assembled in the forum?

    The barbarians are due here today.

Why isn't anything going on in the senate?
Why are the senators sitting there without legislating?

    Because the barbarians are coming today.
    What's the point of senators making laws now?
    Once the barbarians are here, they'll do the legislating.

Why did our emperor get up so early,
and why is he sitting enthroned at the city's main gate,
in state, wearing the crown?

    Because the barbarians are coming today
    and the emperor's waiting to receive their leader.
    He's even got a scroll to give him,
    loaded with titles, with imposing names.

Why have our two consuls and praetors come out today
wearing their embroidered, their scarlet togas?
Why have they put on bracelets with so many amethysts,
rings sparkling with magnificent emeralds?
Why are they carrying elegant canes
beautifully worked in silver and gold?

    Because the barbarians are coming today
    and things like that dazzle the barbarians.

Why don't our distinguished orators turn up as usual
to make their speeches, say what they have to say?

    Because the barbarians are coming today
    and they're bored by rhetoric and public speaking.

Why this sudden bewilderment, this confusion?
(How serious people's faces have become.)
Why are the streets and squares emptying so rapidly,
everyone going home lost in thought?

    Because night has fallen and the barbarians haven't come.
    And some of our men just in from the border say
    there are no barbarians any longer.

Now what's going to happen to us without barbarians?
Those people were a kind of solution.

Constantine P Cavafy (1863–1933)
Translated by Edmund Keeley and Philip Sherrard

MOYA CANNON 417

Dear Ewan Gibson, Áine Jackson, Christopher Pillow,

Many thanks for your letter and apologies for not having replied until now. Like most people I have many favourite poems and it is difficult to choose one. However 'Thalassa' by Louis MacNeice is certainly very high on my list of touchstone poems.

I love it for its evocation of courage, not only in the face of external circumstances, but also within the context of profound self doubt. Our freedom is hampered not only by the external 'adverse forces' with which we contend but by the 'ruined churches' of our own hearts and minds. There is also great truth in the exhortation to 'Let your poison be your cure'. The aspects of our natures, the sensitivities, which cause pain to us and to those around us are precisely the same aspects of our natures which when eventually turned outwards instead of inwards, allow for real communication, creativity and change.

Congratulations on the previous success of Lifelines, *and the very best of luck with the next issue.*

Very best wishes,
Moya Cannon

Thalassa

Run out the boat, my broken comrades;
Let the old seaweed crack, the surge
Burgeon oblivious of the last
Embarkation of feckless men,
Let every adverse force converge —
Here we must needs embark again.

Run up the sail, my heartsick comrades;
Let each horizon tilt and lurch —
You know the worst: your wills are fickle,
Your values blurred, your hearts impure
And your past life a ruined church —
But let your poison be your cure.

Put out to sea, ignoble comrades,
Whose record shall be noble yet;
Butting through scarps of moving marble
The narwhal dares us to be free;
By a high star our course is set,
Our end is Life. Put out to sea.

Louis MacNeice (1907–1963)

JOHN MacKENNA   418

8 January 1994

Dear Áine, Ewan and Christopher,

Thank you for your letter and kind invitation to nominate some poem/poems for the new Lifelines. *I hope it is every bit as successful as the previous editions. I'm enclosing two poems — if you are stuck for space I'd go with the John Clare poem 'I Am'. I might have nominated two others — Byron's 'We'll go no more a roving' and Tennyson's 'Crossing the bar' — and, I think, the Lord's Prayer but I'm moving towards taking up more than enough space in that!*

The John Clare poem was the piece that inspired me to write the novel Clare *about his life. I think its strength is its honesty. It comes from the heart and isn't at all self-pitying. It tells his story briefly and bitterly. The Raymond Carver poem closes his posthumous collection* A New Path to the Waterfall *and was written in his last days. It speaks so much of hope and life and optimism and satisfaction. I think it's wonderful.*

All the best, again, with your book — may it sell a million.

Good things,
John MacKenna

I Am

I am: yet what I am none cares or knows,
    My friends forsake me like a memory lost;
I am the self-consumer of my woes,
    They rise and vanish in oblivious host,
Like shades in love and death's oblivion lost;
And yet I am, and live with shadows tost

Into the nothingness of scorn and noise,
    Into the living sea of waking dreams,
Where there is neither sense of life nor joys,
    But the vast shipwreck of my life's esteems;
And een the dearest — that I loved the best —
Are strange — nay, rather stranger than the rest.

I long for scenes where man has never trod;
    A place where woman never smiled or wept;
There to abide with my Creator, GOD,
    And sleep as I in childhood sweetly slept:
Untroubling and untroubled where I lie;
The grass below — above the vaulted sky.

John Clare (1793–1864)

So We'll Go No More a Roving

So we'll go no more a roving
    So late into the night,
Though the heart be still as loving,
    And the moon be still as bright.

For the sword outwears the sheath,
    And the soul wears out the breast,
And the heart must pause to breathe,
    And Love itself have rest.

Though the night was made for loving,
    And the day returns too soon,
Yet we'll go no more a roving
    By the light of the moon.

George Gordon, Lord Byron (1788–1824)

Crossing the Bar

Sunset and evening star,
    And one clear call for me!
And may there be no moaning of the bar,
    When I put out to sea.

But such a tide as moving seems asleep,
    Too full for sound and foam,
When that which drew from out the boundless deep
    Turns again home.

Twilight and evening bell,
    And after that the dark!
And may there be no sadness of farewell,
    When I embark;

For though from out our bourne of Time and Place
    The flood may bear me far,
I hope to see my Pilot face to face
    When I have crost the bar.

Alfred, Lord Tennyson (1809–1892)

The Lord's Prayer

Our Father, who art in heaven,
hallowed be thy Name;
thy kingdom come;
thy will be done;
on earth as it is in heaven.
Give us this day our daily bread.
And forgive us our trespasses,

as we forgive those who trespass against us.
And lead us not into temptation;
but deliver us from evil.
For thine is the kingdom,
the power, and the glory,
for ever and ever.

Amen.

Late Fragment

And did you get what
you wanted from this life, even so?
I did.
And what did you want?
To call myself beloved, to feel myself
beloved on the earth.

Raymond Carver (1939–1988)

Notes on the contributors (in alphabetical order)

Bertie Ahern TD (p10) — Politician, Minister for Finance in the Irish government; **Paul Andrews SJ** (p245) — Psychologist and educator; **John Arden** (p179) — Playwright (*All Fall Down; The Waters of Babylon; Sergeant Musgrave's Dance; The Non-Stop Connolly Show* — in collaboration with Margaretta D'Arcy), essayist (*To Present the Pretence*) and novelist (*Silence Among the Weapons; Books of Bale*); **Neil Astley** (p17) — Director of Bloodaxe Books; **Vincent Banville** (p169) — Writer, critic and novelist for adults (*An End to Flight*) and teenagers (*Hennessy; Hennessy Goes West; Hennessy in Africa*); **Leland Bardwell** (p60) — Poet (*The Mad Cyclist; The Fly and the Bed Bug*), novelist (*Girl on a Bicycle; The Home*), short story writer (*Different Kinds of Love*); **Ben Barnes** (p46) — Theatre director and director of The Gaiety Theatre, Dublin; **Kevin Barry** (p85) — Professor of English Literature, University College Galway, critic and writer; **Bibi Baskin** (p56) — Broadcaster on RTE television; **John Behan** (p295) — Sculptor; **Ciarán Benson** (p160) — Chairperson of The Arts Council/An Chomhairle Ealaíon; **Steven Berkoff** (p26) — Playwright (*East; Greek; Decadence; Kvetch; Acapulco*), actor, director and travel writer (*Overview*); **Agnes Bernelle** (p154) — Singer, songwriter, performer, actor; **Wendell Berry** (p68) — American poet (*Openings; The Country of Marriage; Clearing; Sabbaths*), essayist (*The Unsettling of America; Standing by Words*) and short story writer (*The Wild Birds*); **Harold Bloom** (p161) — Sterling Professor of the Humanities, Yale. Critic and author (*Shelley's Mythmaking; The Visionary Company; Blake's Apocalypse; A Map of Misreading; The Anxiety of Influence*); **Seoirse Bodley** (p188) — Composer; **Veronica Bolay** (p291) — Artist; **Brian Bourke** (p216) — Artist; **Brian Boydell** (p106) — Composer; **Charles Brady** (p148) — Artist; **Conor Brady** (p194) — Editor, *The Irish Times*; **Cecily Brennan** (p32) — Artist; **Rory Brennan** (p199) — Poet (*The Sun on Fire; The Walking Wounded*) and broadcaster; **Joseph Brodsky** (p187) — Russian poet (*A Part of Speech; To Urania*), winner of the 1987 Nobel Prize for literature; **Denis Brown** (p107) — Artist and calligrapher. Calligraphic work includes *The Great Book of Ireland*; **Terence Brown** (p197) — Professor of English, Trinity College Dublin. Critic and writer; **John Bruton TD** (p238) — Leader of Fine Gael; **Julie Burchill** (p260) — Journalist and novelist (*Ambition; No Exit*). Film critic with *The Sunday Times*; **Donald Caird** (p36) — Church of Ireland Archbishop of Dublin; **Ciana Campbell** (p129) — Broadcaster and presenter of 'Teletalk' on RTE television; **Moya Cannon** (p304) — Poet (*Oar*); **John Carey** (p179) — Professor of English, Merton College, Oxford. Critic and writer (*The Intellectuals and the Masses*); **Eithne Carr** (p286) — Artist; **Ciaran Carson** (p140) — Poet (*The New Estate; The Irish for No; Belfast Confetti; First Language*). Winner of the T S Eliot Prize for Poetry 1994. Author (*The Pocket Guide to Irish Traditional Music*); **Charles Causley** (p182) — Poet (*Farewell, Aggie Weston; Under the Water; A Field of Vision; Collected Poems*), playwright and writer of children's stories. Winner of the Queen's Gold Medal for Poetry 1967; **Jung Chang** (p1) — Chinese writer (*Wild Swans*); **Siobhán Cleary** (p90) — Broadcaster. Presenter of 'Check Up' on RTE. Lecturer in communications skills; **Michael Coady** (p7) — Poet (*Two for a Woman, Three for a Man; Oven Lane*). Winner of the Patrick Kavanagh Award 1979; **Paddy Cole** (p21) — Musician; **Michael Colgan** (p49) — Director of the Gate Theatre; **Evelyn Conlon** (p173) — Novelist (*Stars in the Daytime*), short story writer (*My Head is Opening; Crimson Houses; Taking Scarlet as a Real Colour*) and broadcaster; **Marita Conlon-McKenna** (p22) — Novelist for teenagers (*Under the Hawthorn; No Goodbye; The Blue Horse; Tree; Wildflower Girl*); **Róisín Conroy** (p195) — Co-founder and publisher of Attic Press. Author (*So You Want To Be Published?*); **Barrie Cooke** (p41) — Artist; **Emma Cooke** (p153) —

Novelist (*A Single Sensation; Wedlocked*) and short story writer (*Female Forms*); **Art Cosgrove** (p275) — President of University College Dublin; **Ingrid Craigie** (p18) — Actor; **John Creedon** (p246) — Broadcaster on RTE radio (*Rise 'n Time*) and television; **Jeananne Crowley** (p5) — Actor; **Margrit Cruikshank** (p237) — Author for children and teenagers (the S.K.U.N.K. books, including *S.K.U.N.K. and the Freak Flood Fiasco; A Monster Called Charlie* and *Circling the Triangle*); **Pádraig J Daly** (p118) — Poet (*Poems, New and Selected; Out of Silence*) and Augustinian priest; **Brian D'Arcy** (p99) — Priest, journalist and broadcaster. Columnist with *The Sunday World;* **Michael Davitt** (p13) — Poet (*Gleann ar Ghleann; Bligeard Sráide*) and broadcaster; **Gerald Dawe** (p211) — Poet (*Sheltering Places; The Lundys Letter; Sunday School*) and editor (*The Younger Irish Poets*); **Éamon de Buitléar** (p100) — Film-maker, naturalist, author (*Ireland's Wild Countryside*); Eilís Dillon (deceased) (p141) — Novelist (*Across the Bitter Sea; Blood Relations*). Author of *Inside Ireland.* Novelist for teenagers (*The Island of Horses; Children of Bach*); **Brian Dobson** (p146) — Newscaster, journalist and broadcaster; **Terry Dolan** (p251) — Professor of Old and Middle English, University College Dublin. Writer, editor and broadcaster; **Emma Donoghue** (p188) — Novelist (*Stir Fry*), playwright (*I Know My Own Heart*), writer (*Passion Between Women*) and broadcaster; **Katie Donovan** (p272) — Author (*Irish Women Writers: Marginalised by Whom?*), poet (*Watermelon Man*), journalist, selector — with Brendan Kennelly and A N Jeffares — of *Ireland's Women, Writers Past and Present;* **Mary Dorcey** (p283) — Poet (*Moving into the Space Cleared by Our Mothers*), short story writer (*A Noise from the Woodshed*) and novelist; **Avril Doyle** (p159) — Politician; **Rose Doyle** (p1) — Novelist (*Images; Kimbay*), writer of novels for teenagers (*The Invisible Monk; Goodbye, Summer, Goodbye*) and journalist; **Carol Ann Duffy** (p176) — Poet (*Standing Female Nude; Selling Manhattan; The Other Country; Mean Time*); **Joe Duffy** (p115) — Broadcaster and journalist; **Anne Dunlop** (p205) — Novelist (*The Pineapple Tart; A Soft Touch; The Dolly Holiday*); **Helen Dunmore** (p137) — Poet (*The Apple Fall; The Sea Skater; The Raw Garden*), novelist (*Zennor in Darkness; Burning Bright*) and short story writer; **Sean Dunne** (p157) — Poet (*Against the Storm; The Sheltered Nest*), writer (*In My Father's House*), journalist and critic. Literary Editor of *The Cork Examiner;* **Alison Dye** (p277) — Novelist (*The Sense of Things*); **Desmond Egan** (p189) — Poet (*Woodcutter; A Song for My Father; Peninsula; Collected Poems*) and writer (*The Death of Metaphor*); **Conor Fallon** (p8) — Sculptor; **Bernard Farrell** (p175) — Playwright (*Happy Birthday Dear Alice; I Do Not Like Thee Dr Fell; The Last Apache Reunion*); **Eithne Fitzgerald** (p247) — Minister of State at the Department of Finance; **Gabriel Fitzmaurice** (p270) — Poet (*The Father's Part*), teacher, editor (*Irish Poetry Now*) and broadcaster; **Christopher Fitz-Simon** (p2) — Literary manager of the Abbey Theatre, Dublin. Writer and biographer (*The Boys — a biography of Micheál MacLiammóir and Hilton Edwards*); **Roy Foster** (p43) — Professor of Irish History at Oxford. Writer (*Charles Stewart Parnell: The Man and His Family; Lord Randolph Churchill: A Political Life; Modern Ireland 1600-1972*). Authorised biographer of W B Yeats; **Maureen Gaffney** (p66) — Chairperson of the National Economic and Social Forum, member of the Law Reform Commission, senior lecturer in psychology, Trinity College Dublin. *Irish Times* columnist ('Living and Loving'); **Tess Gallagher** (p248) — American poet (*Stepping Outside; Instructions to the Double; Willingly; Amplitude: New and Selected Poems*) and short story writer (*The Lover of Horses*); **Trevor Geoghegan** (p300) — Artist; **Máire Geoghegan-Quinn** (p302) — Minister for Justice in the Irish government; **Allen Ginsberg** (p50) — American poet (*Howl and Other Poems; Kaddish and Other Poems; TV Baby Poems; The Fall of America: Poems of These States*); **Louise Glück** (p19) — American poet (*Firstborn; The House on Marshland; Descending Figure; The Wild Iris*). Winner of the Pulitzer

Prize; **Richard Gorman** (p198) — Artist; **Tim Goulding** (p241) — Artist; **Bernadette Greevy** (p218) — Singer. Contralto. Has given recitals and performed operatic roles worldwide; **Eamon Grennan** (p219) — Poet (*Wildly for Days; What Light There Is; As If It Matters*); **Vona Groarke** (p224) — Poet (*Shale*) and curator of Newman House, Dublin; **Donald Hall** (p221) — Poet (*The Happy Man; Kicking the Leaves; Great Days in the Cow House*). Critic, essayist (*Fathers Playing Catch with Sons; Remembering Poets; The One Day*), editor, anthologist and short story writer (*The Ideal Bakery*); **Daniel Halpern** (p287) — Founder — with Paul Bowles — of Antaeus. Editor-in-chief of The Ecco Press. Poet (*Seasonal Rights; Tango; Foreign Neon*), editor (*The American Poetry Anthology; The Art of the Tale; An International Anthology of Short Stories*); **James Hanley** (p87) — Artist; **Nigel Hawthorne** (p208) — Actor. Celebrated roles include George III in *The Madness of George III*; **Michael D Higgins** (p200) — Poet (*The Betrayal: The Season of Fire*). Minister for Arts, Culture and the Gaeltacht in the Irish government; **Kathryn Holmquist** (p203) — Writer (*A Good Daughter*), journalist (*The Irish Times*), critic and broadcaster; **Nick Hornby** (p230) — Arsenal football fan, writer (*Fever Pitch*) and critic; **Kevin Hough** (p15) — Presenter of 'Theatre Nights' on RTE Radio I. Producer with RTE; **Sean Hughes** (p110) — Comedian. Writer (*Sean's Book*). Columnist with *The Sunday Times;* **Ted Hughes** (p91) — Poet Laureate since 1984. Poet (*Poetry in the Making; The Hawk in the Rain; Lupercal, Crow*), essayist (*Winter Pollen*); **Gemma Hussey** (p12) — Former politician and Minister for Education in the Irish government. Author (*Ireland Today*); **Garry Hynes** (p38) — Founder of the Druid Theatre, Galway, and former director of the Abbey Theatre, Dublin; **Neil Jordan** (p12) — Novelist (*The Past; The Dream of a Beast*), short story writer (*Night in Tunisia*) and film director (*Angel; Company of Wolves; Mona Lisa; The Crying Game*); **Jenny Joseph** (p297) — Poet (*The Unlooked-for Season; The Thinking Heart; Beyond Descartes; Selected Poems*); **Mark Joyce** (p271) — Artist; **Madeleine Keane** (p94) — Journalist, critic and broadcaster; **Brian Keenan** (p61) — Writer (*An Evil Cradling*) and lecturer in English; **Eamon Kelly** (p128) — Storyteller, author (*In My Father's Time*) and actor (played S B O'Donnell in the first production of Brian Friel's *Philadelphia Here I Come!*, September 1964; **Maeve Kelly** (p150) — Short story writer (*A Life of Her Own*), poet (*Resolution*) and novelist (*Necessary Treasons; Florrie's Girls*); **Jim Kemmy** (p33) — Politician. Chairperson of the Labour Party; **Anne Kennedy** (p301) — Poet (*Buck Mountain Poems; The Dog Kubla Dreams; no; My Life*), broadcaster and photographer; **Brian P Kennedy** (p77) — Assistant director of the National Gallery of Ireland. Author (*Irish Painting; Jack B Yeats*) and editor (— with Raymond Gillespie — *Ireland: Art into History*); **Mary Kennedy** (p207) — Newscaster, presenter of 'Words and Music' on RTE Radio I; **Jean Kennedy Smith** (p117) — American ambassador to Ireland; **Philip King** (p290) — Musician, singer, songwriter and film-maker (work includes *Bringing It All Back Home*); **Penelope Leach** (p79) — Child psychologist, writer (*Babyhood; Baby and Child; The Parents' A-Z; Children First*). Founder of EPOCH — End Physical Punishment Of Children; **Hermione Lee** (p9) — Critic, broadcaster, lecturer in English at York University. Author of books on Virginia Woolf, Elizabeth Bowen, Philip Roth, Willa Cather; **Anne Le Marquand Hartigan** (p258) — Poet (*Long Tongue; Return Single; Now is a Moveable Feast; Immortal Sins*), playwright (*Beds; La Corbière*), artist; **Brian Leyden** (p234) — Short story writer (*Departures*) and broadcaster (*No Meadows in Manhattan*); **Edna Longley** (p4) — Professor of English, Queen's University Belfast. Essayist (*The Living Stream*) and critic (*Poetry in the Wars; Louis MacNeice*); **Seán Lysaght** (p125) — Poet (*Noah's Irish Ark; The Clare Island Survey*); **Sam McAughtry** (p185) — Novelist (*The Sinking of the Kenbane Head*), short story writer, travel writer, broadcaster and journalist; **Eugene McCabe** (p137) — Playwright

(*Breakdown; Pull Down a Horseman; King of the Castle*), novelist (*Victims; Death and Nightingales*) and short story writer; **Patrick McCabe** (p121) — Novelist (*The Butcher Boy, Music on Clinton Street; Carn*); **Catherine Phil MacCarthy** (p172) — Poet (*This Hour of the Tide*); **Moy McCrory** (p168) — Short story writer (*The Water's Edge; Bleeding Sinners; Those Sailing Ships of His Boyhood Dreams*) and novelist (*The Fading Shrine*); **Steve MacDonogh** (p219) — Poet (*By Dingle Bay; Blasket Sound*) and publisher (Brandon Books); **Eleanor McEvoy** (p296) — Singer, songwriter, musician; **Barry McGovern** (p286) — Actor. Celebrated roles include the one-man show *I'll Go On* based on the writing of Samuel Beckett; **Jamie McKendrick** (p58) — Poet (*The Sirocco Room; The Kiosk on the Brink*); **John MacKenna** (p305) — Writer (*The Occasional Optimist; Castledermot and Kilkea; The Lost Village*), short story writer (*The Fallen*) and novelist (*Clare*); **Liz McManus** (p98) — Politician and novelist (*Acts of Subversion*); **Ciarán Mac Mathúna** (p235) — Presenter of 'Mo Cheol Thú' on RTE Radio I. Producer; **Deirdre Madden** (p44) — Novelist (*The Birds of the Innocent Wood; Remembering Light and Stone; Nothing is Black*) and short story writer (*Hidden Symptoms*); **Anne Madden Le Brocquy** (p182) — Artist and writer (*Seeing His Way* — a biography of Louis Le Brocquy); **David Malouf** (p47) — Novelist (*An Imaginary Life; Fly Away Peter; Remembering Babylon*) and poet (*First Things Last; Wild Lemons*); **David Marcus** (p178) — Former editor of 'New Irish Writing', *The Irish Press*. Editor of numerous anthologies, including *Modern Irish Love Stories and Alternative Love: Irish Lesbian and Gay Short Stories*). Novelist (*A Land Not Theirs; A Land in Flames*); **Jim Mays** (p186) — Professor of Modern English and American Literature at University College Dublin. Writer, editor and critic; **Leonard Michaels** (p158) — Author of two collections of stories (*Going Places; I Would Have Saved Them If I Could*), novelist (*The Men's Club*), Professor of English at the University of California, Berkeley, and editor (with Christopher Ricks, of *The State of the Language*). **Áine Miller** (p281) — Poet (*Goldfish in a Baby Bath*). Winner of the 1992 Patrick Kavanagh Award; **Mary Morrissey** (p244) — Short story writer (*A Lazy Eye*). *Irish Times* journalist and critic; **Michael Mortell** (p234) — Fashion designer; **Paul Muldoon** (p196) — Poet (*New Weather; Mules; Why Brownlee Left; Meeting the British; Madoc: A Mystery; The Annals of Chile*) and editor (*The Faber Book of Contemporary Irish Poetry*); **Jimmy Murphy** (p171) — Playwright (*Brothers of the Brush*); **Gloria Naylor** (p193) — African-American novelist (*The Women of Brewster Place; Linden Hills; Mama Day; Bailey's Café*); **Eilís Ní Dhuibhne** (p231) — Short story writer (*Blood and Water; Eating Women is not Recommended*) and novelist (*The Bray House*). Chairperson of Irish Writers' Union; **Christopher Nolan** (p212) — Poet (*Dam Burst of Dreams*) and novelist (*Under the Eye of the Clock*); **Sharon O'Brien** (p267) — Professor of English and American Studies, Dickinson College, Carlisle, Pennsylvania. Critic, short story writer and biographer (*Willa Cather: The Emerging Voice*); **Conor O'Callaghan** (p192) — Poet (*The History of Rain*). Winner of the Patrick Kavanagh Award 1993; **Gwen O'Dowd** (p104) — Artist; **Proinnsías Ó Duinn** (p242) — Principal conductor with the RTE Concert Orchestra. Composer. **Macdara Ó Fátharta** (p124) — Actor and translator; **Colm O'Gaora** (p181) — Short story writer (*Giving Ground*); **Fionn O'Leary** (p201) — Broadcaster on RTE Radio 1, FM3, and presenter of 'Sounds Classical'; **Olivia O'Leary** (p217) — Political journalist and broadcaster; **Jane O'Malley** (p206) — Artist; **Mary O'Malley** (p213) — Poet (*A Consideration of Silk; Where the Rocks Float*); **Brendan O'Reilly** (p84) — Sports commentator, broadcaster, poet (*Across the Spectrum; The Great Explosion*), songwriter, film and stage actor and cabaret artist; **Emily O'Reilly** (p64) — Journalist, broadcaster and writer (*Candidate; Masterminds of the Right*) and political editor of *The Sunday Business Post*; **Cathal Ó Searcaigh** (p209) — Playwright and poet (*Súile Shuibhne; Ag Tnúth Leis an tSolas*); **Micheál Ó Súilleabháin** (p198) — **Composer and musician. Professor of**

Music at the University of Limerick; **Seán Ó Tuama** (p225) — Poet, critic and Professor of Irish at University College Cork. Editor — with Thomas Kinsella — of *An Duanaire, 1600-1900: Poems of the Dispossessed*; **Jay Parini** (p202) — American poet (*Singing in Time; Town Life*), novelist (*The Love Run; The Patch Boys; The Last Station*) and biographer (*John Steinbeck*); **Don Paterson** (p24) — Poet (*Nil Nil*) and winner of The Arvon Poetry Prize 1993; **Tom Paulin** (p240) — Poet (*Liberty Tree; Fivemiletown; Selected Poems 1972-1990; Walking a Line*), editor (*The Faber Book of Political Verse; The Faber Book of Vernacular Verse*); **Tim Pigott-Smith** (p260) — Actor of television, stage and screen (*The Remains of the Day*); **Robert Pinsky** (p92) — American poet (*Sadness and Happiness; An Exploration of America; History of My Heart*) and critic (*The Situation of Poetry*); **E Annie Proulx** (p126) — Short story writer (*Heart Songs*), novelist (*Postcards; The Shipping News*) and winner of the Pulitzer Prize; **John Quinn** (p59) — Novelist for teenagers (*The Summer of Lily and Esme*), broadcaster and producer with RTE; **Richard W Riley** (p152) — Education secretary in President Clinton's Cabinet. Former governor of South Carolina; **Lilian Roberts Finlay** (p116) — Short story writer (*A Bona Fide Husband*) and novelist (*Always in My Mind; Stella*); **Michèle Roberts** (p42) — Novelist (*A Piece of the Night; The Witch Girl; Daughters of the House*), poet (*Touch Papers; The Mirror of the Mother*) and short story writer; **Adi Roche** (p138) — National secretary of the Irish Campaign for Nuclear Disarmament; director of the Chernobyl Children's Project; **Gabriel Rosenstock** (p143) — Chairperson of Éigse Éireann/Poetry Ireland. Author/translator of over forty books, most recently *Ní Mian Léi an Fhilíocht Níos Mó*; **Carol Rumens** (p120) — Poet (*A Strange Girl in Bright Colours; Unplayed Music; Star Whisper; Direct Dialling*); **James Scanlon** (p59) — Sculptor; **Vikram Seth** (p264) — Novelist (*The Golden Gate; A Suitable Boy*), poet (*Mappings; The Humble Administrator's Garden; All You Who Sleep Tonight*), travel writer (*From Heaven Lake: Travels through Sinkiang and Tibet*); **John Shinnors** (p293) — Artist; **Jo Slade** (p95) — Poet (*In Fields I Hear Them Sing; The Vigilant One*) and artist; **Art Spiegelman** (p95) — American cartoonist, illustrator and writer (*Maus*); **Dick Spring** (p65) — Leader of the Labour Party. Tánaiste and Minister for Foreign Affairs; **Niall Stokes** (p279) — Editor of *Hot Press* and chairperson of IRTC (Independent Radio and Television Commission); **Eithne Strong** (p49) — Novelist (*Degrees of Kindred*), poet (*Spatial Nosing — New and Selected Poems*), short story writer (*Patterns*); **Imogen Stuart** (p292) — Sculptor; **Matthew Sweeney** (p16) — Poet (*A Dream of Maps; A Round House; The Lame Waltzer; Blue Shoes*, and for younger readers *The Flying Spring Onion*) and fiction writer for children (*The Chinese Dressing Gown*); **R S Thomas** (p249) — Welsh poet (*Song at the Year's Turning; The Bread of Truth; H'm; Mass for Hard Times*) and Anglican priest. Winner of the Queen's Gold Medal for Poetry in 1964; **Carl Tighe** (p131) — Writer for radio and the stage and author of *Rejoice!*, a collection of short stories; **Maura Treacy** (p25) — Novelist (*Scenes From a Country Wedding*) and short story writer (*Sixpence in Her Shoe and Other Stories*); **Charles Tyrrell** (p250) — Artist; **Jean Valentine** (p156) — American poet (*Dream Breaker; Ordinary Things; Home • Deep • Blue; The River at Wolf*); **Edward Walsh** (p191) — President of the University of Limerick; **Dolores Walshe** (p114) — Poet, playwright, novelist (*Where the Trees Weep*) and short story writer (*Moon Mad*); **John Waters** (p145) — *Irish Times* journalist and writer (*Jiving at the Crossroads*); **Fay Weldon** (p239) — Novelist (*Praxis; Affliction*); **Hugo Williams** (p35) — Poet (*Symptoms of Loss; Sugar Daddy; Some Sweet Day; Love-Life; Writing Home; Self-Portrait with a Slide; Dock Leaves*) and writer (*All the Time in the World*); **Judith Woodworth** (p234) — Director of The National Concert Hall; **Charles Wright** (p269) — American poet (*Hard Freight; Country Music; Zone Journals*). Professor of English at the University of Virginia; **Nancy Wynne-Jones** (p63) — Artist.

Index of poets and their works

Index of titles

Index of first lines

Contributors to the first Lifelines

Fleur Adcock, Darina Allen, Sir Kingsley Amis, Martin Amis, Lord Jeffrey Archer, Simon Armitage, Margaret Atwood, Robert Ballagh, Mary Banotti, MEP, John Banville, Lynn Barber, Julian Barnes, Gerald Barry, Sebastian Barry, John Bayley, Mary Beckett, Emmet Bergin, Sara Berkeley, Pauline Bewick, Maeve Binchy, Kenneth Blackmore, Michael Blumenthal, Eavan Boland, Ken Bourke, Clare Boylan, Alicia Boyle, Kenneth Branagh, Richard Branson, Séamus Brennan, TD, Noël Browne, Helen Lucy Burke, Barbara Bush, A S Byatt, CBE, Gay Byrne, Ollie Campbell, Noelle Campbell-Sharp, Bunny Carr, Amy Clampitt, Anthony Clare, Adam Clayton, Don Cockburn, Shane Connaughton, Jilly Cooper, Elizabeth Cope, Wendy Cope, Anthony Cronin, William Crozier , Dorothy Cross, Cyril Cusack (deceased), Niamh Cusack, Cardinal Cahal Daly, Ita Daly, Derek Davis, Treasa Davison, Seamus Deane, Greg Delanty, Dame Judi Dench, Thomas Docherty, Patricia Donlon, Theo Dorgan, Anne Doyle, Maria Doyle, Margaret Drabble, CBE, Alan Dukes, TD, Myles Dungan, Eileen Dunne, Paul Durcan, Archbishop Robin Eames, Lauris Edmond, Felim Egan, Ben Elton, Peter Fallon, Brian Farrell, Desmond Fennell, Anne Fine, Mr Justice Thomas A Finlay, Garret FitzGerald, Mary FitzGerald, Theodora FitzGibbon (deceased), T P Flanagan, Bob Gallico, Sir John Gielgud, Ellen Gilchrist, Larry Gogan, Patrick Graham, Victor Griffin, Hugo Hamilton, Eithne Hand, Mary Harney, TD, Charles Haughey, Isabel Healy, Seamus Heaney, Margaret Heckler, Chaim Herzog, Tom Hickey, Rita Ann Higgins, Desmond Hogan, Alan Hollinghurst, Michael Holroyd, Miroslav Holub, Patricia Hurl, Jeremy Irons, Glenda Jackson, MP, Jennifer Johnston, Rónán Johnston, John Kavanagh, John B Keane, Richard Kearney, Sr Stanislaus Kennedy, Brendan Kennelly, Pat Kenny, Declan Kiberd, Benedict Kiely, Galway Kinnell, Thomas Kinsella, Mick Lally, Barry Lang, Mary Lavin, Sue Lawley, David Leavitt, Louis Le Brocquy, Laurie Lee, Mary Leland, Brian Lenihan TD, Hugh Leonard, Doris Lessing, Rosaleen Linehan, David Lodge, Michael Longley, Seán Lucy, Joe Lynch, Ferdia MacAnna, Joan McBreen, Nell McCafferty, Mr Justice Niall McCarthy (deceased), Thomas McCarthy, Tom McCaughren, Margaret MacCurtain (Sr Benvenuta), Mary McEvoy, Michael McGlynn, Medbh McGuckian, Frank McGuinness, Sir Ian McKellen, Bernard MacLaverty, Bryan MacMahon, Sean McMahon, Flo McSweeney, Jimmy Magee, Alice Maher, Derek Mahon, Thelma Mansfield, Augustine Martin, Maxi, Paula Meehan, Máire Mhac an tSaoi, Sue Miller, John Montague, Mary Mooney, Christy Moore, Brian Moore, Andrew Motion, Dame Iris Murdoch, Mike Murphy, Richard Murphy, Tom Murphy, Kevin Myers, Doireann Ní Bhriain, Eiléan Ní Chuilleanáin, Nuala Ní Dhomhnaill, David Norris, Conor Cruise O'Brien, Julie O'Callaghan, Eilís O'Connell, Joseph O'Connor, Ulick O'Connor, Mary O'Donnell, Dennis O'Driscoll, Cardinal Tomás Ó Fiaich (deceased), Emer O'Kelly, Sharon Olds, Michael O'Loughlin, Andy O'Mahony, Tony O'Malley, Liam Ó Murchú, Joseph O'Neill, Hilary Orpen, Micheal O'Siadhail, Fintan O'Toole, Lord David Owen, Geraldine Plunkett, James Plunkett, Maureen Potter, Kathy Prendergast, Sir V S Pritchett, Deirdre Purcell, Marian Richardson, Christopher Ricks, Vivienne Roche, Neil Rudenstine, Patricia Scanlan, Anna Scher, Fiona Shaw, Antony Sher, James Simmons, Archbishop George Otto Simms (deceased), Maria Simonds-Gooding, Ailbhe Smyth, Camille Souter, Michele Souter, Alan Stanford, Amelia Stein, Francis Stuart, Alice Taylor, Mother Teresa, Sue Townsend, William Trevor, Gerrit van Gelderen, Helen Vendler, Michael Viney, Martin Waddell, Kathleen Watkins, Padraic White, Macdara Woods.

Acknowledgements

A note from the editor and compilers
Thank you to Kate Bateman, Sara Berkeley, Kenneth Blackmore, Frank Cinnamond, Mary Clayton, Greg Delanty, Dorrie Dowling, Melissa Hammerle, Mavis Johnson, Marybeth Joyce, Catherine La Farge, John Leeson, Linda Miller, Kate O'Carroll, Dennis O'Driscoll, Rosemary Roe, Sandra Williams. A special thanks to Treasa Coady, Elaine Campion and Bernie Daly of Town House and Country House.

For permission to reprint copyright material, the compilers, editor and publishers are grateful to the following:

John Murray (Publishers) Ltd for 'The Cottage Hospital' by John Betjeman; Farrar, Straus & Giroux Inc for 'Manners' from *The Complete Poems 1927-1979* by Elizabeth Bishop, © 1979, 1983 by Alice Helen Methfessel; Carcanet Press Ltd for 'The Pomegrante' and 'Night Feed' from *Selected Poems* by Eavan Boland; Carcanet Press Ltd for 'Poem' from *Collected Poems* by William Carlos Williams; New Directions Publishing Company, 80 Eighth Avenue, New York 10011 for 'The Whole Mess . . . Almost' by Gregory Corse from *Herald of the Autochthonic Spirit*, © 1981 by Gregory Corso; W W Norton & Company for 'Buffalo Bill's' from *Complete Poems 1904-1962* by E E Cummings, edited by George J Firmage, © 1923, 1951, 1991 by the Trustees for the E E Cummings Trust; W W Norton & Company for 'mr youse needn't be so spry' from *Complete Poems 1904-1962* by E E Cummings, edited by George J Firmage © 1926, 1954, 1991 by the Trustees for the E E Cummings Trust; W W Norton & Company for 'this is a rubbish of human rind' from *Complete Poems 1904-1962* by E E Cummings, edited by George J Firmage, © 1947, 1975, 1991; Michael Davitt for 'Urnaí Maidne' by Michael Davitt, published by Coiscéim (1983), and 'Morning Prayer' translated by Philip Casey, published by Raven Arts Press in *Michael Davitt, Selected Poems* (1987); Greg Delanty for 'The Fable of Swans'; Eileán Ní Chuilleanáin for 'Caoineadh Airt Uí Laoghaire' - an excerpt - translated by Eilís Dillon, © the estate of Eilís Dillon; Salmon Publishing, a division of Poolbeg Enterprises Ltd, for 'If Only She Had Told You Beforehand' by Mary Dorcey from *Moving Into the Space Cleared by Our Mothers*, © Mary Dorcey 1991, 1994; Anvil Press Poetry Ltd for 'Prayer' by Carol Ann Duffy from *Mean Time* (published 1993); Oliver Dunne for 'Uh-Oh'; The Blackstaff Press for 'Felicity in Turin' by Paul Durcan from *Daddy, Daddy*; Paul Durcan for 'The Mantelpiece' and 'A Cornfield with Cypresses' from *Give Me Your Hand*; Desmond Egan for 'Peace' from *Poems for Peace*, published by AFRI, © Desmond Egan, 1986; Faber and Faber Ltd for 'Ash Wednesday' from *Collected Poems 1909-1962* by T S Eliot; Brian Fallon and the estate of Padraic Fallon for 'The Skellig Way' by Padraic Fallon from *Collected Poems*, Carcanet/Gallery Press 1990; Gabriel Fitzmaurice for 'Galvin and Vicars' from *The Space Between: New and Selected Poems*, Cló Iar Chonnachta, Conamara; Oxford University Press for 'Pangur Bán' from *The Irish Tradition* by Robin Flower (1947); Random House UK Ltd for 'Mowing', 'Desert Places' and 'After Apple-Picking' from *The Poetry of Robert Frost*, edited by Edward Connery Lathem; A P Watt Ltd on behalf of The Trustees of the Robert Graves Copyright Trust for 'Symptoms of Love' from *Collected Poems 1975* by Robert Graves; Faber and Faber Ltd for 'Lightenings viii' from *Seeing Things* by Seamus Heaney, for 'Digging' from *Death of a Naturalist* by Seamus Heaney, for 'Clearances' from *The Haw Lantern* by Seamus Heaney, for 'A Constable Calls' from *North* by Seamus Heaney, and for 'Limbo' from *Wintering Out* by Seamus Heaney; Salmon Publishing, a division of Poolbeg Enterprises Ltd for 'Between Them' by Rita Ann Higgins from *Philomena's Revenge*, © Rita Ann Higgins, 1992; Bloodaxe Books Ltd for 'The Door' by Miroslav Holub, translated by Ian Milner, from *Miroslav Holub: Poems Before and After: Collected English Translations* (Bloodaxe Books, 1990), Bloodaxe Books Ltd for 'Rain – Birdoswald' by Frances Horovitz, from *Frances*